Raising and Educating a Deaf Child

Raising and Educating a Deaf Child

*A Comprehensive Guide
to the Choices, Controversies,
and Decisions Faced
by Parents and Educators*

SECOND EDITION

Marc Marschark

OXFORD
UNIVERSITY PRESS
2007

OXFORD
UNIVERSITY PRESS

Oxford University Press, Inc., publishes works that further
Oxford University's objective of excellence
in research, scholarship, and education.

Oxford   New York
Auckland   Cape Town   Dar es Salaam   Hong Kong   Karachi
Kuala Lumpur   Madrid   Melbourne   Mexico City   Nairobi
New Delhi   Shanghai   Taipei   Toronto

With offices in
Argentina   Austria   Brazil   Chile   Czech Republic   France   Greece
Guatemala   Hungary   Italy   Japan   Poland   Portugal   Singapore
South Korea   Switzerland   Thailand   Turkey   Ukraine   Vietnam

Published by Oxford University Press, Inc.
198 Madison Avenue, New York, New York 10016

www.oup.com

Oxford is a registered trademark of Oxford University Press

Library of Congress Cataloging-in-Publication Data
Marschark, Marc.
Raising and educating a deaf child: a comprehensive guide to choices, controversies,
and decisions faced by parents and educators / Marc Marschark.—2nd ed.
p. cm.
ISBN-13 978-0-19-531458-8
ISBN 0-19-531458-1
1. Deaf children.   2. Deaf children—Language.   3. Parents of deaf children.   I. Title.
HV2391.M26 2007
649'.1512—dc22   2006014127

9 8 7 6 5 4 3 2 1

Printed in the United States of America
on acid-free paper

In memory of my father (and role model),

Herbert L. Marschark

Foreword

Six years ago, when we adopted our first deaf child, we felt we had a pretty good idea of what we were getting into. If there are such things as the "typical" parents of deaf children, we are not it. We are the parents of six children ranging in age from 6 to 24. Our younger four (ages 6, 11, 12, and 13) are deaf. Sherry is a teacher of the deaf and Roger works as a social worker in the Deaf community. We decided to adopt our younger children when we were faced with the challenge of finding appropriate foster homes for deaf children in our area. You might think that this would somehow make raising a deaf child an easy task for us. Unfortunately, nothing could be further from the truth. Despite long experience in deafness and deaf education, formal training in the field, and contacts in the community, we find ourselves stuck at many of the same dilemmas that all parents of deaf children face:

- Should our children go to a mainstream, day, or residential school? How do we give them the best education possible?
- Should our children get cochlear implants?
- What is the best way to deal with our extended family?
- How do we deal with a child who is not only deaf but has other disabilities?

In trying to wade our way through a sea of confusing and conflicting information, our knowledge about the "ideal" environment provided us with little assistance in negotiating the "real" world in which we were seeking an education for our children. Our contacts in the field confirmed what we already knew—that resources were limited and that the "best" choices might not be available in our area.

Our children are a never-ending source of joy and laughter (not to mention the occasional frustration and exasperation), but what were simple questions for our hearing children are still unanswered, and we spend much time trying to determine our future plans.

So it was with great delight that we had the opportunity to review a draft of the book you hold in front of you, the second edition of *Raising and Educating a Deaf Child.* In the very opening of the book, Marc Marschark captured our frustrations (and our unrealistic desire for simple objective answers). As co-presidents of the American Society for Deaf Children, we are often asked for answers to these questions, and many others. As much as we might like, Marc does not provide simple answers to these complex questions. However, as in no other book that we have read, he does give a balanced perspective on the questions, providing up-to-date information in a concise and readable format. As parents, we cannot easily know all the current research and latest news in the field of deafness and deaf education. If your experience is anything like ours, your time at home is probably spent figuring out how to cook supper, discuss the school day, do homework, and get children ready for bed. By the time we do that with the four younger children still at home, we do not have the energy or the time to do the research needed to keep abreast of developments.

Raising and Educating a Deaf Child provides a broad review of those developments. It offers the parent or the professional working with parents a resource that focuses on the very tasks that occupy most of our time. When we meet with other parents and discuss the challenges we all face, we discuss the very topics that Marc has chosen to explore and for which he provides if not answers, at least guidance. He does not shy away from the controversies that, at times, overshadow the universal goal we all share of raising children who reach their potential. He tackles these controversies with an understandable review of the literature and, where there is no clear-cut answer (as is all too often the case), provides parents with at least enough information to help them formulate an opinion as to what is right for them and their child.

While we are experienced parents, having raised our two hearing children to be happy self-sufficient adults, and while we are already familiar with the field of deafness, we are aware that many readers are probably new parents, struggling with the idea of raising a deaf child and wondering where to go and if you are doing the right thing for your child. You will experience a lot of frustration with "the system" and with professionals who give conflicting information on how best to raise your child, and you will steer your way through the communication minefield, trying to get appropriate services from an educational system that is all too often focused on providing the bare minimum of services with a limited budget. If you are lucky enough to live in an area with a wealth of resources, the choices can be overwhelming. If, like us, you live in an area with scant resources, it is a Hobson's choice with no easy options.

We strongly recommend this book, which is an updated edition of the first one published in 1997, to parents and professionals. Back in 1997, we did not have the body of research on the long-range effects of cochlear implants or cued speech on the language and social development of deaf children. Marc has evolved and refined some of his ideas during these past nine years. We look forward to seeing future editions as more research is done into the needs of deaf children and as more definitive answers can be provided to those questions that plague us all.

In the meantime, enjoy this book. It is easy to read and while there will undoubtedly be people who do not agree with some parts, you will be better informed for having read it. Enjoy your children. They are our future. Without them, you wouldn't be reading this book and learning about topics which may never have even crossed your mind before.

> Roger & Sherry Williams
> Co-Presidents
> American Society for Deaf Children

Preface

A preface is something that comes at the beginning of a book, but it is invariably something that the author writes last. I suppose that's a good thing, because it allows one to look back and reflect on all of the work that has gone into the book and to look ahead, with hope, to how it will be received. I guess it is a little like being a parent. I have watched this book develop for years, I see how different it is from its older sister (the first edition), and now, with some trepidation, I have to give up control and send it out into the world. I suppose it is time to get some perspective.

Looking back, I wrote the first edition of this book because I felt that, despite all of the excellent research (past and present) relevant to children who are deaf, very little of the resulting information "trickled down" to the people who needed it most: parents, teachers, and other professionals involved with deaf children on a day-to-day basis. My goal, therefore, was to take what we know from a wide variety of investigations and explain it in everyday language. Because of my own perspective of the field and the needs and sensitivities of many people who I hope will read this book, that turned out to be rather more time consuming and difficult than I originally expected. I wanted to be sure that readers got "the whole truth and nothing but the truth," but that sometimes required a decision about whether it was worth even starting on some issues that might seem trivial unless they were put in what would be a rather complex context.

Surprisingly, I went through it all again with this second edition. The bridge between research and practice is still a fragile one, but I think it has made some progress over the past 10 years. At the same time, however, the need is also greater, as many parents have become more aware of the fact that they are not getting all the information they need, and that some of what they are getting is patently biased. I wanted this edition of the book to have even less of my own bias (which I really thought I had eliminated in the first edition) and to include several issues that were, for whatever reason, underserved in the first one, topics like cochlear implants, mental health, and spoken language. I also struggled with the fact that although this book was originally intended for parents and teachers, the first edition was sometimes used as a textbook, a purpose for which I believe it was ill suited. Readers thus will see that this edition has been expanded quite a bit and includes reference citations to key journal articles, chapters, and books that provide background reading or the original sources for research findings. Hopefully, all of this will make the book more useful for some audiences without being too overwhelming. Most readers can comfortably ignore all of those references, but they are there if you need them.

Another struggle I confronted in this book, quite different from the situation in most of my scientific writing, was balancing the needs and sensitivities of parents of deaf children. When I write a journal article, I can be confident that the people reading it will understand the nuances of scientific language and the importance of issues like statistical significance, reliability, and validity. Scientific writing lays bare the essence of a research project or an area of scholarly interest, whereas writing for anxious parents and frustrated teachers carries a different kind of responsibility. Rest assured that, regardless of what anyone might claim, this book is as free of "spin" as I can make it, recognizing that generalities about deaf children are extremely difficult and conclusions that seem obvious today might change tomorrow. As always, therefore, compromises were necessary, and I owe a great debt to the many people who helped me to work through these sometimes complicated and sensitive issues. I was also helped by something I read years ago, written by Albert Einstein in 1948, but still true today:

> Anyone who has ever tried to present a rather abstract scientific subject in a popular manner knows the great difficulties of such an attempt. Either he succeeds in being intelligible by concealing the core of the problem and by offering to the reader only superficial aspects or vague allusions, thus deceiving the reader by arousing in him the deceptive illusion of comprehension; or else he gives an expert account of the problem, but in such a fashion that the untrained reader is unable to follow the exposition and becomes discouraged from reading any further.

If these two categories are omitted from today's popular
scientific literature, surprisingly little remains . . . It is of great
importance that the general public be given an opportunity to
experience—consciously and intelligently—the efforts and
results of scientific research. It is not sufficient that each result
be taken up, elaborated, and applied by a few specialists in the
field. (Einstein, 1948, p. 9)

Taking heed of Einstein's cautions, I have tried to summarize what we know
from research concerning deaf children and deaf education, what we don't
know, and what we think we know but really don't. Throughout, I have
sought to remain true to the original significance and generality of the findings (if perhaps not always to what the original author had in mind). I fully
admit that, in the process, I raise as many questions as I answer. As I emphasize repeatedly, however, there are few "right" answers in this field,
and what is "right" for one child may be wrong for another. So, my goal
has been to show what kinds of questions we should be asking and where
to look for the answers. Perhaps most importantly, I argue for the need to
accept the many differences among deaf children and between deaf and
hearing children without viewing these differences as deficiencies or disabilities that need to be "corrected."

As a final disclaimer, this book is in no way intended to be a "how-to"
manual. Instead, I have focused on broad issues like alternatives for effective communication, the importance of diverse social experiences, and the
need for consistency in parenting. In a variety of situations, I have been
quite specific, but only going so far as I could with confidence. For example,
it should not seem odd to parents and teachers when I suggest that they
need to read to their children and students. Nor should it surprise anyone
when I suggest that this activity is all the more important for deaf children, who may lack other opportunities for exposure to English. Hopefully
I have explained clearly why these are so.

I learned a lot from writing this book the first time. I learned even more
in doing so the second time. Some things I learned from doing background
research in areas with which I was less familiar. Other things I learned by
discussing issues with deaf friends and colleagues and with teachers of deaf
learners of all ages. Most importantly, perhaps, I have learned from meeting and talking with parents of deaf children. I admit to awkward moments
and feelings of inadequacy when parents have looked to me for answers
that I feel wholly unprepared to provide. Hopefully, I have at least set them
on the right course, in roughly the right direction. My interactions with
parents and teachers, as well as with many deaf children, also have helped
me to challenge my own assumptions and beliefs about raising and educating a deaf child. Nothing could be healthier! It turns out that some of
the "facts" I had previously held were not really facts at all, but assump-

tions that I either made myself or accepted from others. Which of these situations were my own fault and which were someone else's is not really important. What is important is that no amount of "book learning" can substitute for being involved with deaf children, the Deaf community, and deaf education in both mainstream and separate settings. I am delighted that I learn something new almost every day and that I am constantly learning that I really did not know as much as I thought I did. I do not feel embarrassed about that, nor should parents or teachers of deaf children ever look back and feel ashamed of what they did not know. We are always learning. Those of us willing to accept a role in the lives of deaf children constantly have to challenge assumptions about what deaf children can and cannot do, and we must explore new avenues to allow them to reach their potentials. Therein lies the pursuit of excellence both for deaf children and those who love them.

Acknowledgments

A variety of individuals were involved in shepherding me through this project, including the many people I thanked in the first edition. In preparing both editions, many people shared with me their specific expertise and experiences (whether they knew it or not) and *Deaf Life* Magazine, Sugar Sign Press, the National Information Center on Deafness, National Captioning Institute, National Cued Speech Association, and Advanced Bionics all allowed the reprinting of various materials as noted throughout this edition and the earlier one.

The second edition also benefited from the feedback I have received from dozens of people in the years since the first edition in 1997. In particular, I appreciate the input from all those parents who told me things they wished I had included in the first edition, the colleagues who pointed out topics I had missed (to put it politely), and everyone who has helped me to see how the field has changed and how my perception of the field has changed. My friends at the National Technical Institute for the Deaf, the Western Pennsylvania School for the Deaf (Pittsburgh, Pennsylvania), the Royal Institute for Deaf and Blind Children (Sydney, Australia), Viataal (The Netherlands), and in other schools and organizations around the world are owed a great debt for the education they have provided for me and their willingness to share their knowledge and offer me their honesty. Students in my graduate and undergraduate courses on the development of deaf children did me the great service of using various drafts of this book as their text and pointing out the confusing bits and the many errors (some rather funny) that were created by my use of voice recognition software.

I would be remiss if I did not thank some of the people who (whether they know it or not) have really sharpened my thinking about the development of education of deaf children, sometimes by offering new perspectives, sometimes by showing me how wrong I was, and sometimes by just helping to "round out my rough edges." These patient people are too numerous to name, but they include Lou Abbate, Stephen Aldersley, Sue Archbold, Carol Convertino, Vince Daniele, Alan Hurwitz Harry Knoors, Harry Lang, Greg Leigh, Chris Licata, Connie Mayer, Barbara Raimando, Cathy and Don Rhoten, Patty Sapere, Patricia Spencer, and Brenda Schick. Particularly thanks in this respect are due to Irene Leigh and Leeanne Seaver, who provided me with line-by-line comments on a draft of the book, offered me their insights, and pointed out some glaring "concerns." This book is much better for their time and effort. Special mention—and warm appreciation—also goes to Catharine Carlin and Oxford University Press for their continuing support in our collaborations and their understanding when this book was delayed by the fact that writing books is only my hobby, and I actually have had to attend to my day job(s). Finally, I thank my wife, Janie Runion, for her never-ending patience and encouragement as I pursue goals that I hope will always be just out of my reach.

Contents

Raising and Educating a Deaf Child

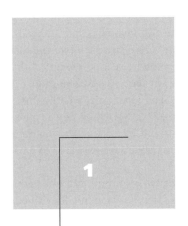

1

People with opinions just go around
bothering one another.
—The Buddha

ONE

A Deaf Child
in the Family

Parents of a deaf child, like the parents of any child who has special needs, want answers to what seem to be some simple and straightforward questions—questions like "What kind of language experience is best for my child, speech or sign language?" "Will my child ever learn to speak normally?" "What kind of school is best?" "Does being deaf affect how smart a child is?" and "Will my child be able to get a good job?" Regrettably, these questions are not as simple as they might appear, and parents may sometimes get contradictory information from professionals who are expected to have the answers.

At times, such contradictions arise because we simply do not know the answers. Consider, for example, progress that has been made with cochlear implants. When the first edition of this book was published, we had no idea how implants would affect deaf children's language development, even while research was demonstrating significant improvement to speech and hearing (later we will see the differences between these). As the second edition is being written, there is still relatively little research to indicate how implants will affect deaf children's long-term educational success, and even that is contradictory. Even deaf children who are considered "successful" implant users hear only about as much as hard-of-hearing children. Is that enough to offer them sufficient access to communication in the classroom? How should we teach children with implants? We do not yet know.

Another frequent cause of confusion is simply that opinions and personal beliefs often get in the way of facts—or at least our best understanding of the facts at any given time. Consider two examples that may confront parents of deaf children.

First, there has never been an real evidence that learning to sign interferes with deaf children's learning to speak. In fact, early sign language consistently has been shown to have beneficial effects on learning spoken language. Meanwhile, exposure only to spoken language typically results in significant delays in language development from early childhood continuing through the high school years (Calderon & Greenberg, 1997; Geers, 2006). Yet, those who advocate for spoken language for deaf children rarely concede these well-established facts.

Second, there is no evidence that deaf children with cochlear implants will find themselves, as some had warned, "stuck between two worlds" (hearing and deaf) and not fully a member of either. Some deaf and hard-of-hearing people feel that they live in two worlds and wonder how much time they should spend in each in order to satisfy themselves and others in their lives. But, there is no evidence that implants make this dilemma any worse—or any better (Spencer & Marschark, 2003). We do not really know how well children with cochlear implants are accepted by either hearing or deaf peers. Cochlear implants do identify deaf children as being "different," but we do not yet know whether having an implant has a greater or lesser effect on social and emotional development than not having one.

If these two examples seem a bit disheartening, the fact that we can now lay them aside is one indicator that the situation has improved. Great strides have been made over the last 25 years in our understanding of language, cognitive, and social development of children who are deaf. Deaf people have never before had as much access to education and employment, and we have never been in a better position to overcome the remaining academic challenges facing deaf children. Deaf children will be just as happy, smart, and successful as hearing children, as long as they are given equal opportunities.

Throughout this book, it is important to keep in mind that every child is different, every family is different, and every school is different. For every general finding described here, someone will be able to offer a counterexample (either positive or negative). Nevertheless, there is enough good information available about the growth and education of deaf children to allow parents to make enlightened decisions. Not all of those decisions will be easy, and some of them may turn out to have been wrong. Parents unfamiliar with deafness will have particular challenges in raising their deaf children, and they will vary widely in how they respond to the situation. Some will take the initiative and become active in fostering their children's development, spending extra time with them on school work, language skills, and in play. Those parents will do whatever they need to do in order to ensure that they have effective communication with their deaf child beginning with the identification of hearing loss or soon afterwards.

Effective parent-child communication early on is easily the best single predictor of success in virtually all areas of deaf children's development, including academic achievement. Many parents thus will learn sign language and, as we will see in chapter 3, they need not be overly concerned with the fact that their children soon will be more skilled at it than they. An increasing number of parents will opt for a cochlear implant for their children and encourage the use of spoken language, with or without sign language. Regardless of which means of communication is found to be most effective, their deaf children will be involved in most of the normal activities of young kids, from dinner table conversation to Girl Scouts. As a result, those children will have essentially all of the learning opportunities of their hearing peers in both social and academic areas.

Other parents leave the initiative in decision making up to schools and to those professionals "who should know." They will follow available advice for the most part, but they often will be hesitant or unable to seek out new information and new strategies. Either they will fear that they might make matters worse, or they will not be able to imagine that they could do much to make matters better. Such parents typically will not take the time to learn and consistently use alternative methods of communication, even when they are clearly needed. They are less likely to make other modifications in day-to-day family life such as installing visual doorbells or turning on television captioning (see chapter 2).

It is understandable that parents frequently go through considerable emotional distress in finding ways to cope with having a deaf or hard-of-hearing child. Social support from family, friends, and other parents of deaf children eventually will help them tremendously. In the meantime, they may not realize how much they can do to help their children succeed. And that is what this book is all about.

It is surprising to many people that over 95 percent of deaf children have hearing parents (Mitchell & Karchmer, 2004). For those parents and other hearing people in a deaf child's life, there is often considerable anxiety, simply because they do not know what to expect. Most hearing people know little more about being deaf and about deaf people than what they have seen in movies like *The Miracle Worker* and *Children of a Lesser God* or what they have gleaned from popular television shows. Other people have had personal contact with someone who is deaf—often a member of their extended family or a child in the neighborhood. When I meet a hearing person who says she "knows" a deaf person, I wonder about how well they communicate with each other. Although many deaf people do have some speech production skills, speech reception is much more difficult—and lipreading is not as easy as most people assume. What kind of relationship can you have with someone when you do not share a common language? What must it be like to grow up unable to have regular conversations with your parents—not to be able to talk to them about school, about love, or about God?

Given the diversity among deaf individuals, their communication preferences, and their social orientations, it is not a simple matter to fully understand what it means to be deaf, but if we are willing to expend the time and energy to learn, most deaf people are willing to aid in our education. There is also a wealth of recent literature that offers a window into the lives of deaf people, mostly those who are members of the Deaf community. For parents desiring "hard data," the task is somewhat more difficult. Some of the information they need is published in scientific journals with jargon not easily understood by lay readers, and most books on the subject of deaf children are written for academic audiences. Furthermore, some of the available research, particularly older work, simply is not very good. It is often lacking in *reliability* (generality across individuals and situations) and *validity* (actually showing what the investigators claim that it does). This situation sometimes arises as a result of conscious or unconscious bias on the part of the investigators, who often seem only to obtain findings that support their positions. Other times it simply reflects a lack of appropriate research methods or training. A primary goal of this book, therefore, is to provide a description of recent advances in research and practice concerning deaf children and deaf education in an objective and understandable manner. In so doing, readers hopefully will gain a better understanding of the context, strengths, and needs of deaf children, with an eye toward improving their opportunities and the likelihood of their success.

The chapters that follow will provide different perspectives on the development of deaf children, no one of which will give a complete view of the whole story. Taken together, however, they will provide a broad view of what we know about the growth and education of deaf children and what parents and teachers can do to optimize them.

A View From Within

Before talking about what it is like to grow up deaf, it is important to clarify some basic terminology and issues as they are perceived from both Deaf and hearing communities. Only then can we avoid the kinds of overgeneralizations and faulty assumptions that have plagued the field in the past and seem to persist despite the extensive availability of information on hearing loss today.

First, a word of caution on the notion of "a view from within." The more years I spend in Rochester, New York (with perhaps the highest per capita deaf population of any city in the world), with deaf friends, and involved in deaf education and the Deaf community, the more I realize how much of an outsider I really am. Simply put, as a hearing person I can never truly understand what it means to be Deaf or to grow up (deaf or hearing) in the Deaf community. I may be welcomed, and I may know more about deafness than many other people, but I still have to understand Deaf people and the Deaf community from my hearing perspective. Some of the differences are minor, such as the kinds of humor than I encounter from hearing and deaf friends. Other differences are more significant and, although unexplored through research, run more deeply through individuals and a community that is often conflicted about its status. For example, the way Deaf people identify themselves as users of American Sign Language (ASL) or spoken language is well recognized as important to their social-emotional functioning. Little is known, however, about how or when language orientation affects deaf children's self-identities or consciously influences their social behavior.

Whether deaf individuals view themselves as members of a linguistic-cultural minority deserving recognition as such, disabled and deserving of appropriate government support/intervention, or neither, they are constantly reminded of their differences. Even when those differences are irrelevant, or are at most inconvenient for hearing individuals with whom they interact, deaf adults and children usually will be seen as being on the other side of some divide. Yet in many ways, technology, legislation, and education are narrowing the gap between deaf and hearing individuals, and children are the major beneficiaries. We have not resolved all of the challenges associated with being deaf, but the progress has been palpable.

This book will describe many similarities and differences between deaf and hearing children. Its goal, however, is not to argue for one view of deaf people or another, to advocate for a particular mode of communication, or to claim that one kind of educational system is generally better for deaf children. Raising and educating a deaf child is about making choices that will help them to fulfill their potential and provide them with environments that are as supportive, nurturing, and demanding as those available to hearing children. In the end, deaf children's needs are little different than those of hearing children, even if sometimes we have to find different ways to satisfy them. With this view in mind, we turn to the contexts in which deaf children grow up.

Big D and Little d

Let us start with the fact that the word "deaf" appeared in both capitalized and uncapitalized form in the preceding section. Most commonly, *Deaf* is used as an adjective, referring to people who see themselves as part of a community bound together by historical successes and challenges and a common language, whether it be ASL, British Sign Language (BSL), Croatian Sign Language (*Hrvatski Znakovni Jezik* or HZJ), or Australian Sign Language (*Auslan*).[1] References both to the Deaf community and to Deaf culture thus are typically written in the capitalized form. The Deaf community also has a rich history including art, humor, and literature in addition to sharing most of those enjoyed by hearing people. In this sense, it offers the same kind of cultural diversity available in the United States to African-American, Hispanic, or Jewish families who can appreciate both mainstream American culture and a link to a special heritage. Although *deaf* is sometimes used as a generic adjective, many people now use it in the audiological sense, to refer only to lack of hearing, preferring to use *Deaf* as a more restricted sociocultural term. Many deaf people thus do not consider themselves Deaf.

Being Big D Deaf   The Deaf community may only have come into public awareness relatively recently, but it has existed for a long time. Still, it is rarely seen by most hearing people, and many do not know anything about it other than what they glean from an occasional newspaper article or events during Deaf Awareness Week (the last full week in September).[2] In part, this situation follows from the nature of our society and the practicalities of being deaf in a largely hearing world. Most deaf adults and their children are part of a social group that is relatively more restricted or at least

more clearly bounded than other groups defined by, say, religious affiliation, political interests, or race. Such "separateness" should not be too
surprising. Why would anyone choose to be with people with whom they
could communicate only with great difficulty?

Like any other subculture, the Deaf community has its own social structures, organizations, attitudes, and values. The National Association of the
Deaf (NAD) has been in existence since 1880, but recent years have seen
the mobilization of a variety of other groups and greater political activity
by them and the NAD. Among the results of such activities are the Americans with Disabilities Act of 1990 and the creation of the National Institute on Deafness and Other Communication Disorders (a division of the
National Institutes of Health) which plays an important role in promoting
quality research relating to hearing loss and deaf children. These changes
are primarily reforms to the hearing culture in which the Deaf community
is immersed. But, they are providing a new understanding of deaf people
by hearing people through the improvement of deaf people's access to
public and private services and to new employment opportunities, and
through investigations of sign language, communication technologies, and
cognitive functioning of deaf adults and children.

Members of the Deaf community are defined primarily by their fluent
use of a natural sign language, such as ASL or BSL, but knowledge of the
rich cultural tradition of the community is also essential. This situation is
consistent with the *Oxford English Dictionary* definition of an ethnic group
as one delineated by a cultural background and claiming official recognition of their group identity. From this perspective, some hearing children
of deaf parents also are part of the Deaf ethnic group, even though they are
not deaf.

For deaf children of deaf parents, growing up in the context of this
social group has some specific consequences. Later chapters will consider
claims that deaf children of deaf parents may have some advantages over
deaf children of hearing parents. At the same time, this cultural and language-based separation can create some natural barriers between deaf and
hearing individuals similar to but perhaps more pronounced than those
that characterize other ethnic groups. In order to decipher the effects of
growing up deaf within hearing and Deaf cultures, we need to pay closer
attention to issues surrounding communication than we normally do with
hearing children. We also have to consider the special situation encountered by deaf children in hearing families, where parents may be unable
to communicate effectively with them. These topics, together with descriptions of sign language and several alternative communication systems are
the subjects of chapter 3.

Part of the reason for devoting so much attention to this issue of cultural identity comes from the fact that people who are deaf have long been
described in medical terms rather than as a people who share a language

and community. For similar reasons, the term "deafness" is frowned upon by some Deaf people who argue that it carries a connotation of pathology, even if the National Association of the Deaf uses the term quite freely in its publications.[3] It is difficult to talk about the field without a noun, however, as can be seen by the fact that the word has slipped into this chapter occasionally despite my efforts to use alternatives. It is also important to note that not all deaf people see themselves as part of a linguistic-cultural group separate from hearing people. Deaf people who grow up using spoken language often strive to be part of the hearing community and do not learn to sign. Others may sign in some situations but prefer to speak in others. Like those who consider themselves Deaf, "oral" deaf people have deaf, hearing, and hard-of-hearing friends with similar lifestyle preferences. Many join advocacy and social organizations comparable to those of the Deaf community, while others seek roles in multiple communities. Both Deaf and deaf people share many concerns and issues, particularly relating to communication access and equal opportunity. They may have differing opinions on other topics relating to deaf children and deaf education. As with anyone else, differences of opinion are expected and contribute to a healthy diversity of views.

What, then, exactly is meant by *deaf*? Hearing losses are not all-or-none; there is a continuum of hearing loss from those so subtle that they might not be noticed to losses so severe that hearing aids and other amplification devices are of little use. In this book, I will not use the word *deaf* to refer either to people who have lost some of their hearing as a normal part of growing older or to people who might have slight hearing losses, perhaps from ear infections as toddlers. Consistent with the primary focus of the book, I will apply it only to those children and adults with hearing losses that are classified as *severe* to *profound*—hearing losses that largely eliminate the use of speech and hearing for all of the practical purposes of day-to-day life (see chapter 2).

Hearing Loss Versus Hearing Impairment

For most hearing parents of deaf children, their child's hearing loss is at first seen as a major challenge, a problem that will interfere with family life, education, and potential success. Although family life certainly *is* different when hearing parents have a deaf child, there is no reason why hearing loss should create any insurmountable obstacles to developmental, educational, or career success. Some parents of deaf children will be told about all the things their child supposedly cannot do, but most educators of deaf children, as well as deaf people themselves, do not see hearing loss in the same light. The term *hearing impaired* is one that is used frequently, although less so in the United States than elsewhere. In 1991, a joint statement by the World Federation of the Deaf and the International Federation of Hard of Hearing People rejected *hearing-impaired* in favor of *deaf and hard of hearing,* but it remains popular in the United Kingdom, Australia, and elsewhere.

According to the World Health Organization (WHO), an *impairment* is any loss of physiological or psychological structure or function considered normal for human beings, whereas a *disability* is any restriction or lack of ability to perform "normally" due to an impairment (where "normally" simply means "like the majority of people"). A *handicap* is a disadvantage for a particular individual that results from an impairment or disability and that limits or prevents their full functioning in appropriate social and career roles (WHO, 1992). By these medical definitions, all deaf children have impairments, most have disabilities, and in the reality of today's world many will be handicapped, even if unnecessarily. An alternative and more accurate description, however, is that because of their hearing losses, deaf children lack full access to information and opportunities normally available to hearing children. Some of those experiences can be made available through cochlear implants or sign language, but not all (Spencer & Marschark, 2003). To the extent that the absence of particular kinds of experience affects deaf children's learning or behavior, there may be consequences for other aspects of development. But, whether or not such differences will have a lasting impact in the grand scheme of growing up is separate from the semantic issue of the terms we use to describe them. In other words, *differences* between deaf and hearing children need not imply *deficiencies.*

Although the above definitions are intended as medical descriptions, they have become generic labels that are applied to deaf children and deaf people at large. Many members of the Deaf community resent those labels, and the community prides itself as being unique among groups that normally would be considered "handicapped." Consistent with this community self-image, some investigators have argued that the best way to optimize the academic, career, and social success of deaf children is to consider them part of that linguistic-cultural minority deserving appropriate educational considerations. The reasons for this situation and its implications will require several more chapters to explain. Meanwhile, my goal is to emphasize the potential of deaf children, not traditional labels. It therefore will be important to remember that although deaf children can be members of multiple cultures, their development and education clearly depends on experiences that may not be available to them from hearing environments if special accommodations are not made. There is no value judgment implied here; it is simply a statement of fact, regardless of whether a deaf child wears a hearing aid, has a cochlear implant, or neither, and independent of one's beliefs and preferences about educating deaf students.

Sign Language

One final terminological distinction we have to make is that between the generic term "sign language" and natural signed languages like American Sign Language or ASL (once called "Ameslan"). The issue will be discussed in depth later, but for the moment we can use "sign language" to refer to any language that makes primary use of the hands and face to communicate grammatically through visual-spatial means. ASL, in contrast, refers to a specific language, used in the United States and in English-speaking parts of Canada. There is no universal sign language any more than there is a universal spoken language. Attempts in this regard, like *Gestuno* or *International Sign Language* (both used by signing deaf people in multi-national settings), have been no more successful than Esperanto, which was developed to become the universal spoken language. In the following sections, I will remain true to the above terminology in the hope of keeping some difficult issues from becoming confused. Rest assured that the distinctions are important and will surface again later. Meanwhile, I will choose my words carefully.

A Deaf Child in the Family

Imagine for the moment a hearing American couple adopting an 18-month-old hearing toddler from Korea. Bridging the language gap with children younger than 18 months seems like it would be relatively easy: The child will have some words and a few simple sentences in Korean, but not too many. The new family and the community then flood the child with language, both intentionally and unintentionally, and eventually she becomes fluent in English rather than Korean. At the same time, of course, she learns more than just a particular language. Through the spoken language that she hears, the child also learns who people are, about social rules and customs, about objects and events in the world, and about the uses of communication. This same process occurs quite naturally for the vast majority of young children in essentially all cultures. Language learning in more "natural" situations may be a bit less contrived and explicit than in the case of an international adoption—after all, most parent-child interactions involve language, regardless of which language it is—but the process is fundamentally the same.

Now consider the situation of a child who cannot hear. Hearing losses in children who are not considered "at risk" are quite rare. As a result, in the absence of universal newborn hearing screening, diagnosis typically does not occur until a deaf child is between 2 and 3 years of age, when his language has fallen noticeably behind his playmates or when the preschool teacher suggests that something might be wrong. Boys are only slightly more likely to have serious hearing losses than girls, but the warning signs of hearing loss are often recognized later for them, because boys are notorious as slower language learners.[4]

Relatively late diagnoses of hearing loss, on average, might be viewed two ways. From one perspective, if it takes 2 to 3 years to discover that a child is deaf, perhaps hearing loss does not have much of an impact during the first months of life. After all, how much hearing does a child need at that age? From another perspective, and the one that turns out to be correct, the late discovery of a hearing loss can have significant and far-reaching consequences. Late diagnoses mean that for the first months of life, when most infants are hearing and beginning to learn the sounds of their native language, deaf children are not. Deaf infants do not hear their mothers coming down the hall nor do they turn to look when she enters the room. Those children are not soothed by their mother's voice and do not respond to their to parents' attempts to have "baby talk" conversations. While these might seem like relatively minor problems, they will have a lasting impact on the children, their parents, and on the relationships between them.

There are, of course, ways other than speech in which parents can communicate with their deaf children. Within the first 24 hours after birth, for example, babies can distinguish their mothers from other women by how they smell, and by 3 days after birth, they can recognize their mothers by sight.[5] On the mother's side, several investigations have found that hearing mothers with deaf babies touch them more than do mothers with hearing infants. They also use more frequent and more exaggerated facial expression with their deaf infants, and they bring more things into their babies' lines of sight so that they can share experiences and play together. But our knowledge about this apparent compensation for the lack of hearing in mother-child interactions comes from observing mothers who already know that their infants are deaf and therefore recognize the need to do something more than talk to their babies.

Our naive assumption might be that hearing parents who unexpectedly have a deaf baby would go through a fairly long period of unintentionally treating him as though he could hear. They would talk to him and expect him to respond with attention, smiling, and his own share of gurgling and cooing. It likely would not take most parents very long to discover that talking to their baby is not as soothing as holding and stroking them, and those parents might be quickly "trained" by their babies to use more physical contact and face-to-face communication, even if they are unaware of it. Unfortunately, there is no way to evaluate this possibility, because as soon as a baby is identified as deaf, parents are likely to change their behavior.

During the first year or so of life, babies normally experience a variety of things that will have important consequences for language, social, and cognitive development. In the case of deaf babies of hearing parents, their early understanding of the world will be somewhat different from hearing babies and different from other deaf babies who have deaf parents. Later chapters will consider various aspects of deaf children growing up in a hearing families, as most do. First, however, it will be worthwhile to consider several different perspectives on deaf children and to get some background on relevant issues.

The Importance of Language

For those children whose hearing losses are sufficient to prevent their efficiently learning an oral (speaking) and aural (hearing) language, sign language can provide a viable alternative method for communication. The dilemma for many parents is deciding when hearing losses are "that severe" (see chapter 2). For many, learning sign language seems like a drastic step. Perhaps it is not quite as drastic as it would be if they were told they had to learn Chinese and use it all of the time, because you cannot speak Chinese and English at the same time. However, learning to sign and using it all the time is not an easy feat; and even those parents who sign and speak simultaneously have no guarantees that their children will be

either fluent signers or fluent users of English (see chapter 3).

The question *To sign or not to sign?* is just one of many issues facing the family of a deaf child, but it is perhaps the most central one. From soon after birth, and maybe even before (see chapter 4), language plays an essential role in parent-child relationships. Contrary to some popular beliefs, sign language works every bit as well as spoken language in educational

settings and social relationships, except perhaps with regard to reading and writing. That issue is a rather complex one, however, which will be held until chapter 7. Meanwhile, parents need to recognize that the majority of children who have profound hearing losses are unlikely to develop spoken language skills comparable to their hearing siblings. A study conducted in Colorado is informative in the regard, because that state has perhaps the most advanced program for early identification and intervention in the United States. Yet, even there, only about 25 percent of the children with profound hearing losses were found have intelligible speech by the time they were 5 to 6 years of age, despite having been identified at birth and receiving early intervention services from birth to 3 years of age. Seventy-five percent of children with mild to severe hearing losses were found to have intelligible speech by that age, in contrast, even when their hearing losses were discovered much later (Yoshinaga-Itano, 2006).

With regard to comprehension rather than production, *speechreading* or lipreading is much less efficient than is typically assumed, even if it can support speech reception for those children with lesser hearing losses and cochlear implants. Nevertheless, the average deaf adult with years of speechreading practice does not read lips much better than the average hearing adult. I know that this is counterintuitive. I once described the finding to a class of Italian special education students who would eventually be working with deaf children. My interpreter, an Italian educator familiar with deaf children in that country, was so convinced of the effectiveness of speechreading that she refused to translate my assertion to the contrary. She could not bring herself to tell those future teachers of deaf children something she "knew" was false! After finishing the lecture on my own in my poor Italian, I suggested that anyone who wanted to see how difficult it is to read lips should try a very simple experiment (one that readers can also try at home). In another room, we found a television set. We watched it first with normal volume, then with very low volume, and then with the volume off. While comprehension was still perfect at low volume, everyone was surprised when it suddenly became impossible when the volume was turned off. My colleague, for her part, never brought up the topic again.

It is important to raise another counterintuitive finding at this point, relating to speaking, hearing, and cochlear implants. As indicated in the preface, recent evidence has demonstrated the utility of cochlear implants for many, if not most, deaf children. As chapter 2 will show, however, children's speech reception and production with implants vary widely. In particular, although cochlear implantation often facilitates a child's receptive language through hearing in one-on-one settings, it is often less helpful in noisy (normal) classroom settings or without face-to-face contact. One of the best predictors of speech abilities after implantation is a child's prior expressive language ability, and it does not matter whether that expressive language is spoken or signed. That is, to the extent that sign language is easier for a young deaf child to learn than spoken language, early signing skill and early spoken language skill may be equally good predictors of later spoken language abilities. This suggestion is based on indirect evidence, however, and the issue will have to await further investigation.

Interestingly, in his classic pamphlet in support of "the oral method" for deaf children, Alexander Graham Bell (1898/2005) commented on the difference in the early ability to learn sign language (earlier championed by Charles Michel Abbé de l'Épée, in Paris):

It has been claimed that the de l'Épée language is an easier
language to learn than English. This may be so, but is that a

> sufficient reason for its use? Italian is probably easier than English; but that is no reason why we should make Italian the vernacular of an American child. That is no reason why we should teach him English by means of Italian. The very ease with which the de l'Épée Sign-language is acquired affords an explanation of the curious fact that it often usurps the place of English, as the vernacular of the deaf child, in spite of exclusion from the schoolroom, and against the wishes of the teachers. (p. 120)

Although there has never been any evidence that signing "usurps the place of English," we can agree with Bell that ease of learning alone is insufficient grounds to support signing over spoken language. As chapter 3 will reveal, however, there are other reasons that might favor signing for many children.

Perhaps most important in this context, the presence or absence of effective communication in early and later childhood has broad consequences for development. For deaf children with greater hearing losses, this situation may well mean that signing—with or without spoken language—is preferred to spoken language alone, at least during the early years. There is considerable evidence that deaf children who learn to sign at a young age tend to be better adjusted emotionally, have higher academic achievement during the early school years, and have better social relationships with parents and peers relative to deaf children raised in speech-only environments (Calderon & Greenberg, 1997). Both the available research findings and their conclusions are considerably more complex than this generalization would suggest, and we do not yet know whether cochlear implants will produce comparable effects. But, again, effective access to language is the key, and an early base in communication often is more easily and fully established via signing than via spoken language, at least for those children with greater hearing losses. The situation is more cloudy for those children with mild to moderate hearing losses, either "naturally" or through the aid of cochlear implants, who may learn spoken language more easily. The large variability among those children in both the degree of hearing loss and the sound frequencies of their losses (see chapter 2) means that it is difficult to make general statements about them. We can make one, however: all children need language models and the ability to make use of them—and the earlier the better!

Regrettably, many parents still complain that they have trouble getting information and advice about the "pros and cons" of spoken language and sign language. Some of this difficulty might result from parents being understandably sensitive and confused when they first learn that their child is deaf. Still, I have heard too many stories of audiologists leaving parents standing in clinic hallways with mouths open and heads buzzing and of misdiagnoses or denials of early hearing losses by trusted pediatricians.

Growing Up Deaf: Differences Versus Deficiencies

Family doctors are most accustomed to dealing with hearing children. The frequency of severe to profound hearing loss in the general population is so low that most pediatricians encounter deaf children only rarely if ever. Moreover, *congenital* (from birth) and *early onset* hearing losses are not so easily noticed unless one is looking for them. When physicians do encounter young children with serious hearing losses, they tend to view them in terms of the "pathology model" acquired during their medical school training. From that perspective, being deaf is considered a serious handicap and an impediment to normal development. True, being deaf deprives children of some of the experiences available to normally hearing children, like the enjoyment of music or the sound of oncoming cars, although powerful hearing aids and cochlear implants can give deaf children some access to these sounds. Other experiences may simply be different than they would be if their hearing were intact, like the rules of children's games or the way they learn to read. Anyone who has ever watched a basketball game between two schools for the deaf or the enthusiasm fostered by their cheerleaders, however, knows that some things are always the same.

The different experiences of hearing and deaf children, language related or not, will affect how they view and interact with the world in a variety of subtle and not-so-subtle ways. In the case of deaf children of deaf parents, their full range of "natural" experiences will lead to their passing through most developmental stages at the same rate as hearing children. For deaf children of hearing parents, early experiences may not blend so readily into the background of family and community life. For them, the potentially limited or atypical nature of their experiences can lead to differences in their social, language, and perhaps their intellectual functioning relative to hearing children. But wait, there is more!

My primary reason for emphasizing differences between deaf and hearing children at this point is a practical one. There is an understandable impulse on the part of many of us to deny or minimize handicaps that are not visible. A Deaf man once told me that deaf people do not receive as much understanding or consideration as those with other handicaps because deaf people "look too normal." Indeed, it is easier for most people to recognize and accept the obstacles faced by someone in a wheelchair than someone with a learning disability, or by someone who is blind than someone who is deaf. But, denying a child's hearing loss or any other possible impediment to full access, no matter how stress reducing to parents or grandparents in the short run, does no one any good in the long run. Eventually, overlooking children's difficulties catches up with them, with their parents, and with society. Sometimes the realization comes too late; it always comes at a higher price.

Let us return to the language-learning issue as an example. It is easy enough to understand the desire of most hearing parents to have a normally speaking and acting child. The truth is, the majority of deaf children will never sound like their hearing brothers and sisters, no matter how much speech therapy they have and whether or not they have a cochlear implant. Delaying decisions about learning sign language or getting an implant can make matters more difficult for both children and their parents. The first years of life are when basic language skills develop, and the first 2 to 3 years are generally recognized as very important for language learning. There is no substitute for natural language learning, and language acquisition that begins at age 4 or 5 is not natural. Similarly, we will see later that the age of cochlear implantation (<3 years, 3–5 years, or older than 5 years) will have a significant effect on reading ability many years later (Archbold, Nikolopoulos, O'Donoghue, & White, 2006).

It should be apparent by this point that the necessity of early language—any language—is an assumption that guides most of our thinking about the normal development of all children. For centuries, philosophers and scientists have sought to understand the relation between language and thinking (see chapter 8 and Marschark & Spencer, 2006). This debate was a particularly popular pastime during the eighteenth and nineteenth centuries, with deaf individuals being used as examples on both sides of the argument! We now know that although the language we use does not *determine* the way we think, the language that children learn and the context in which they learn it will affect the way that they view the world. It is not just the explicit teaching in the classroom that requires and contributes to fluency in language. In addition, the vast majority of most children's experience comes in the form of language or accompanied by language. Our perceptions and conceptions of the world will be colored just as much by the way something is described as by its factual content.

Most of young children's experiences in the world thus will be shaped by the language of parents who are communicating with a particular purpose in mind. It does not matter much if the parents are using English, Japanese, ASL, or Auslan; the content and effects of that communication are always present. Therefore, if a child does not receive any language or receives only impoverished language input, an essential component of development will be missing. Parents of deaf children with greater hearing losses can compensate for their children's lack of hearing once they become aware of the loss through newborn hearing screening or later audiological assessment. In many countries (and not so long ago in the United States), however, hearing parents are often unaware that their child is deaf. The primary issues we need to consider thus will concern how parents normally interact with their deaf infants, both before and after the diagnoses of their hearing losses, and the consequences of those interactions throughout childhood.

Family Adjustment to Early Childhood Hearing Loss

The diagnosis of a significant hearing loss in a young child and a hearing family's adjustment to its new situation have a variety of ramifications. One of the most important things to keep in mind is that the entire family is affected by having a deaf child. Although mothers tend to take the greater share of responsibility for dealing with the added necessities of a deaf child (or any other child with special needs), the effects of such changes are felt by each member of the family. Frequently forgotten in the new and sometimes stressful situation are the older children, who now are likely to receive somewhat less attention than they did prior to their sibling's diagnosis (see chapter 9). I knew one couple who avoided this problem by putting a note on their door requesting visitors to remember to pay attention to the hearing 4-year-old sister of a deaf toddler. Whatever the methods, the goal of parents and children alike in this situation should be to maintain comfortable and "normal" interactions within the home. In this, the whole family is involved and has to work together with patience and understanding.

It is well worth emphasizing that no matter how anxious or guilty a hearing couple may feel when they discover that their child is deaf, those feelings do pass. Any stress between the parents because of their different ways of responding to the situation also will dissipate, and there is no evidence that having a deaf child impacts a marriage in any way that affects its success or failure. Once the initial shock passes, parents start to collect useful information on what it means to be deaf and how to accommodate their child's hearing loss. Things that initially may have seemed overwhelming are recognized as being less burdensome than they originally appeared. This is not to say that gathering unbiased information is easy. Many parents report feeling bewildered when they first receive a diagnosis of hearing loss in their young child and all too often complain about an apparent lack of sensitivity on the part of medical professionals about their need for advice on where to start their search for information and support services.

An example of this situation was recounted by two of my colleagues (Hurwitz & Hurwitz, 2004). When they noticed that their 3-year-old son Bernard was not playing with other children and his teacher reported that he was not talking to anyone in school, they had his hearing tested (this was before newborn hearing screening in their state). During the visit, an audiologist took Bernard to his office while his parents sat in the waiting room. Approximately 15 minutes later, the audiologist came back dragging Bernard, who was crying. He told the parents that he could do nothing with the child, who he said was not cooperative during the test. The audiologist told the parents to bring the child back when he was "good and ready." The parents were furious at the way Bernard was handled and demanded that the audiologist do the test again in their presence and with their assistance. At first, the audiologist hesitated to comply with their request, but he finally relented to their persistence. In the testing room, the audiologist handed Bernard an abacus with colored beads for him to slide from one side to another each time he heard a sound. There was no communication or explanation from the audiologist to Bernard. Bernard was hesitant and frightened at not understanding what was expected of him.

At this point, the father intervened, and turned the testing session into a game which his son clearly enjoyed. To the surprise of the audiologist, the test was now completed smoothly. It showed that Bernard had a significant hearing loss. Then, the doctor appeared on the scene:

> The doctor told us that Bernard had "inner ear deafness." We asked for further explanation about the nature of the deafness and what recourse, if any, we had. At that point, a hearing aid dealer came into the office to talk with the doctor, and as he left, the doctor told us he had to leave for lunch. We were dumbfounded with his rudeness in leaving us alone, so we demanded the time to speak with him. He simply told us to go to a hearing and speech clinic and then left. We sat in the office in a daze.

Unfortunately, this kind of experience is not unusual, and you can imagine the hurt and anger experienced by the parents. Actually, these parents are deaf. Imagine what the experience would have been like for hearing parents who would have had almost no idea what the audiologist and otolaryngologist were talking about!

Not surprisingly, research has shown that parents who receive emotional and practical support from their family and friends are best able to cope with the demands of having a deaf child. This finding reinforces the notion that support groups and early intervention services involving other parents and professionals involved with young deaf children are invaluable resources. In fact, one of the best (and simplest) predictors of how well a child will fare with a cochlear implant is how much time parents spend gathering information on the subject. This positive relationship comes about partly because well-informed parents have a pretty good idea of whether their child is likely to be a good candidate and thus are less likely to implant a child who is not. Being well-informed also allows parents to have reasonable expectations for themselves and their deaf child. Information gathering, of course, is not just pertinent in the case of cochlear implants, but is an essential responsibility of parents who have a deaf child, especially during the first months of life.

Down the road, parents' abilities to function and deal with their children's being deaf will affect the child in a variety of ways. Those parents who are more secure and confident about themselves tend to treat their deaf children in ways that lead to better social and emotional adjustment in childhood and eventually doing better in school. Findings of this sort clearly indicate the need for greater training for hearing parents throughout their deaf children's formative years. Parents need to be educated about childhood hearing loss and its consequences, about the possible special needs of deaf children to ensure normal development, and about the educational alternatives open to deaf children and their families.

Just as the causes and characteristics of childhood deafness vary widely, so do the early experiences of deaf children and the abilities of parents and families to adapt to the changes that accompany having a deaf child. These changes are not always dramatic and need not be negative. Nevertheless, parental acceptance of children's hearing losses and adjustment to their needs are essential for a normal childhood. This understanding has implications not only for parents and teachers of deaf children, but also for anyone who has contact with deaf children or with children who are academically—or emotionally—challenged for any reason.

It is essential to remember that, as with most generalities, those that are applied to deaf children in this book are rarely accurate in individual cases. The strengths and needs of each child must be considered, and we must be aware that deaf children likely are even more variable than hearing children (who clearly differ considerably from each other even within families). Perhaps most important, parents should be wary of taking advice about deaf children from people who are not knowledgeable about deafness or do not have first-hand experience. In this situation, "knowledgeable" does not necessarily refer to those of us who are trained in a relevant field and have diplomas or certificates hanging on the office wall. Professionals will be able to provide important information related to language, hearing aids, and so on. However, we often have our own biases, usually based on where and how we were trained. I therefore believe that because we are *authorities,* parents and teachers sometimes may be too quick to accept our advice as necessarily the "only true path." To really understand what it means to have a deaf child, there is no substitute for chatting with other parents who have been or are currently working their ways through similar issues. At this juncture, local groups or national organizations like the American Society for Deaf Children or Hands and Voices can be important sources of information and support. Early intervention programming for deaf children and their parents also will play a central role in helping the family adjust to having a deaf child and establishing a context for healthy development.

Early Intervention

Early intervention programs are often assumed to be for deaf children, but they are just as important to parents of young deaf children. For that reason, many of those programs are now referred to as *parent-infant programs* instead. Such programs focus on language development, parent-child communication, social skills, and appropriate support for any residual hearing children might have, as well as testing and evaluation for hearing aids and cochlear implants. Parent-infant interventionists provide parents with strategies for enhancing their children's development, including instruction in sign language, speech training, or both, depending on the particular program. They usually are designed to accommodate youngsters from birth until their entry into preschool (see chapter 6).

As our understanding of the role of the environment in development and learning by deaf children has improved, greater attention has been given to the social-emotional mosaic of the family and the deaf child's place in it, with parent-infant programs at the forefront. Chapter 2 will emphasize that having a deaf child changes the dynamics of the entire family, and recently there has been an emphasis on *family-centered* early intervention programs for deaf children (Brown & Nott, 2006; Sass-Lehrer & Bodner-Johnson, 2003). Family-centered intervention emphasizes the strength of the family in making decisions and collaborating with relevant professionals, and it typically involves working with children and their parents in the home instead of, or in addition to, other settings. Parents in the United States were given a greater role in making educational decisions for their deaf child under the Education of All Handicapped Children Act (PL 94-142) in 1975, and 20 years later the importance of family-centered programming gained a central place under IDEA (PL 99-457, Part C, Early Intervention Program for Infants and Toddlers).

Family-centered intervention has been particularly important with regard to providing families with information and the skills necessary to support the development of communication and language in deaf children. Programs emphasizing visual communication (Mohay, Milton, Hindmarsh, & Ganley, 1998), spoken language (Brown & Nott, 2006), or both encourage communication between parents and their deaf child in the context of day-to-day activities, fostering child learning and parent confidence. The result is greater parental involvement (but less intrusiveness) in their children's activities, a situation known to enhance both early language development and later academic achievement. Indeed, family involvement has been found to be a stronger predictor of early language development than either the age at which early intervention begins or a child's degree of hearing loss (Moeller, 2000).

As with most early intervention programs, family-centered programs are about much more than just language. Because they are able to take into account the specific needs of parents and siblings as well as the deaf child, such programs can have a more holistic view of the family dynamic. Language can be considered in the context of social-emotional development and cognitive development, recognizing their mutual effects on each other and on early experience. Most importantly, this sort of programming emphasizes that each family is different in its needs, priorities, and methods of coping. For children who have multiple handicaps, family-centered intervention provides a means of integrating support for children's diverse needs within the realistic constraints of the home environment. With the recent expansion of universal newborn hearing screening, we have the opportunity for seamless support for deaf children and their families from birth onward. Not everyone has access to such opportunities, but as new early intervention programs are established, a family-oriented perspective helps to optimize opportunities and outcomes.

Final Comments

The vast majority of deaf children have hearing parents, and those parents usually are unprepared to deal with the emotional and practical issues related to having a deaf child. Whether due to denial or misunderstanding, without newborn hearing screening, diagnoses of hearing losses in children who are not seen as "at risk" frequently do not occur until two to three years of age. Resulting delays in deaf children's access to language during the critical stages of development (the first 2 to 3 years) have a variety of consequences in social, language, and academic areas. Newborn hearing screening (see chapter 2) and early intervention can help to support deaf infants and their families, but neither they nor implants make deaf children into hearing children

Sign language can provide deaf children with access to the "information flow" of people around them, providing that their parents and teachers are consistent signers—even if they are not fluent. Learning to sign as an adult is as difficult as learning any foreign language, however, and some people have considerable difficulty in learning a second language, whether spoken or signed. This situation may be even more complex for hearing parents who have discovered that their child is deaf and who may be receiving conflicting or incomplete advice.

Although many hearing parents will view their deaf child as disabled, the vast majority of deaf people are fully normal, contributing members of the community. Within the Deaf community, art, Deaf history, and Deaf culture provide people with a unique identity and a network of friends, but they are simultaneously part of the larger inclusive community. Other deaf people choose to assimilate within the hearing community, do not sign (or do so rarely), and are involved with groups like the Alexander Graham Bell Association of the Deaf and Hard of Hearing, and Self-Help for the Hard of Hearing (SHHH). Therefore, most deaf people, regardless of their identification with one community or other, resent patronizing attitudes that suggest that their lives are any less full or successful than those of hearing people.

In the spirit of avoiding some of the common overgeneralizations about early childhood hearing loss, let us look at some of them. Most of these are discussed at various places later in this book, and some have already been mentioned. Just to clear up some of the inaccurate claims at the outset, however, it generally is *not* true that:

- Deaf children who learn to sign will not learn to speak.
- Deaf children and adults are very quiet.
- Hearing aids and cochlear implants enable deaf children to understand speech (they do help them to hear speech, but understanding it is a different matter).
- All deaf children can be taught to "read lips."
- Deaf children are less intelligent than hearing children.
- Deaf children have more emotional difficulties than hearing children.
- *Mainstreaming* (placement in a local public school classroom rather than a special setting) is the best way to educate all deaf children.
- Deaf children will not have many friends.
- American Sign Language is a form of English.
- All deaf people use sign language.
- Deaf people cannot drive cars because they cannot hear.

It generally *is* true that:

- Deaf children usually cannot hear how much noise they are making.
- Hearing aids may enable some deaf children to understand speech.
- Children with cochlear implants, on average, hear as well as hard-of-hearing children.
- Speechreading is very difficult, especially in English.
- Deaf children tend to have more academic difficulty than hearing children, especially in learning to read and write.
- Deaf children may have behavioral problems in school, but these usually are traceable to home environments or medical issues and are not due to their hearing losses.
- Placement in integrated public school classrooms works for some deaf children but not others.
- American Sign Language is a language in its own right and differs from English in grammar and vocabulary.
- Most deaf people hold regular jobs and are fully functioning members of society.
- Most deaf people resent the patronizing attitudes of hearing people.

In most respects, then, deaf and hearing children are much the same. Like hearing children, deaf children's success begins with acceptance and communication at home. Attention to their special needs acknowledges that deaf children may be different from hearing peers, but those differences should not be taken to mean that deaf children are in any way "defective." Instead, it is essential that we recognize that deaf children vary greatly—just like hearing children—and we have to treat them as individuals. Optimizing their opportunities in school and the social world requires a more complete understanding of deaf people and related issues than most hearing people will ever obtain in their own communities. The remainder of this book therefore will provide a survey of what we currently know about the language, social, and intellectual development of deaf children and will extensively consider the educational and practical issues confronting them and their families. First, we will consider characteristics of deaf children—and of the deaf population in general—as well as several issues relating to communication and language, whether signed or spoken.

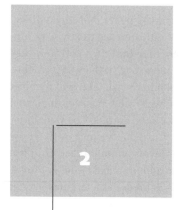

I never knew air conditioning makes noise!
—A friend with a new cochlear implant

Practical Aspects
of Being Deaf

In chapter 1, we touched on the kinds of adjustments that may be necessary for parents of deaf children. If we really want to understand the development of deaf children, however, we need a feeling for the worlds they grow up in and the various factors that shape their futures. Before considering the details of deaf children's early development within either hearing or deaf families, it will be helpful to consider some of the practical aspects of being deaf.

In the Lands of the Deaf

During the 1960s, when I was growing up just outside Washington, D.C., I knew about Gallaudet University (then Gallaudet College), which is the only free-standing liberal arts college for deaf students in the United States. My only experience on the campus—attending basketball games—impressed me primarily because they were so noisy. I noticed a lot of hearing aids at the games, but I do not recall their making much of an impact on me at the time. My mother once explained that because most of the students could not hear, the vibrations of the big bass drum in the bleachers were just as important as its sound. I am sure that she meant it both as a science lesson and cultural lesson, but all it meant to me was that I could join in, stamping my feet and cheering as much as I wanted—no one seemed to notice.

Living now in Rochester, New York, where there are about 10,000 people who are deaf and another 60,000 who are hard of hearing,[1] it is easy for me to forget how difficult it must be for the only deaf child in a town or county that has scarce resources and little understanding of what it means to be deaf. A colleague who grew up deaf in Kansas captured this well when he told me, "There were only three interpreters in the whole state when I was growing up. When one of them was out on disability, it was a big deal. Medical, legal, and educational activities all were disrupted." Today, in contrast, Rochester, New York, alone has over 250 interpreters!

Most deaf children and their parents will have experiences more like that of my Kansas friend than a child lucky enough to grow up deaf in Washington, D.C., or Rochester, New York.[2] Unless they happen to live in a metropolitan area or a city that has a school for the deaf, children and their parents are unlikely to interact with—much less really get to know—any other deaf children or deaf adults. This situation has implications not only for interpreting and other services, but also for the availability of deaf role models and sign language teachers for deaf children and their parents.

Although a variety of early intervention programs are available in this country (see chapter 6), many hearing parents of deaf children initially have to rely on their own resources and those of a variety of public and private groups. Local school boards also may be helpful, but parents first have to understand the issues and know the right questions to ask. The remainder of this chapter therefore provides preliminary information about the frequency and causes of various kinds of hearing loss and the kinds of technology that help to support hearing.

Describing the Deaf Population

Any attempt to provide complete and precise descriptions of "deaf people" or "deaf children" is unlikely to succeed. Like the members of any other group, deaf individuals in the United States vary widely. In some ways, they vary even more widely than the population of hearing individuals. In the case of the deaf children, there is variation contributed by differences in whether their hearing losses are *congenital* (present at birth) or *adventitious* (acquired), *acute* (sudden) or *progressive* (increasing over time), caused by medical or genetic factors, by whether they are born into deaf or hearing families, and by the quality and type of education they receive. Whether or not these variables are any more important than the many factors that affect hearing children, they are in addition to the normal sources of variation that can influence development and as such seem destined to make for a more diverse population.

As will become clear through the rest of this book, it appears that several direct and indirect effects of hearing loss have a greater impact on deaf children's development than anything experienced by most hearing children. To the extent that deaf children begin their lives by heading down somewhat different roads than hearing children, simple comparisons between the two groups will yield only partial information—and can lead to misleading conclusions. Consideration of differences among deaf children will be more informative in many cases, especially insofar as they point up aspects of children's situations that are particularly influential for fostering subsequent development. Because of variability within this group, expressions like "the typical deaf child" will be of little use. At the same time, while trying to avoid unfounded stereotypes, it must be acknowledged that they usually are the result of how individuals within a group are perceived. Stereotypes thus are often rooted in fact, even if they are not universally applicable.

In order to understand the influences of individual differences among children who are growing up deaf, it is important to examine the character of the community in which they are immersed. The definitions and the demographics relating to hearing loss have to be considered together in this context for the simple reason that the number of people counted as *deaf* will depend on how the term is defined. In part this situation arises because there is no legal definition of deafness comparable to the legal definition for blindness. Recent figures from the (U.S.) National Center for Health Statistics (NCHS), however, indicate that over 35 million people, more than 10 percent of the population have some difficulty hearing (although various other estimates put the number anywhere from 10 million to 38 million). Over half of those people, however, have age-related hearing losses. About 6,000,000 people in the United States (2.2 percent of the population) report having "a lot of trouble" hearing, and another 600,000 are described as "deaf." These numbers make deafness easily the single most prevalent, chronic, physical disability in the United States. The problem is that these broad categories include both people like my father, who had a hearing loss that interfered with his conversations in moderately noisy rooms but not on the telephone,[3] and people like my racquetball partner, who has no hearing at all.

Approximately one in 1000 infants is born with a hearing loss greater than or equal to 70 dB (*decibels,* see below) in the better ear. *Bilateral* (in both ears) hearing losses ≤ 35dB occur about once in every 750 births, on average, still a surprisingly high *prevalence* (frequency) for a condition considered potentially disabling (Cone-Wesson, 2003). This rate of congenital hearing loss plus the frequency of acquired hearing losses suggests there may be more than 100,000 children in the United States with some degree of loss, and more than 70,000 have hearing losses of sufficient severity to have received related special education services. The prevalence of hearing loss in young children thus remains a significant issue in the United States, medical advances notwithstanding. The situation is surely more varied and complex elsewhere. Among Australian indigenous children, for example, who are both prone to middle ear infections (otitis media) and often live in remote areas where medical treatment and antibiotics are in short supply, 25–30 percent have been reported to have significant hearing losses! Similar numbers have been suggested by colleagues working with Inuit children in northern Canada.

According to government data for the general population in the United States, males are about 30 percent more likely to be deaf than females, whites are about twice as likely as African-Americans to be deaf, and non-Hispanics are about twice as likely as Hispanics/Latinos to be deaf. The extent to which these differences are due to environmental versus genetic factors remains uncertain. Among American deaf children, 54 percent are males, 50 to 60 percent are reported to be white, approximately 16 percent are Hispanic/Latino, and 10 percent are African American. Overall, about 20 percent of individuals who are categorized as having significant hearing loss in the United States experienced the onset of those losses prior to age 18 years; about 5.5 percent of those prior to age 3.

Causes and Consequences of Early Hearing Loss

Before discussing hearing loss, let us consider hearing. This section is somewhat technical, and some readers may wish to skip it and come back to it later, if necessary, as a reference. In either case, after treatments of hearing and hearing loss, we will be in a position to consider the early identification of hearing losses and various aids to support hearing after those losses are determined.

Mechanisms of Hearing

Sound   If a tree falls in the forest and there is no one to hear it, does it make a sound? Technically, according to a (deaf) physicist I know, the fact that a falling tree sets up a *compressional wave train* that *could be* heard makes the answer "yes." In order for sounds to be heard, however, there has to be a force that sets up vibrations (perhaps a falling tree) in a medium (like air or water) that conducts the vibrations to a receiver who can "decode" the *acoustic* (physical) vibrations into an *auditory* (perceptual) event. If we were actually standing in the forest when the tree fell, pressure waves caused by the tree hitting the ground would create vibrations in the air molecules around it, and those vibrations—or sound waves— would wash over us and travel some distance until they faded out. Our perception of the sound would vary both in loudness (related to the amount of pressure) and in pitch (related to the wavelength, the distance between waves).

The decibel (dB) is the common unit of measurement for the intensity of sounds, perceived as loudness. For example, the loudness of normal speech in an otherwise quiet environment is about 60–65 dB. The music of rock bands begins at about 85–90 dB and goes up to 115 dB. This volume is 10 percent louder than a jackhammer, and many of our more senior rock musicians now have significant hearing losses. Traveling in a car at 55 miles per hour, with the windows rolled up, air conditioning and heat off, and no one talking produces background noise of about 80 dB. NASCAR drivers, in contrast, are constantly bombarded with noise up to 100 dB and more, perhaps explaining why some of them have apparent hearing losses and affections for loud country music. Equally loud automobile noise also can be caused by three children, a dog, and a radio in an air conditioned car on the way to the beach. Luckily, that noise does not last long, and its effects are only temporary.

Intensity is not the only factor affecting whether we can hear speech, because the particular frequency or pitch of a sound makes a big difference in what is heard. Normally, humans can hear sounds in the range of 20 to 20,000 hertz (Hz). Dogs can hear sounds over 30,000 Hz; hence the effectiveness of "silent" dog whistles too high-pitched for us to hear. When it comes to human speech, losses that affect hearing in the range of 500 Hz to 2000 Hz are those that are most troublesome, because those are the frequencies at which the important features of spoken language are expressed. Vowels tend to fall in the lower frequency range, while consonants fall in the higher frequency range. Vowels are also louder than consonants, but they are not as important for distinguishing one word from another; and hearing a word is not the same as being able to understand it.

For children with hearing losses already present at birth or appearing soon thereafter, the particular frequencies affected can vary considerably, with a comparably broad range of implications. Thus, while the severity of hearing loss is usually given in terms of decibel loss or the hearing threshold in the better ear across all frequencies, referred to as their *PTA* or *pure tone average* (the average threshold or loss across all sound frequencies), consideration of any individual child must focus on qualitative as well as quantitative aspects of auditory loss and any remaining ability to discriminate sounds. This caution is especially important with milder hearing losses, in which the patterns of frequency loss tend to vary the widest. The hearing losses most frequently seen in older adults, in contrast, tend to affect the ability to hear sounds at higher frequencies before the lower frequencies. This explains why your grandfather often can hear his (male) friends' voices but not your grandmother's (even if she thinks he does it on purpose!).

With this background, the physics of sound and hearing becomes relatively straightforward: To say that a sound has a higher frequency means that more waves occur per unit of time. If you imagine blowing into a 2-liter soda bottle filled half-way with water, it will make a higher-pitched sound than blowing into an empty container. When there is water in the bottle, the vibrations created in the bottle neck do not have as much room to expand in the smaller areas, resulting in smaller wavelengths and the higher frequency sounds. Similarly, the shorter vocal cords and smaller chest volumes of most children and females compared to adult males usually makes their voices higher in frequency. Different "production devices" thus have different characteristic frequencies of sound, and the same device often can be made to make higher or lower frequency sounds by changing their shapes—like a slide whistle or a trombone. To perceive the full range of sound, "reception devices" (like ears) have to be able to be sensitive to and respond appropriately to that variability.

Ears   How do we hear? The *auricle or pinna* (outer ear) funnels vibrations in the air through the *external auditory meatus* (ear canal) to the *tympanic membrane* (eardrum), which vibrates in response to the changing pressure (see Figure 2–1). That vibration causes small movements in the three-bone chain of the *malleus* (hammer), *incus* (anvil), and *stapes* (stirrup) of the middle ear, the smallest bones in the human body. The linked movement of the hammer, anvil, and stirrup (collectively known as the *ossicles*) transmits the vibrations through its connection to the *oval window* (actually, another membrane, like the eardrum), which causes vibrations in the inner ear fluids that lie on its other side. Higher frequencies have shorter distances between waves and therefore make for faster vibrations that are passed along this chain.

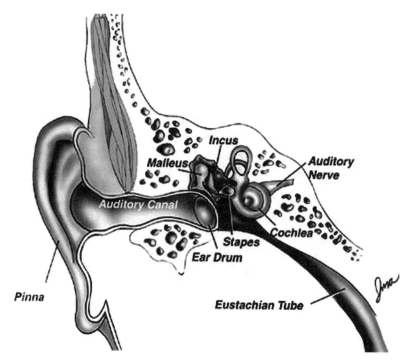

Figure 2–1. Schematic diagram of the human ear (Courtesy National Institutes of Health)

The inner ear houses both the organs of balance, most notably the *semicircular canals* (involved in balance) and the *cochlea*. The snail-like spiral of the cochlea contains, among other things, the *basilar membrane*, a soft tube that holds the sensory cells that actually "receive" sound. The sensory cells themselves are actually four parallel rows of more than 20,000 hair cells. The outer spiral of the cochlea responds to the lowest frequency sounds, with reception of higher and higher frequencies as the cochlea spirals inward. When the oval window creates movement in the fluids of the inner ear, the basilar membrane rubs against an adjacent (*tectorial*) membrane, creating a shearing force on the hair cells similar to the feeling of rubbing your hand back and forth on velvet. This stimulation of the cells, in turn, creates nerve impulses that are carried to the auditory centers of the brain by the auditory nerve . . . at least in most people.[4]

Mechanisms of Hearing Loss

When illness, accident, or hereditary factors reduce the amount of hearing someone has, the resulting losses generally are categorized as *conductive, sensorineural* (or *sensory-neural*), or *central*.

Conductive Hearing Loss   *Conductive* hearing losses are those that hinder the transmission of vibrations through the mechanism of the middle ear. Usually, the damage is to either the eardrum or the ossicles, which restricts the vibration of the bones against the oval window, although conductive losses also can include blockage of the ear canal. Some children are born with or develop severe problems with their eardrums, and occasionally one or more ossicles may be missing or malformed. Most frequently, conductive losses are the result of severe or repeated middle ear infections, collectively referred to as *otitis media,* that inflame and damage the eardrum or the ossicles, reducing the perceived intensity of sound. Otitis media accounts for over 10 million visits to the family doctor each year in this country. Many children have repeated bouts of ear infections that can temporarily impair their eardrums and their hearing. Repeated cases can sometimes lead to speech impediments which usually disappear with speech therapy. More severe cases lead to varying degrees of permanent hearing loss, making otitis media one of the most common nongenetic causes of hearing loss seen in infants and children.

Sensorineural and Central Hearing Loss   *Sensorineural* hearing losses, which can be either congenital or acquired, typically involve the cochlea or its connections to the auditory nerve (from "sensory" to "neural"). *Central* or *cortical* hearing losses involve auditory centers of the brain or the "brain end" (rather than the "ear end") of the auditory nerve. Both kinds of losses usually affect particular frequencies of sound—unfortunately, precisely those frequencies needed to hear speech. Because sensorineural and central hearing losses actually reduce or eliminate the transmission or reception of nerve impulses "representing" sound, people with such hearing losses cannot benefit from bone conduction, and they cannot hear their own voices. As will be described in a later section of this chapter, it is here that cochlear implants have their primary benefit.

Tinnitus, a condition most common in older adults, may occur in individuals with sensorineural hearing losses. It is often referred to as "ringing in the ears," although some people hear hissing, roaring, whistling, chirping, or clicking. Tinnitus can be so intense as to be confused with telephones or doorbells (at least by hearing people). On reading this description in the first edition, one deaf friend wrote of tinnitus: "I've had it consistently for 30 years. It screams at me like a music that haunts." In fact, tinnitus is a general term referring to the perception of sound in one or both ears or in the head when no external sound is present. It can be intermittent or constant—with single or multiple tones—and its perceived volume can range from subtle to shattering. According to the American Tinnitus Association, over 50 million people in the United States have some degree of tinnitus; and about 12 million have sufficiently severe symptoms that they seek medical attention. Perhaps 2 million people have tinnitus so severe that they cannot function normally on day-to-day basis. Although the cause of tinnitus is unclear, it can be triggered or worsened by exposure to loud noise, wax build-up in the ear canal, or damage caused by drugs, infections, head injuries, or jaw misalignment.

Degrees of Hearing Loss

When a hearing loss affects only the intensity of sound perception, amplification can improve reception if the loss is not too great. Loss of intensity frequently is not uniform across all frequencies, however, and as I have already noted, higher frequencies usually are affected more than lower frequencies. For this reason, digital hearing aids, which can be adjusted to augment particular frequencies, are often more helpful than analog hearing aids, which equally amplify sounds at all frequencies (see below).

Regardless of the kind or cause of childhood hearing loss, the measurement of most practical interest is the pure tone hearing threshold in the better ear. This is essentially the limit of potential hearing in any particular frequency range. Hearing is considered normal with losses up to 25 decibels (dB) in the better ear. Losses from 26 to 40 dB are *mild,* those from 41–55 dB are *moderate,* and those from 56–70 dB are *moderately severe.* Hearing losses from 71–90 dB are *severe* and those over 91 dB in the better ear are considered *profound.* Most frequently, conductive hearing losses are less severe, ranging up to about 60 dB. Hearing losses above that level typically are of the sensorineural variety and are the ones that cause difficulty for children growing up in hearing environments. It will be useful to keep these broad categories in mind (or turn over the corner of this page) when reading the following sections. It also will be helpful to keep in mind that both intensity and frequency affect whether and what we hear. Even children with profound hearing losses can have some residual hearing. The most important question is whether it is in a frequency range relevant to speech perception.

Hard of hearing is a term frequently encountered in reference to hearing loss. To most people, "hard of hearing people" represent a larger group than "deaf people." *Deaf* people are usually thought of as those who do not have sufficient hearing for it to play a role in day-to-day life. Hard-of-hearing people, in contrast, are people like our parents or grandparents who simply do not hear quite as much as they used to. Some educators and public officials describe hard-of-hearing people not as those with a broader range of hearing losses, but as those who have been able to acquire a spoken language, regardless of the extent of their hearing losses. The most interesting aspect of this distinction is that, rightly or wrongly, it highlights the frequent centrality of spoken language in deciding who is deaf and who is not. In most cases, those children who show the greatest skill for acquisition of a spoken language will be those who have more *residual* (remaining) hearing. It seems odd, however, that two children with identical hearing losses might be differentially identified as "deaf" and "hard of hearing" solely because of the emphasis their parents have placed on sign language or spoken language, respectively. Similarly, two people may have comparable hearing losses, but one may have excellent lipreading skills while the other does not. The former thus may appear to be hard of hearing, but the difference between the two is unrelated to hearing per se. In the present context therefore, the term "hard of hearing" will be avoided, and references to various degrees of hearing loss, where necessary, will be based on *audiological* (hearing-related) definitions. Generally, though, people with *mild* to *moderate* hearing losses are considered hard of hearing.

Causes of Hearing Loss

Etiologies (or causes) of hearing loss in children vary widely, although accurate data are difficult to find. According to one recent survey, almost half of the cases of significant hearing losses in children were present at birth. Another 23 percent had onsets after birth, with the remainder unknown or not reported. Among those children for whom the causes of their hearing losses were reported, 13 percent were linked to hereditary factors, 8.7 percent to pregnancy or birth complications such as prematurity and Rh incompatibility, 8.1 percent to meningitis, and 4.0 percent to infections/fevers including measles and mumps. Some etiologies are never discovered. It is noteworthy that bacterial meningitis is more likely to cause permanent hearing loss than viral meningitis. Hearing losses linked to meningitis occur more frequently in minority populations, presumably due to reduced access to health care. At one time, *maternal rubella* (or German measles) was the single greatest cause of hearing loss in children, culminating in the rubella epidemic of 1963–1965, which led to 30,000–40,000 babies being born deaf. With the development of a rubella vaccine in 1969, rubella has receded as a major cause of congenital and early onset deafness, and it now accounts for only about 2 percent of the cases.

Congenital hearing losses can result from illnesses prior to birth on the part of either mother or fetus, illnesses during childhood, or from hereditary (genetic) factors that are not yet fully understood. It long was assumed that heredity accounted for about 20–30 percent of all childhood deafness. With recent advances in genetics, we now know that although only 25 percent of deaf children come from families with histories of hearing loss, approximately 80 percent of the cases of childhood hearing loss have a genetic component (Arnos & Pandya, 2003). Indeed, recent studies have identified several dozen genes involved in deafness, and 50–60 percent of all moderate to profound sensorineural hearing losses in young children now appear to result from more than 400 different forms of hereditary deafness. Such *syndromic* hearing losses (that is, hearing loss as part of a larger syndrome with other characteristics as well) may be either acute or progressive. Progressive hearing losses may not be detectable in newborn hearing screening. Chronic otitis media and other illnesses similarly can create hearing losses during the first year or two, even when earlier testing correctly indicated that an infant had normal hearing.

The variety of causes of congenital or early onset hearing loss clearly contributes to diversity in the development of those children. Hearing losses associated with illness or accidents carry the risk of damage to other sensory systems or of related neurological effects, and one third of all types of hereditary deafness also have associated medical or physical implications. Approximately half of children with *cytomegalovirus* (CMV), a virus that causes "holes" in brain tissue, have multiple disabilities. Premature birth also is associated with disabilities beyond hearing loss, including a higher frequency of behavioral problems, delays in language and cognitive development, and delays in physical and motor development.

Various estimates suggest that 30–40 percent of all deaf children have associated psychological, neurological, or physical conditions, although that proportion includes all correlates, whether or not they are obvious or affect behavior. Reports of psychological or behavioral differences between deaf and hearing children therefore need to be considered with some caution. Differences that might be described as "due to deafness" may well be the result of other factors, particularly neurological factors. It also is important to note that statistics concerning the academic success of deaf children, literacy rates, intelligence, and so on will include a variety of children and do not reflect only implications of hearing loss. In short, because deaf children vary so widely—and for so many reasons—it is important that their needs be evaluated carefully so as to offer them the most beneficial environments for growth and learning.

Deaf Children With Other Needs

Being the parent of a deaf child is even more challenging when the child has multiple handicaps. Depending on their etiology, age of onset, and severity, hearing losses may be a greater or lesser issue for such children. Deaf babies who also have medical difficulties sometimes slip through the cracks during hearing screening, simply because so many other things are happening that seem to have a higher priority. New parents may not know how to soothe a crying deaf infant or how to establish a channel of communication, and medical personnel may overlook the fact that without access to communication and language, deaf children with multiple handicaps cannot understand what is happening to them and what others want from them. Communication must be a high priority with such children, not something to take care of later. Otherwise, behavioral difficulties may remain even when medical issues are resolved.

When people refer to "multiple handicaps" or "multiple disabilities," they may be referring to physical disabilities such as vision impairment, severe emotional or behavioral problems, or psychological disorders such as mental retardation or autism (see chapter 9). In the United States, a recent survey indicated that close to 40 percent of deaf students (ranging from "under 3 years" to "18 years and older") were reported to have an *additional disability*, while approximately 70 percent were reported to have one or more *functional limitations* aside from hearing loss (Gallaudet Research Institute, 2003). Additional disabilities ranged from learning disability (10.2 percent) and mental retardation (9.6 percent) to attention deficit disorder (6.6 percent), low vision and blindness (4.4 percent), cerebral palsy (3.3 percent), and emotional disorders (1.8 percent); "other disorders" were reported for 12.7 percent of deaf children nationwide. Functional limitations included both physical limitations (e.g., balance, or use of the limbs) and behavioral/psychological challenges such as difficulties in expressive or receptive communication in social interaction, maintaining attention, and thinking/reasoning skills.

Perhaps best documented among multiple disabilities is the co-occurrence of hearing loss and vision loss. The challenges of being *deafblind* are such that this group of children has received considerable attention (Knoors & Vervloed, 2003). Being deafblind does not necessarily mean that an individual is profoundly deaf and totally blind; the term usually means having insufficient vision to compensate for hearing loss and insufficient hearing to compensate for vision loss. Importantly, the loss of both vision and hearing is synergistic, meaning that together they create a disability more severe than "vision loss plus hearing loss."

Mental retardation is defined as having significant limitations of intellectual functioning and in everyday social, practical, and conceptual skills, with an onset during childhood (Knoors & Vervloed, 2003). Mental retardation and learning disability are often confused in deaf children, at least in part because the definitions are rather fuzzy and overlapping. Mental retardation, however, typically results from congenital infections and premature birth, whereas most learning disabilities appear to have developmental origins. Hearing loss and mental retardation frequently co-occur in children with Down syndrome, a group which is also prone to otitis media.

There is also overlap in symptoms among mental retardation, learning disability, and *autism,* with the last of these usually defined in terms of an inability to develop and maintain social relationships, difficulty in adjusting to environmental change, inadequate communication and language, and frequent stereotyped or repetitive behaviors. Deaf children frequently have been misdiagnosed as having autism, as well as mental retardation, because of the communication barriers associated with hearing loss. It remains unclear, however, whether autism is overdiagnosed or underdiagnosed in deaf children today, and the direction might vary by country and the presence of other disabilities.

This is not the place and I am not the person to help parents and teachers sort out diagnoses of additional disabilities and deaf children. Given that deaf children are at risk for physiological or psychological challenges, however, surprisingly little appears to be known about possible compounding effects of multiple disabilities, and the considerable variability among deaf children with disabilities makes it difficult to draw any strong conclusions about either etiology or the best support services. If it is suspected that a particular child has difficulties beyond those that can be attributed to hearing loss, it is important that the child have a thorough examination by someone familiar with deaf children, alternative modes of communication, and psychological assessment.

Early Identification of Hearing Losses

Hearing losses that have onsets after early hearing screening often are not recognized immediately but are suspected only when a child fails to meet certain milestones for language and social development. In those cases, traditionally representing about 70 percent of all children with hearing losses, it is the parents who recognize that something is "wrong" and eventually seek out an audiologist to check their child's hearing or an otolaryngologist, an "ear, nose, and throat doctor," to determine the reasons for the problem. Other parents may first look to psychologists to explain their children's behavior problems! Some later onset hearing losses and even congenital losses in children who live in places that do not have newborn hearing screening may not be detected until children are screened as part of school placement. The sad part is that they could be detected even before a newborn leaves the hospital.

As recently as the first edition of this book, in 1997, the average age for detection of childhood hearing losses in the United States was between 2 and 3 years, with reports of averages closer to 5 years of age in some states. At that time, the only babies screened for hearing loss at the time of birth were those who are considered "high-risk" due to premature birth, maternal illness, multiple handicaps, or other factors. Fifty to 70 percent of the congenital hearing losses thus were missed. Significant progress is now being made in the United States, as most of the states now mandate newborn hearing screening, and it has been widely available in the United Kingdom for many years. Identification in such places now averages weeks rather than years. The impact on early language development is just beginning to be documented, but it is already clear that infants whose hearing losses are identified and who begin intervention prior to 6 months of age show language gains superior to those who are identified after 6 months

(Yoshinaga-Itano, 2006). As simple and cost-effective as the process is, the United States has been slow in embracing it. Newborn hearing screening should be viewed in the same way as childhood immunizations: simple, cost-effective, and necessary.

Identifying Hearing Loss Early

For many years, hearing screening for babies consisted of little more than a pediatrician trying to elicit a startle response by making a loud noise outside of the baby's view. Fortunately, this haphazard assessment has given way to more accurate, automated tools such as *otoacoustic emissions* (OAE) and *auditory brainstem response* (ABR).

There are several different kinds of otoacoustic emission procedures. The more popular ones all have in common the use of a sensitive microphone that can pick up both externally generated sounds and inner ear responses to them. Evoked otoacoustic emissions (EOAEs) take advantage of the mechanical functioning of the cochlea. Invented in the United Kingdom in the mid-1970s, it has only recently become popular in the United States. EAOE requires less than 1 minute per ear, and provides a full assessment and documentation in 3 minutes. Testing involves fitting the newborn with a soft-tipped combination earphone/microphone that sends out either tone bursts or a "click" containing several tone frequencies. When the vibrations reach the cochlea, movement of the fluid and hair cells create detectable sound. The probe then records the slight changes in air pressure inside the ear canal that result from both the sound and its "echo." The pattern and intensity of the echo provides information on the healthiness of the middle and inner ear and likelihood of hearing loss.

Auditory brainstem responses (ABR) have been used for over 30 years as a test of auditory activity in the auditory nerve and brain, that is, beyond the cochlea. ABR involves rapidly sending thousands of tone bursts consisting of a broad range of frequencies and measuring the response of cells in the brainstem using electrodes placed on the scalp. Because the tone bursts are very brief and the responses small, ABR is best used with a relaxed or sleeping baby. Recently, procedures been developed that allow assessments of particular frequencies (e.g., those most important for hearing speech) rather than multi-frequency tones, giving the test greater utility. If an ABR indicates lack of a normal brainstem response to a sound, follow-up testing can expand the screening in order to specify whether the problem is at the level of the auditory nerve, the cochlea, or elsewhere. The infant may "pass" a second screening, or maybe a third, when more careful and precise measures are employed.

It is interesting to note that these "hearing screening tests" do not actually test hearing, but rather the functioning of various parts of the auditory system that are normally associated with hearing. Even if all of the "hardware" is working normally, there still may be central or cortical hearing loss (e.g., *auditory neuropathy*). EOAE and ABR testing also may suggest a severe hearing loss while the child functionally has only a mild or moderate hearing loss, thanks to the ability of the brain to interpret degraded neural signals.

Universal Newborn Hearing Screening Challenges

Delays in adopting universal newborn hearing screening (UNHS) in the United States and other countries were partly due to cost, which has come down significantly since automated systems have been developed that do not require administration by physicians or other highly trained individuals. A considerable part of the resistance, however, was concern about the accuracy of such tests and the potential of inaccurate results to affect early parent-child interactions. According to a colleague who served on the government panel that originally called for UNHS in the United States, the primary impediment to wider testing at the time was the issue of ABR and OAE yielding "false positives." The problem is that some babies who test positive—that is, indicating a hearing loss—actually will have normal hearing. According to my friend, there was concern on the panel that telling parents that they have a deaf baby when they really do not would cause too much mental anguish for parents. Several authors subsequently argued that concern about their infants would result in mothers being more hesitant in early interactions, and might disrupt the mother-infant bond (very important to later development, as we shall see). The long-term effects of such a situation were simply unknown.

Depending on one's perspective, such occasional anguish may be well worth the price; certainly there is nothing that a parent would do for a deaf baby that would in any way be disadvantageous for a hearing baby. Nevertheless, while those tests were producing false positives of perhaps 10 percent in the early 1990s, the rate is now down to around 2 percent, and most parents report that any short-term anxiety produced by testing is more than outweighed by the avoidance of the parental guilt that often follows late diagnoses of hearing loss (Young & Andrews, 2001). In most studies, parental approval rate for the screening is above 90 percent, supported both by parents whose babies "passed" the screening and those who were identified as having hearing losses. As it turns out, it is pediatricians who most often attribute anxiety and distress to parents with regard to hearing screening. Parents themselves almost universally support it, and I know of no data indicating any adverse effects of screening or false positives on mothers, infants, or their relationships.

Importantly, the testing that happens before a newborn leaves the hospital is not supposed to be an end to the screening process, but is considered only the first stage. In the second stage, those infants who have been identified as possibly having a hearing loss return for additional test-ing as soon as possible. Because of scheduling issues and the many things to be done when a new baby comes home, however, the second stage of screening often is not conducted for weeks, during which time parents might indeed be anxious about the possible outcomes. Yet, if anything, the greater problem seems to be parents who do not return for follow-up test-ing after their infants have been identified as at-risk by screening. In vari-ous studies, the failure to return for follow-up testing has been found to be as high as 30–50 percent, depending on the community, hospital, and demographic characteristics of parents involved. Hopefully, as newborn hearing screening becomes more common, it will be seen as part of the ordinary, postnatal routine like immunizations and monitoring of early growth.

Hearing Aids and Related Technology

As I described in previous sections, some kinds of hearing loss involve the reduced intensity of sound across a broad range of frequencies, a situation that often can be improved through the use of some amplification device—that is, by making everything louder. Other hearing losses are more com-plex, involving losses of particular frequencies or damage to the nerves that carry sound-related impulses to the brain.

Deaf individuals with severe to profound hearing losses often wear hearing aids as well, but their utility will vary widely, with the particular frequencies of their losses. Even when someone has a profound hearing loss at the frequencies important for speech reception, amplification still may be useful. Hearing aids can serve a signaling function in those cases, letting the user know when some sound-related event is happening, when some-one is approaching, or when someone is speaking to them even if they can-not understand what is being said. In children, hearing aids also are of critical importance for two other reasons, even if they do not allow the child to perceive speech well enough to understand it. First, connecting sounds with events in the environment plays an important role of cognitive development. Through such associations, children learn about cause and effect (a falling dish breaks *and* makes a noise), about the nature of things (air conditioning makes a constant, neutral sound—it must be a machine), and about the na-ture of communication. In this last case, when mother makes a noise (e.g., through speaking) and points to a toy, the connection between things and references to them gradually becomes part of the behavioral interactions of mother and infant. Eventually, the link of things and their names will be-come clear, giving arbitrary symbols (words and signs) meaning.

Even if hearing aids do not always appear to be useful, they may also serve as a kind of insurance policy in young children. In humans, the auditory system and related connections to the brain have an early flexibility, which appears to last until children are about 8 years old. As we will see in the next section, this *plasticity* helps to explain why both the age of children when they receive cochlear implants and the length of time between onset of their hearing losses and implantation are predictors of success with the implant. For children who *may* be candidates for implants in the future, stimulation of the auditory nerve with a hearing aid helps to keep the nerve itself healthy. Admittedly, providing early auditory stimulation for deaf children prior to implantation complicates the explanation of results from *clinical trials* or implant studies involving such children (that is, relating to the amount of nerve stimulation received prior to the implant), but that is a problem for researchers to worry about.

Hearing Aids

Hearing aids come in a variety of styles, models, and even colors, but they are all relatively simple devices. Regardless of whether they fit behind the ear, in the ear, or strapped to a child's chest, hearing aids consist of a microphone, a receiver/amplifier with volume control, a miniature speaker, a battery, and an acoustically designed earmold (see Figure 2–2). Amplified sound picked up by the microphone passes from the receiver to the speaker, through a tube, and into the plastic earmold that is custom molded for each user to ensure a snug fit.

Even in the simplest cases, the use of technology for improving hearing is not as straightforward as it might seem. Comprehension is a process that happens in the brain, not in the ear. The listener has to have sufficient information from the ear to analyze several different kinds of information in order to understand what is spoken. If a particular deaf child does not understand English speech, hearing aids will help his understanding to the same extent as speaking louder to someone who does not speak English—not at all. Further, as noted in the preceding section, most hearing aids are not specifically tuned to speech sounds the way that (functioning) human ears are. The common analog-type hearing aid amplifies all sounds equally, so background noise is made louder along with whatever it is the person is actually trying to hear (voices, music, and so on). The newer digital hearing aids, in contrast, are designed to amplify only those frequencies that correspond to an individual child's hearing loss, so the *signal* but not the *noise* is amplified. Digital aids are still quite expensive compared to the traditional analog aids, but prices continue to fall.

Some people with greater hearing losses do not find hearing aids worth the small amount of information they gain. A recent study found that deaf children of deaf parents were only half as likely as deaf children of hearing parents to wear hearing aids, even when their hearing losses were the same, so necessity is clearly not the only factor involved. For some people,

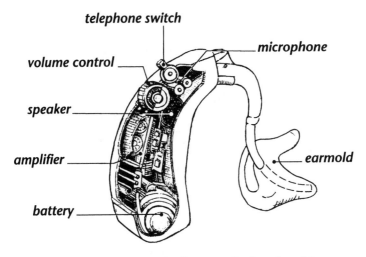

telephone switch

microphone

volume control

speaker

amplifier

earmold

battery

Figure 2–2. Schematic diagram of a hearing aid

hearing aids may be a matter of habit (like professional tennis players wearing their watches during championship matches). For others, there are personal or social reasons for wearing or not wearing them. A few deaf people prefer not to use hearing aids on principle, feeling that it would compromise their Deaf identities; but these are exceptions, and most Deaf people who would benefit from hearing aids wear them. Yet others prefer not to wear hearing aids for cosmetic reasons. A teacher at a school for the deaf once told me that her students did not like wearing their hearing aids because they "weren't sexy." A boy in the class quickly corrected her, however, saying he did not mind wearing them at school, but he would never wear them if he was "trying to pick up hearing girls."

For children, the use of hearing aids can be very important. Not only do they provide children with access to the language of their (usually) hearing parents and siblings, but in cases of progressive hearing loss they can provide a temporary bridge that will allow those children to more easily acquire sign language and reading skills in addition to speech skills. Hearing aids must be approached cautiously with very young children, because too much amplification can damage the young ear, perhaps speeding up or causing more hearing loss.

Loop, Infrared, and FM Systems

Most hearing aids include special circuitry and a "T" (telephone) switch that improves their operation with telephones and in large meeting rooms, theaters, and religious buildings equipped with *loop systems*.[5] The essence of loop circuitry is an electronic telecoil in the hearing aid that picks up magnetic signals generated by a telephone handset or closed-circuit loop system and feeds them directly to the hearing aid receiver, something like using a direct-connect computer modem rather than an old acoustic coupler. "Loop" refers to the fact that most such systems have a wire loop in the ceiling or under the floor that generates the sound signals. Alternatively, similar systems can use infrared signals from centrally located transmitters (requiring a clear line of sight). In classrooms, FM systems are frequently used: The teacher uses a microphone attached to an FM transmitter, while the children each have FM receivers attached to their hearing aids. In all cases, these systems provide a "cleaner" source of sound, improving its quality in situations where it normally would suffer, thus providing access to more information.

Everything You Always Wanted to Know About Cochlear Implants

At the time of the first edition of this book, the use of cochlear implants by children was still relatively new, and there was little research concerning their effects.[6] Available evidence showed implants to be very successful for late-deafened adults, but results were more equivocal for children with congenital or early-onset hearing losses, who often appeared to do as well with hearing aids as with implants. For that reason, together with my orientation as a researcher who needed hard evidence, I was not a supporter of implantation for children in 1997. But the situation now has changed, and advances in implant technology and strong evidence for their effectiveness have changed my perspective. Today, the increasing popularity of cochlear implants is altering the face of deafness (if not Deafness), and research published over the past few years has provided a wealth of information about the implications of implantation for speech, hearing, and language. Studies concerning social and cognitive development, as well as effects on schooling, are also now beginning to appear, although there are still large gaps in our knowledge, most notably concerning the best way to educate children with implants. The following sections provide an overview of what we currently know about cochlear implants for children, holding technical details to a minimum.

How Implants Work

A cochlear implant has two primary parts, one that is implanted in the head and one worn outside, connected by a magnet. (There are no wires poking through the scalp!) The external part of the implant is much like a hearing aid, including a microphone and a receiver that can be worn behind the ear or attached to clothing (see Figure 2–3). This unit includes a microproces-

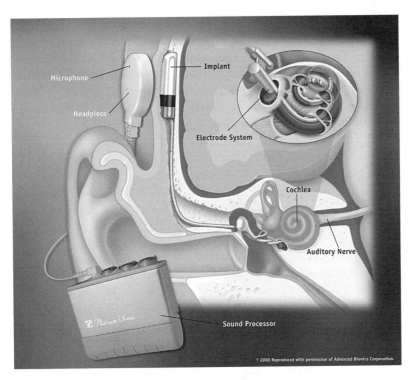

Figure 2-3. Schematic diagram of a cochlear implant (Courtesy Advanced Bionics Corporation).

sor which generates electrical signals of different frequencies, correspond-ing to sounds that vary in pitch and loudness. Finally, a wire attached to the external unit ends in a magnet with a small transmitter. The internal part of the implant consists of a small receiver and a smooth wire contain-ing areas (electrodes) that transmit electrical impulses. Happily, technologi-cal advances in implants primarily involve the external device—primarily the software of the microprocessor—so "upgrades" do not involve additional surgery to change the internal part of the implant system.

Implant surgery involves opening a flap of skin above and behind the ear, and hollowing a small indentation in the skull. The internal receiver fits into the indentation, and the electrode wire is threaded into the spiral of the cochlea. Newer implants have precurved wires, so that the electrodes lie tight against the inner wall of the cochlea, optimizing their function-ing. When activated by sounds picked up by the microphone and analyzed by the processor, the implant system sends signals through the transmit-ter, across to the receiver, and into the electrode array. The electrodes send electrical impulses to the auditory nerve at different points along the co-chlea, corresponding to different sound frequencies, bypassing the hair cells and other parts of the cochlea that might be compromised. In some cases, the electrode wire cannot be fully inserted into the cochlea, which may become *ossified* or hardened after meningitis or years of disuse. In that situation, because of the structure of the cochlea described above (higher frequencies as the cochlea spirals inward), the implant will transmit only lower frequencies. In cases of ossification or malformed cochleas, implants often cannot be used, and each candidate for cochlear implantation must be carefully screened by an audiologist and an implant surgeon.

As soon as the incision has healed, from 2 to 4 weeks after surgery, it is time for the initial *mapping* of the implant, where it is "tuned" to the particular hearing loss profile of the child. Over a series of visits to the audiologist, the tuning will become more precise in terms of both in- tensity and frequencies. The younger the child, typically the more visits are necessary to establish optimal programming, and because responses may change over time, long-term follow-up visits are required. Newer mapping techniques are less dependent on specific responses from the child, and these are proving valuable in setting the processors of very young children. The skill of the audiologist in programming the speech proces- sor thus has a major impact on a child's eventual success in developing speech perception and production skills. I know two families in which there was little progress with their children's implants with their initial audi- ologists, whereas then children blossomed when the parents transferred to different practices (one requiring several hours for the round trip).

Ultimately, the implant will offer several sound processing alterna- tives—separate programs that are best for speech, for music, for television, and so on. All of this mapping takes time and effort, however, and it should not be assumed that the full impact of the implant will be apparent in the first weeks or even months after surgery. It appears that receptive and ex- pressive language continue to improve over at least several years in chil- dren who receive implants, in contrast to late-deafened adults who tend to experience relatively rapid recovery of auditory functioning after im- plantation but reach a point of diminishing returns more quickly.

Before leaving the mechanics of cochlear implants, it is worth noting three more practical issues. First, because of the way that the electrode wire is inserted and wound into the cochlea, remaining hair cells—and residual hearing—are sometimes lost. Implants always used to be inserted in the ear with less hearing for that reason, but many surgeons feel it is no longer an issue. Second, although implants sometimes have to be removed, re- implantation in the same ear is quite common. This can occur in medical emergencies where MRI (magnetic resonance imaging) or other medical imaging is necessary but barred by the metallic internal portion of the implant. Nonmetallic implants are now on the market which should rule out this relatively rare event. Implants, like hearing aids and other tech- nologies, also suffer breakdowns (referred to as *device failure*). Although proponents of implants report failures in the range of 2–3 percent, one recent study found that over 25 percent of implants in children had to be replaced (Beadle, 2005). Third, contrary to some suggestions, the internal portion of an implant does not create any difficulty for swimming or sports. The external portion must be removed in those situations, however, and then, or when the batteries die, a child is once again quite deaf. In fact, some children and adults use their implants selectively, choosing when to be deaf and when to have auditory input.

A Brief History of Cochlear Implant Technology

Over 200 years ago, Alessandro Volta connected a battery to two metal rods inserted in his ears and described receiving a "jolt," a "boom in the head," and a "boiling-type" noise. Not surprisingly, similar reports are rare, but Volta's experiment established that electrical stimulation to peripheral parts of the auditory system can create the perception of sound. Still, not until 1957 was it reported that direct stimulation from an electrode placed to the auditory nerve allowed a patient to discriminate sounds and words. The original goal was simply to provide late-deafened individuals with enough information about speech to supplement and assist speechreading. Expectations quickly increased as rapid advances in microprocessors and software allowed greater specificity in the information received by the auditory nerve.

The original cochlear implant system, developed during the 1970s, consisted of a single active electrode plus a "ground" electrode outside the cochlea. "Single channel" refers to the fact that the original implants had a wire that transmitted only a single frequency. The device thus offered only the equivalent of a single, simple tone, giving information about loudness and the timing of sounds, but nothing more. The United States Food and Drug Administration (FDA) approved the use of a single-channel cochlear implant with adults in 1984, but its benefits were eventually deemed to be minimal, and it was discontinued. Research into more complex implant systems had been continuing around the world, particularly in Australia, and the single-channel implant was quickly replaced by multichannel devices. The newer cochlear implant systems stimulated up to 24 different locations in the cochlea, where the auditory nerve endings are located, corresponding to 24 distinct auditory frequencies. This advance allowed many users to discriminate voices and other sounds, and early trials showed much broader and more successful application of newer cochlear implants than the inventors had ever thought possible.

By the mid-1980s, multichannel cochlear implants were being tested in children, and the FDA formally approved their use with children as young as 2 years of age in 1990 and 18 months in 1998. In 2004, deaf children in the United States were receiving implants as early as 1 year of age, and as young as 6 months if they are part of clinical trials. By 1997, 9000 adults and children worldwide had received cochlear implants, a number that grew to 25,000 by mid-2000, and over 75,000 by 2003. In Australia, fully 80 percent of deaf children now receive cochlear implants, some as early as 2–3 months of age. The surgery is now quite safe, and relatively few medical complications are reported. Binaural implants (one in each ear) thus are becoming more popular. Not only do these provide more, and more accurate auditory information, there is now less worry about "saving one ear" in case something goes wrong. At present, binaural implants are far less popular in the United States than in some other countries, but their numbers are increasing.

As the emphasis in marketing and the use of cochlear implants shifted from adults to children, controversy erupted. Deaf people initially attacked the notion of cochlear implants for children, suggesting that they were insufficiently effective and interfered with children's developing identities as a Deaf people, as well as hindering their acquisition of sign language skills. Perhaps most interesting was the fact that many of the most vehement critics of implants were hearing people.

Since 2001, with the emergence of research showing the value of implants for most deaf children, many criticisms have evaporated. Still, Deaf people in some countries object to public monies being spent to provide individual children with cochlear implant technology while access to other technologies (such as telephone relay systems) that would serve all deaf people are limited. In the United States and elsewhere, some members of the Deaf community and people allied with it argue that the decision by parents to implant their deaf children violates the children's rights by performing unnecessary surgery on them. Moreover, some deaf people who are comfortable with their identities as Deaf believe that "forcing" cochlear implants on children does not allow them the opportunity to develop normal identities and freedom of choice. Having a cochlear implant, in their view, communicates to the child that being deaf is bad and that this message may leave him or her forever caught between Deaf and hearing cultures, a member of neither. Some other Deaf people, admittedly, are threatened by the possible "death by implant" of the Deaf community. These people know what it is like growing up deaf, and also recognize the quality of their lives as Deaf people. These are things that hearing parents can never know.

On the other side, hearing parents know what it is like growing up hearing, and know only the quality of their lives as hearing people. Is it wrong for them to want that for their children? Unfortunately they are often bombarded with propaganda and one-sided arguments from advocates and opponents of cochlear implants that make objective decision-making difficult. Many parents, for example, report being told at the time of newborn hearing screening that cochlear implantation is absolutely necessary if deaf children are ever to be able to acquire language and be educated in school.

Thus far, all of the cochlear implant surgeons I have met have been far more balanced and reasonable than this in advising parents for or against implantation at any particular time. Rather, it is the "front-line" medical and audiological personnel whom parents encounter first who tend to have this all-or-none view of implants and language. This claim clearly is not a valid one, but many people in the speech and hearing field are relatively unfamiliar with people who are comfortable and content with being deaf. They primarily meet people who are unhappy or traumatized by hearing loss and who desire change.

Individuals who have argued against cochlear implants for children have been accused of being short-sighted and focusing on perceived group needs at the expense of the needs of individual children. In fact, they are most often people who desire to maintain a language and culture with a long history. Those who argue for implants, meanwhile, have been called "oppressors," seeking to wipe out the Deaf community in a manner similar to the eugenics movement, which advocated selective breeding and sterilization of people with undesirable characteristics 100 years ago (see Lane, 2005, and the rejoinder by Johnston, 2005). Yet as more and more Deaf adults get implants—and remain part of the Deaf community—the situation is changing, and after their initial opposition, too, the National Association of the Deaf in the United States now supports cochlear implants as one alternative in a range of options for deaf children. Efforts to decrease the emotion and increase the objectivity of the debate through books, conferences, and more objective research seem to be working. Nonetheless, the debate continues, and parents have to carefully navigate the rhetoric that often obscures the facts about this sensitive issue.

Who Benefits From Cochlear Implants?

It is important to remember that even at their best, cochlear implants do not change deaf children into hearing children. Information provided by implants is less precise than that provided by a fully functional cochlea, and what is heard has been described as "coarse" or "degraded" compared to the sounds received by hearing persons. People who have lost their hearing as adults and children who become deaf after having developed a spoken language (*postlingually*) have to learn to associate this new input with their memories of speech and the individual sounds of language. Children who are born deaf or become deaf before spoken language is well established (*prelingually*) have a very different task in learning to understand what they receive from a cochlear implant. Their challenge is to develop auditory-based language using much more limited information than that received by hearing children. Further, most deaf children already have significant delays in spoken language development before obtaining their implant, so they usually lack implicit understanding of the structure of the information they will receive. My colleague Patricia Spencer described the situation this way:

> Asking a child to make sense of, and be able to reproduce, spoken language received only through a cochlear implant is somewhat like asking the child to recognize and draw a picture of an exotic animal they have never seen before that is standing behind a tall picket fence. Only parts of the strange animal are visible through the spaces between the wooden slats of the fence. The child must complete the image in his or her mind, imagining the shape of the parts of the animal that are not directly visible.

Spencer also cautions that the demonstrated advantages for children who receive cochlear implants and are exposed only to spoken language are relative, as they usually are compared only to deaf children who do not have implants. Implants typically do not "level the playing field" with hearing children, and there are a variety of factors that will affect an individual child's degree of success with an implant.

In general, we know that abilities in speech perception, speech production, and language are usually interrelated, and children who progress in one area typically progress in the other two as well. Until 2001, however, most of the evidence about cochlear implantation for children concerned their benefits for speech and hearing (rather than language, social functioning, or learning). This focus was consistent with the fact that the majority of funding for early implant research came primarily from medical sources and, in particular, the manufacturers of implants. Most surgeons viewed the goal of implantation as improving the hearing of individuals with significant hearing losses, leaving language development as the responsibility of parents and teachers.

More recently, investigations have turn to detailed examinations of language development following cochlear implantation, as well as possible preimplantation predictors of success. This research has indicated that generalizations about language development following cochlear implantation must be tempered by recognition of the large individual differences among children and the lack of fully reliable preimplant predictors of outcomes. Nevertheless, there are several variables that have been empirically demonstrated to benefit speech and language performance of children with implants. Most prominent among these are

- length of time since implantation (shorter is better)
- age at implantation (younger is better)
- degree of hearing loss (both in the implanted ear and the other ear)
- age at onset of hearing loss

- amount of language when hearing was lost
- parental support for the child and postimplant therapy
- children's cognitive abilities, and
- the amount and types of postimplantation therapy received.

Some of these factors affect the level of performance achieved while others affect the speed of acquiring various skills, and this may vary across children as well as variables. Additional child, family, and therapy factors likely are also involved, even if their specific effects have not yet been identified, and some parents report better results just from changing from one audiologist to another.

Among the variables that apparently have not been addressed—but eventually will be, given their usual impact on language development in deaf and hearing children—are ease of mother-child communication, parent's level of education, parental hearing status, siblings, child temperament, and specific cognitive abilities. Also still to be determined is the extent to which more positive situations with regard to any of these variables can compensate for less positive situations with regard to others. Finally, even if we were to sort out the various contributions of these factors, we still would be faced with the fact that, at least at this point, most children who are implanted are those who appear best suited to spoken communication in the first place, and children who stop using their implants are rarely included in follow-up studies. As a result, we have essentially no idea how the number of implant "stars" (like those seen on television) compares with the number of implant "failures."

As noted earlier, children's success with implants appears to be enhanced by stimulation of the auditory system prior to implantation, and they also benefit from participation in preschool and/or educational programs that emphasize spoken language. It is with regard to educational programming and the mode(s) of language to which they are exposed after implantation that much of the cultural and emotional debate has ensued. The situation is at the same time both simple and complex. On the simple side is the fact that cochlear implants are designed to facilitate speech and hearing and, thus, it should not be surprising that exposure to spoken language leads to better success. Nonetheless, it remains unclear whether there is some *threshold* for exposure to speech, a minimum level that is necessary or sufficient for development of spoken language. There is no real evidence that signing interferes with the development of spoken language after implantation (or at any other time), and, in fact, earlier use of sign language appears to provide cognitive and linguistic support for the acquisition of auditory language after cochlear implantation. At the same time, because the threshold for spoken language experience is likely to vary across children, it is difficult to know whether too much emphasis on signing could reduce much-needed exposure to speech.

The extent to which a setting that emphasizes spoken language versus *total communication* (combining signing, spoken language, and amplification; see chapter 3) for children with cochlear implants has been the subject of a variety of analyses yielding contradictory results. My own reading of the literature suggests that early (preschool) sign language can facilitate acquisition of spoken language after implantation, but exposure to good spoken language models is also essential for such children. This view is also supported by preliminary data concerning academic achievement (see below). Given that almost 200 years of research and experience in educating deaf children without implants still has not provided an unequivocal answer to such questions, however, it is not at all surprising that the issue continues to be contentious. Unfortunately, proponents on each side of the issue usually cite only the evidence that supports their position, and so parents frequently are denied information necessary in order to make appropriate decisions for their children. Definitive answers to these questions remain, in any case, and they likely will be different for almost every child, no matter what the "experts" tell you.

If all of this seems complicated, I am afraid it is likely to be more so when deaf children have multiple handicaps. How can we decide whether cochlear implants might be useful for such a child? At present, there appears to be little research on the topic, although the increasing popularity of implants and the decreasing risk of the surgery make it likely that more such children will be receiving them in the future. It has been suggested that children with multiple disabilities might even gain greater benefit from implants (Bertram, 2004; Hamzavi et al., 2000). There does not appear to be any comparative research on the topic, however, and because deaf children with multiple handicaps vary even more widely than other deaf children, decisions concerning implantation have to be made on a case-by-case basis. For parents who are considering the possibility, this is one of those areas where I strongly suggest seeking information from other parents who have been similar situations. Their advice likely will depend on the successes of their own children, and considering input from several different families likely is the best idea.

Long-Term Effects of Cochlear Implants

Although some children have greater success with cochlear implants, most profoundly deaf children with implants display language skills comparable to those of children with moderate to severe hearing losses. The *intelligibility* or clarity of their speech varies widely, and even with intensive therapy deaf children who receive implants rarely achieve spoken language skills considered average for hearing children of the same age. Therefore, even if they eventually come to depend more on spoken language than sign language—and some children with implants certainly will not—early access to language is essential for all aspects of development. Hence, I stand by the suggestion of sign language as an alternative available to deaf children and their families.

Research has indicated the potential benefit of sign language for children with implants, and new research is beginning to emerge on how cochlear implants influence academic achievement. Several studies have come from a research group in Iowa, including one that examined the academic achievement of high school students who had received their implants an average of 10 years before as part of one of the first waves of children with implants (Spencer, Gantz, & Knutson, 2004). Most notable is the finding that those students with implants read at levels only slightly below hearing norms, and they had overall academic achievement comparable to them. Importantly, however, although they had been educated in mainstream schools, the students all were supported by sign language interpreters. More recently, a study from a research group in Scotland surveyed essentially all children in that country who had received implants (Thoutenhoofd, 2006). Those children, who mostly depended on spoken language, showed better achievement than peers without implants, functioning at levels comparable to deaf students with moderate hearing losses. Nevertheless, those with cochlear implants still performed below the national average on standardized testing across academic domains, so the study is unlikely to put to rest questions concerning the costs and benefits of implants for education.

With regard to the economic benefits of cochlear implantation, several studies have suggested educating deaf children with cochlear implants costs less than educating deaf peers without implants (Francis, Koch, Wyatt, & Niparko, 1999; O'Neill, O'Donoghue, Archbold, & Normand, 2000; Summerfield, 2004). In particular, they found that length of implant experience predicted whether children were educated in (less costly) local public schools or (more costly) special classrooms, although the strength of that relationship varied considerably. More recent findings indicate that only about one third of the cost of a cochlear implant is recovered in educational savings (Summerfield, 2004). While such issues are still under consideration, it is important to note that investigators and educators have given little attention to the issue of how best to educate children with cochlear implants. Most such children are placed in regular classes, where they still need extra support in order to succeed—at least as much support as any other hard-of-hearing child would require. Such support may well be less expensive than separate schooling for deaf children, depending on factors such as the number of children being served, the presence of multiple disabilities, and so on. Ideally, however, such decisions should be made on educational grounds, not financial grounds. Otherwise, long-term "hidden" costs may well outweigh early savings. We all hear stories of those deaf children with implants who become outstanding students in public school settings, but there is no way to know how common they are compared to students who do not succeed there.

At this juncture, it also is important to recognize that implants might affect development and educational achievement via indirect routes other than language per se. It was noted earlier, for example, that visual attention is especially important to children with hearing losses. Although early studies had reported enhanced visual attention skills in deaf individuals, we now know that it is often sign language skill rather than hearing status that is the important variable in such findings (see Marschark, 2003, for a review). Performance on visual attention tasks also is related to (nonverbal) intelligence, however, so the issue is clearly not a simple one. We therefore will postpone discussion of this topic until chapter 8.

With regard to the social-emotional effects of cochlear implantation, results thus far indicate marked improvement in quality of life for postlingually deafened adults, allowing them to re-establish friendships and social interactions similar to those prior to their hearing losses. In the case of children, there have been concerns that cochlear implantation will have negative effects by interfering with development of their self-image as Deaf persons and damaging self-esteem due to lack of a peer group with which to identify. This situation could be made worse if children are moved from segregated schools or classrooms to mainstream settings where they are the only deaf student in the class. Yet there is no evidence that this situation would be any more difficult if they do not have implants. Is it more awkward to go to school with an implant or an interpreter?

Studies evaluating reported "quality of life" among older deaf children generally have been quite positive. Adolescents and their parents report positive value in the increased awareness of environmental sounds, even if sound sometimes is considered bothersome (some people I know who have implants like to take them off occasionally for "some peace and quiet"). Teens also report that their implants offer access to a wider range of activities, although what they generally like best about their implant was simply being able to hear. According to one large study involving parents of children with cochlear implants, almost all of them indicated that their children used the implant regularly, and 60 percent reported that their children had never refused to use it. Even if these numbers indicate that not all children used their implants all the time, most reported that their children were happier, more independent, and had more self-confidence after receiving their implants. Almost 90 percent said their children socialized more often with hearing children after acquiring their cochlear implants, and many children were seen as becoming more socially comfortable.

Reports from children with implants, rather from their parents, are more mixed. Some studies have shown that deaf children with implants increase their number of friendships with hearing children after receiving a cochlear implant. Others report that implanted deaf children were unlikely to successfully enter into interactions with hearing children regardless of how long they had their implants. Part of the issue here may relate to age, as it appears that older children tend to be more successful than younger children in initiating social contact. In general, however, findings suggest that children who were less social prior to implantation are much the same after implantation (Christiansen & Leigh, 2002). Once again, those who argue for and against implants for children tend only to mention the studies that support their position—but then we are always more receptive to information that is consistent with our beliefs than those which are inconsistent, and no sinister motives should be read into this fact of human nature.

Initial results are also now emerging concerning the impact of cochlear implants on children's peer group identification. One investigation found that deaf adolescents with implants rated qualities associated with being a hearing person more positively than did peers without implants, although that may be an understandable consequence in situations in which children receive implants in the first place (for example, parents' praise of being like a hearing child). Interestingly, both groups gave highest ratings to having a "bicultural" identity, but none of their self-perceptions turned out to be related to how their peers actually viewed them.

Taken together, then, the few studies conducted thus far do not suggest any large effects of cochlear implants, either positively or negatively, on deaf children's social-emotional development, their interactions with hearing peers, or relations with their families. Somewhat more positive effects are reported for adolescents and young adults. Family dynamics and children's social development apparently are too complex to be greatly affected by a cochlear implant alone. Nevertheless, the course of social development for deaf children who are implanted very early and others who do not receive implants are likely to be markedly different. So too will be their language functioning and perhaps their intellectual functioning (largely as a result of language and literacy skills), and it will not be easy to determine the precise nature of the complex interactions of these factors with child temperament, family acceptance of their children's hearing losses, and social attitudes.

One final note: In July 2002, the Food and Drug Administration in the United States announced that approximately 25 people who had received cochlear implants had contracted meningitis, while 26 cases were reported in Western Europe. Meningitis, an infection of tissues and the fluid around the brain, often has hearing loss as a consequence, and the connection to implants already inserted was initially a puzzle. Although 50 cases of meningitis out of the tens of thousands of individuals to have received cochlear implants may not seem high, the situation received a lot of attention in the press, and parents of deaf children were understandably concerned. As it turned out, the culprit turned out to be a mechanism used for insertion of the implant so that it fits tightly to the turns of the cochlea, not the implant itself, and manufacturers quickly modified their construction, apparently eliminating the danger. At the same time, individuals with implants were strongly advised to receive a meningitis vaccination—still not a bad idea, as recent studies have suggested a slightly greater risk of meningitis among children with implants than among those without.

Technological Tools for Deaf People

For children who are identified as having significant hearing losses, there are a variety of technological and educational tools available to them and to their parents and teachers. When people think of the ways in which technology might affect the lives of people who are deaf, they most often think of hearing aids. Technology in this area has seen important advances over the last 20 years, but hearing aids are just one area of several areas that have made great strides. In addition to aids that assist with hearing, there are also a variety of devices that deaf people use to reduce the reliance on hearing. These technological aids are particularly important for people who have little or no residual hearing, providing deaf people with a personal and emotional independence that eliminates the need for them to rely on hearing relatives and friends. In addition, they make life more pleasant and more "normal."

Most of these technological aids provide visual information or signals. There are baby monitors that pick up the sound of crying or other noises and flash signal lights to get the parents' attention. In the home, there are also vibrating alarm clocks and safety alarms (e.g., smoke detectors), lights that flash in place of the doorbell, and lights that indicate when the telephone is ringing. Consider several of the technologies that are currently the most important and popular.

TTYs and Pagers

A *TTY* (or a *minicom* in the United Kingdom) is essentially a visual telephone (with letters, not pictures) for people who are deaf. A caller types in one part of a telephone conversation, a receiver reads it and types a reply, and so on. Basic TTY models consist of a standard ("QWERTY") keyboard, a horizontal window with LED display, and an acoustic coupler. The model now on my desk (a big one, by current standards, at 9" x 9") also includes a printer to keep track of conversations, a "direct connect" plug so that it does not actually require a telephone, and a TTY answering machine. A TTY produces a series of tones when the character keys are pressed. Those tones are picked up via the telephone handset through the acoustic coupler or via the direct connect cord and sent through standard phone lines. At the other end, a phone is placed on a similar coupler, and the tones are decoded into characters and shown on the display. Many companies and essentially all public offices, including 911 in most areas, now have TTY capability. This availability usually is indicated by either separate TTY telephone numbers or the "V/TTY" designation, which means the number handles both voice and TTY calls.

TTYs are relatively inexpensive, and they are available in models ranging from pay TTY telephones in many airports and public buildings to portable versions that are barely bigger than a hand calculator. This was not always the case. It was not until the early 1960s that three deaf men, Robert Weitbrecht, Andrew Saks, and Jim Marsters, invented the acoustic coupler when AT&T and other large companies failed to do so because they felt there was not enough financial incentive. The three men then started hooking couplers up to discarded and refurbished teletypewriter machines (traditionally abbreviated "TTY," hence the name). This breakthrough allowed deaf people to communicate over long distances in "real-time" rather than through letters or telegrams for the first time, and it radically changed their lives, culture, and community (Lang, 2000).

With the increasing popularity of two-way pagers and instant messaging, TTYs are becoming scarce. After reading the penultimate version of this chapter, a deaf colleague e-mailed me:

> I had to laugh at the TTY section. I have more and more people telling me they have no TTY, no longer have alerting light for their TTY, etc. . . . and we were sooooo excited to have the clunkers back in the 1960s, fought for TTY access at airports, etc and now the equipment is ignored in favor of pagers.

Indeed, pagers now provide deaf individuals with the equivalent of cell phone communication, allowing people to stay in touch without the need for TTYs, telephones, or face-to-face communication. The long history of the "deaf grapevine" continues, as important (or personal) information spreads rapidly across the country through an electronic network.

Relay Services and Webcams

Another telecommunication advance for deaf people originally was made possible by the TTY and the cooperation of telephone companies in the United States. For a deaf person who wants to call a hearing person or business that does not have a TTY, or for a hearing person who does not have TTY but wants to call a deaf person, many countries now have nationwide "relay" systems. The relay system involves calling a hearing operator using a toll-free number. The operator reads TTY messages from deaf callers and types spoken messages from hearing callers, and the entire conversation is guaranteed to be confidential. This network has freed deaf people from having to depend on hearing friends to make calls for them or to have to make personal visits when they want to make doctor appointments, reservations, consult lawyers, or inquire about goods or services from companies that do not have TTYs. A good relay operator, like a good sign language interpreter (see chapter 6), will tell the deaf person everything that the hearing person says and often will include information about the emotional state of the person if it is important to the conversation (e.g., "she's crying" or "he's yelling"). Some hearing people apparently are not aware of this fact, however. A deaf friend told me that he saw on his display "I hate getting these calls!" as an operator faithfully typed exactly what his veterinarian's receptionist said when the operator informed her that it was a relay call.

It was an important day in the American Deaf community when President Bill Clinton inaugurated the relay system in 1993 by telephoning Frank Harkin, the deaf brother of U.S. Senator Tom Harkin of Iowa. A large group of hearing and deaf dignitaries, including Senator Harkin, were gathered around the President in the White House when he made the call. Unfortunately, Frank was on the phone at the time, telling a deaf friend that the President was going to be calling him. After the President got a busy signal, Senator Harkin called his brother's neighbor, who went next door and told Frank to get off the phone!

In the United States and elsewhere, *video relay services* (or VRS) are now becoming popular and replacing TTY-based relay services. VRS is the same idea as traditional relay services, except that it involves video instead of text. It uses digital web cameras or dedicated videophone systems and broadband or other high-speed Internet connections. VRS is accessed via the worldwide web. A deaf caller signs to an interpreter who then interprets into spoken language for hearing recipients, and the reverse. VRS thus has an advantage over voice relay in that it allows both participants in a conversation to use their own language. In areas with less up-to-date cable services or during periods of heavy Web usage (that is, when *bandwidth* is limited), the VRS display may have lower resolution, but technological limitations are rapidly disappearing. In addition to VRS services, many deaf people are now using the same systems to communicate directly. Webcams and videophones allow deaf people (or anyone for that matter) to have visual "telephone" conversations comparable to those of hearing individuals. In fact, I have used a Webcam on my computer for calls to hearing people in other countries, just so we can have face-to-face contact. Best of all, VRS equipment is free from service providers, and a communication barrier that confronted deaf people for decades has been eliminated thanks to technology.

Captioning

Most people are familiar with *closed captioning*, even if they do not real-ize that they can utilize it on their own television (my wife and I, both hearing, would not want to live without it!). Closed captioning, in its sim-plest form, is the production of visual text on the screen, either edited or verbatim, representing the spoken messages and other sounds that hear-ing people hear. Using caption decoders or built-in decoder chips, text is available on a variety of television programs, videotapes, and DVDs. De-coders do not "do" the captioning. Rather, someone has to actually type in captions for each program, preferably at the time of the original pro-duction, and the captions are embedded in the television signal. The chip or decoder merely converts the signal to text and displays the message on the television screen.

Captioned programs are not new. "Open captions," meaning ones that are always visible, have been used in foreign films for many years. They are used by local television stations to warn of serious weather or other emergencies without interrupting a broadcast, and are increasingly avail-able at movie theaters in cities with larger deaf populations.[7] In 1971, WGBH, the Public Broadcasting station in Boston, used open captions on an episode of Julia Child's "The French Chef," and in 1973 they started open captioning ABC-TV news and rebroadcasting it for deaf viewers a few hours later. As captioning started to expand, hearing viewers complained that open captions were distracting, and "closed captions" were subse-quently developed. With the help of the National Captioning Institute and the Federal Communications Commission, broadcasters started to include captions on a special signal band of commercial television broadcasts. Since 1990, decoder circuitry has been built into all 13" diagonal or larger tele-visions sold in the United States (at an approximate cost of 25 cents per television set), and they are becoming standard around the world. Caption decoders are still needed for smaller and older television sets.

All kinds of programming are now captioned, either through pre- or post-programming additions of captions or through "real-time" captioning in which the captions are typed in by a captioner as a program is proceed-ing (for example, during special live news and sporting events). This does not mean that all programming is captioned. A 2004 report from the Na-tional Center for Accessible Media reported that although 100 per cent of prime-time programming on Public Broadcasting stations is captioned, captioning is available on only about 36 per cent of the programming on pay channels like HBO and The Disney Channel and 25 percent of local newscasts. Meanwhile, only 5 per cent of the educational and children's programming now being released is captioned. That means that deaf chil-dren will often encounter uncaptioned videos in school and will have no access to the content of most instructional programming.

Captions, when done properly, should not detract from the original audio or video content, and they generally use the original wording. Sometimes, changes are necessary to avoid overwhelming the viewer with captions that are too fast to be able to read them all, and technical, scientific, and other difficult vocabulary may be presented at a slower rate to accommodate viewers' unfamiliarity with the material.

In addition to providing deaf people with access to television broadcasts, captioning is valuable in many other ways. Captioning has been shown to improve reading skills and social communication skills of hearing children learning English as a second language, and similar claims have been made with regard to deaf children. My own reading of that literature, however, indicates that despite all of the statements about captioning improving comprehension and literacy skills of deaf children, there is actually little evidence to support them. What research is available suggests that the problem is not with the captioning, or even with deaf children's reading skills per se. Rather, deaf children develop different information processing skills than hearing children, and they may read captions relatively passively, not using them to activate knowledge they already have on the same topic (chapter 8). We also have to remember that whereas hearing children can hear the words of a television show or film while watching on-screen activity, deaf children have to alternate between two different visual inputs (the activity and the visually presented language), guaranteeing that they will be unable to process either one fully. This issue thus far has not been adequately addressed by research studies, but it suggests that the benefits of captioning for children will be limited unless we can find creative, perhaps interactive, ways to use it.

Closed captioning remains particularly helpful to older adults who have partial hearing losses as a normal part of the aging process. Captions also are useful in noisy environments or where having the sound on a television would be distracting (for example, health clubs and airports), and it has now been accepted by most people. While the value of captioning is just starting to be explored, the battle to have all television and video material captioned continues to be an uphill one. The battle must be won in the end, however, and meanwhile captioners and caption researchers are pushing captioning technology and potential to its limits.

Final Comments

Almost 10 percent of the people in the United States have some degree of hearing loss, most of them older people who have begun to lose what once was normal hearing. Close to a million adults and children have never had normal hearing and consider themselves deaf or hard of hearing. Hearing losses in these people can be from a variety of causes, including infant, childhood, or maternal illness; accidents; or hereditary factors. Genetics appears to account for most cases of childhood hearing loss, even if it is not always apparent.

Being deaf and being Deaf are not the same thing. Capital-d Deaf is applied to people who are part of the historical and cultural community of deaf people and who use a natural sign language, such as American Sign Language or British Sign Language, as their primary means of communication. Over 95 percent of deaf children have hearing parents; for them, access to the Deaf community is something that usually will not start until they are well into their school years. This affiliation is a natural one, and there is nothing that parents either should or can do to stop it. For emotional, social, and academic purposes, parents are much better supporting and perhaps even seeking it out rather than fighting it (see chapter 6). Deaf children of deaf families represent an important core in the Deaf community.

Deaf people are not evenly distributed around the country, but tend to be more populous around residential schools for the deaf, where there are historical and social ties, and in cities like Washington, D.C., Rochester, New York, and Northridge, California, where there are college programs specifically designed for students who are deaf. Within those population centers, parents and teachers are likely to have a variety of sources of information available to them about educational and other options for deaf children, but in outlying areas, information and access may be more limited. I thus have met several families that have moved to a city with a residential school for the deaf, allowing their child to live at home while having the most available options and support.

The causes and extent of hearing losses vary greatly, as do deaf people's use of spoken or signed communication and their involvement in the Deaf community. Deaf children will vary in whether their hearing losses occurred prior to or after they learned spoken language and whether their hearing losses are stable or progressive. These factors, as well as the degree and frequencies of their hearing losses, will play a major role in social, language, and academic development, issues to be considered through the remainder of this book. Most central for development is the fact that the first 3 years of life are the most important for language acquisition, whether spoken or signed. Where newborn hearing screening is not available and in cases where hearing losses occur sometime after birth, diagnoses may not be made until children are in their second or third year. Many deaf children thus lose out on "educational" opportunities that could have been available if they had earlier screening of their hearing and early interventions to support parent-child communication.

There is a variety of strategies and technologies to help deaf people to offset their lack of hearing. Some technologies support hearing (hearing aids, loop systems, cochlear implants), while others rely on vision to make life more comfortable and convenient as well as safer (TTYs, captioning, doorbell lights). Analog hearing aids are most effective when a child has a hearing loss that involves only the *amount* that they can hear, because they amplify all incoming sound equally. Digital hearing aids can be programmed to vary according to the particular frequencies of a child's hearing loss while reducing background noise.

Cochlear implants are becoming increasingly popular for children with more serious hearing losses. Implant surgery entails inserting an electrode wire into the cochlea and sending signals to the auditory nerve by means of an external micro-processor that converts sound to electrical impulses. In recent years, implants have been shown to be of significant benefit to the hearing of most deaf children, with slightly less impact on speech. Evidence thus far suggests that implants have relatively little impact on social-emotional development, which appears to be much the same after implantation as it was before. Studies of their long-term influence on academic achievement and long-term social functioning are just beginning.

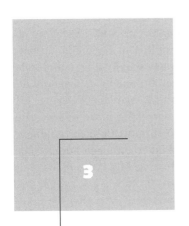

3

I learned ASL before I learned English. . . .
What is important to success is not how
people communicate but the extent to
which they are willing to apply themselves
in pursuit of their life's goals.
—Robert R. Davila, former Assistant
Secretary, U.S. Department of Education

Communicating
With Deaf Children

THREE

To this point, I have described several similarities and differences observed between deaf children and hearing children. Throughout, I have been careful to emphasize that these differences are natural and normal consequences of differences in their early environments and should not be seen as problems to be corrected. Deaf children are not "hearing children who cannot hear," and trying to make them more like hearing children is unlikely to be the best way to support their development and learning. Instead, we have to accommodate their needs and perhaps alter our approaches to education and childrearing. In this regard, it would not be an exaggeration to suggest that most of the ways in which deaf and hearing children are different and the factors on which their success depend revolve around the availability and effectiveness of early communication. Indeed, language is an essential component of normal development for all humans. Numerous studies with hearing children have demonstrated the importance of maternal language to language development, social development, cognitive development, and even the development of visual perception. Deaf children have no lesser needs in these areas, and the goal must be the establishment of an *effective* mode of communication, meaning one that the child can access fully.

Exposure exclusively to spoken language often is not very successful for deaf children who have more severe prelingual hearing losses. This means that even while it is important for parents to strongly support their child's spoken language (if they so desire), it should not be to the exclusion of sign language. Similarly, while it is important for parents to strongly support deaf children's sign language, it should be to the exclusion of spoken language. The important thing is to establish an effective mode of parent-child communication as early as possible. Postponing the beginning of sign language learning until "giving up" on speech training is a common pitfall for parents of deaf children (see chapter 5). It is also one to be avoided unless you want to put all of your eggs into a precarious basket. After exploring the available evidence, we will see that it clearly points to three conclusions: (1) There is no single "correct" answer to the language question that can be applied to all or even most deaf children, (2) there are places for both signed and spoken language in the lives of most deaf children, and (3) sign language will play a vital role in the lives of most deaf children, including many who later rely on spoken language, and its value should not be underestimated. Clearly, I have expressed a bias for using both spoken language and sign language with most deaf children to offer them as much opportunity for normal development as possible. This position comes from my reading of the research literature, however, not any prior philosophical orientation or collection of anecdotes.

Availability of Sign Language for Deaf Children

Surveys conducted during the 1960s indicated that about 90 per cent of hearing parents used only spoken language with their deaf children, while the remainder used some form of "manual communication" (literally, *of the hands*). Since that time, sign languages like American Sign Language (ASL) have been recognized as being full, natural languages, and recent surveys indicate that most deaf students sign at least some of the time. Only about 27 percent of deaf children, however, have families that sign regularly at home (Gallaudet Research Institute, 2003). This situation does not mean that signing is not really necessary, it means that many children and parents are being short-changed in their interactions.

As emphasized in chapter 1, there is no real evidence to support claims that the early use of manual communication (signs or gestures) by deaf children hampers their development of skills in spoken language or in any other area. Gestures, in fact, appear to be an essential prelude to both spoken and signed language development, establishing the rules and contexts of interpersonal communication for both deaf and hearing children (Marschark, 1994). Denying the use of gestures to deaf children, as is done in many programs emphasizing spoken language, thus seems more likely to hurt them rather than to help them.[1] Moreover, the available evidence clearly indicates that, all other things being equal (and they rarely are), deaf children who learn sign language as preschoolers show better progress in development, education, and social adjustment during the school years than children raised in oral-only settings. Those children who are exposed to both sign language and spoken/written language also are the ones who show the best progress in learning to read and write (Akamatsu, Musselman, & Zweibel, 2000; Brasel & Quigley, 1977; see chapter 7).[2] Children who are born to hearing parents and who become deaf after learning language also tend to exhibit better academic and social abilities than children who became deaf prior to learning language. Thus, the important factor is not necessarily the ability to speak, but the ability to communicate through language, whatever its form, from an early age.

Over 50 percent of American schoolchildren identified by the Gallaudet University Annual Survey of Deaf and Hard-of-Hearing Children and Youth now receive some kind of sign language education in school (Gallaudet Research Institute, 2003). Because most hearing parents cannot communicate fully and comfortably with their deaf children, schools for the deaf and other special programs have long been important environments where these children learn a large part of their social skills and social roles as well as academic subjects. Although the proportion of children enrolled in separate versus regular mainstream school programs has changed dramatically in the last 25 years—from 80 percent attending separate school programs to 80 percent attending mainstream programs (see chapter 6)—sign language continues to play an important role in the lives of most deaf children. Deaf children born to deaf parents who use sign language, of course, will be exposed to language from the beginning of their lives—a language that serves both social and educational functions. Most deaf children of deaf parents[3] thus learn about life and about "who they are" at home and in the context of the Deaf community, whereas deaf children of hearing parents often depend more on (signing) individuals outside the home to fill in the gaps left by limited communication with their parents.

The following sections describe several forms of signing used by deaf children in various settings, as well as methods of teaching spoken language to deaf children. Before describing sign language, however, some important groundwork is necessary. First, I need to distinguish what is meant by *manual communication* versus *sign language,* and how each relates to the language actually experienced by deaf children. "Manual communication" is now recognized as somewhat of a misnomer, even though it is often used in contrast to "spoken communication." The error here is that although many people who learn to sign only use their hands (and most hearing people only notice the hands), true sign languages like ASL include a variety of other features as well. Facial expression is particularly important in the way it carries grammatical information including questions and indication of the topic of an utterance. Emotion is communicated by signing rate and size as well as by facial expression and sign selection. Even talking about deaf children learning "sign language" rather than "manual communication" is somewhat misleading, because it is extremely rare that deaf children are exposed exclusively to sign language. Some deaf adults rely solely on ASL in communication among themselves, but their communication with deaf children and hearing individuals frequently includes mouth movements and sign modifications that increase the number of "comprehension cues" available to the receiver. Some of these are actually part of ASL, but others are included to ensure communication with less-than-fluent language users (Marschark, LePoutre, & Bement, 1998).

In educational settings, a multiplicity of language cues for deaf children is made quite explicit through artificial means, and most "sign-language-oriented" programs for deaf children actually employ either *simultaneous communication* (SimCom) or *total communication* (TC). Simultaneous communication refers to the concurrent production of both sign and speech and is the most common means of educational communication between deaf children and those hearing individuals who can sign. Within the classroom, many schools make use of total communication, which argues for the utilization of all potentially available sources of linguistic communication, including sign, speech, and amplification through the use of hearing aids (Spencer & Tomblin, 2006). Total communication is an educational philosophy that supports deaf children acquiring spoken language, sign language, or both—whatever best allows them to communicate in educational and social settings. While SimCom and TC are designed to give deaf children access to as much information as possible, it should not be assumed that they result in deaf children who are fluent in both ASL and English, or either one. The signing used in SimCom and TC are not the same as ASL, any more than it is the same as English. Fluency in natural languages like ASL or English will require exposure to them and considerable instruction if they are not learned naturally.

This issue raises another important distinction to keep in mind, that between natural languages, such as English or ASL, and the gestures and pantomime that accompany them both. Gestures and "body language" are normally used to facilitate both signed and spoken communication. Complex gesture and pantomime also have been shown to develop out of necessity when deaf children grow up in hearing families without the benefit of exposure to sign language, although they are insufficient to communicate more than the most basic information between child and parent.

The relation of gestures and signs as they are used and understood by young deaf children will be considered in chapter 5. Looking ahead, deaf and hearing children tend to use many of the same gestures, both before they actually learn a signed or spoken language and in their day-to-day use of language as they get older. If these gestures are common to speakers of both sign language and English, clearly they cannot be said to be part of ASL any more than they are part of English. It just happens that hearing people tend not to notice how frequently they use gestures—an oversight that can be remedied by careful observation during any 5-minute conversation (even of someone on the telephone).

About Signed Languages

Like a spoken language, a signed language consists of a large vocabulary of arbitrary signs,[4] together with a set of implicit rules, or a *grammar,* that govern both the formation of individual signs and combinations of signs into phrases and sentences. In addition to the repertoire of formalized signs, signed languages contain number signs (Figure 3–1) and a manual alphabet (Figure 3–2). Note that whereas that alphabet used in the United States and many other countries is one-handed, the United Kingdom and Australia make use of a two-handed alphabet. (In the descriptions to follow, English and ASL are still used generically, and the discussion could be about any spoken language and the natural sign language used by Deaf people in the same culture.) Number signs are used just as they are in spoken language: The signs represent number concepts just as the words "ten" and "ten million" do.

As in the case of spoken languages, ASL and other sign languages are quite distinct from each other. Signers of ASL and British Sign Language

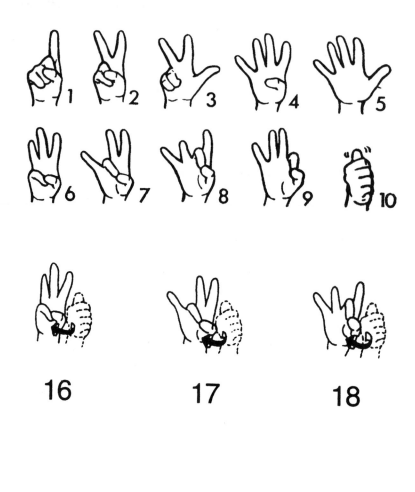

16 17 18

21 100

Figure 3–1. ASL number signs (Courtesy Sugar Sign Press)

Figure 3–2. One-handed manual alphabet (used in the United States and France (Courtesy Sugar Sign Press))

(BSL), for example, are no more likely to understand each other than are speakers of English and Chinese. What is formally called *Signed English* also should not be confused with any of the naturally-occurring sign languages like ASL. Signed English is an artificial signing system combining the signs of ASL and the grammatical structure of English (see discussion later in this chapter). Although it is taught to deaf children attending some programs, Signed English is not used in day-to-day conversations among deaf adults, and children who use it in school typically do not use it in other settings. There is also a generic use of the term *signed English* (or *sign-supported English* in Australia and the UK), which simply refers to signing that retains many features of ASL, but uses English word order. Far more common than the formal Signed English, signed English is just that: English, signed. When produced by a sign language interpreter, it is known as *transliteration*. Parallel forms of signing exist in many other countries. I was once embroiled in a related argument in Warsaw, Poland, where I was making a presentation about language development in deaf children. Members of the Deaf community wanted my presentation interpreted in Polish Sign Language, while audience members closer to the hearing community demanded transliteration using signed Polish. After an animated discussion and a brief delay, both alternatives were offered, but an argument about which interpreter should be positioned on the stage and which should have to be on floor level indicated the significance of the issue for the participants.

The goal of Signed English and other hybridized forms of English/sign language is clear enough: They seek to facilitate signed communication for deaf children while also encouraging acquisition of the English structure necessary for reading, writing, and possibly speech. After more than a century of debate concerning whether deaf children should be taught signed or spoken communication, there is also an educational debate about whether deaf students should continue to be taught using systems like Signed English or taught in ASL instead. Teaching ASL would contribute to the preservation and extension of Deaf culture and provide deaf children with a natural language that "holds together" (making it more learnable) in a way that artificial systems and combinations cannot. Some authors also claim that learning ASL can facilitate deaf children's learning to read and write. This argument may seem to have some credibility, because sign language is more accessible to young deaf children than spoken language if their parents know it and use it consistently. Because ASL bears no resemblance to English or any other written language, however, it should not contribute to reading English any more than would the learning any other language (Mayer & Akamatsu, 2003). Because of the complexity of this issue, discussion of it will be held until chapter 7.

The artificial nature of English-based sign systems may make them less effective than other alternatives as a foundation for natural language development (Schick, 2003). While the jury is still out on this issue, normal development clearly demands the availability of some early language. ASL and similar sign languages clearly are viable alternatives to spoken language, even if they do not contribute directly to children's English literacy skills. At the same time, early learning of ASL may provide deaf children with proficiency in at least one language, and with that comes access to information that will contribute to subsequent development in other domains, including spoken language. Acquisition of ASL or another natural sign language also gives children a sense of mastery and control that is important to subsequent academic success.

A Brief History of American Sign Language

From both practical and educational perspectives, it is difficult to understand how any informed observer could claim that a natural sign language like ASL is anything but a true language. Historically, extensive vocabularies of signs appear to have existed in Spain as early as the 16th century, but it was not until 200 years later that signs were combined with rules for their combination, or *grammars,* and sign language moved into the classroom. This shift, and accompanying changes within the Deaf community, also moved signing from a "gestural system" to a full-fledged language.

The distinction of being the first to take the important step of combining signs with a signing grammar is usually ascribed to the French educator Abbé Charles Michel de l'Épée (1712–1789). Some years later, it was Thomas Hopkins Gallaudet (1787–1851) and Laurent Clerc (1786–1869) who brought Abbé de l'Épée's sign language to America and opened the first public school for deaf children, in Hartford, Connecticut (now the American School for the Deaf). At that point, de l'Épée's sign system was blended with many of the signs that were already in common usage by American deaf people, and ASL was born.[5] One suspects that the resulting change in education of the deaf and in the communication between deaf children and their parents must have opened new horizons of interpersonal contact not much less dramatic than the classic scene in *The Miracle Worker* in which the deaf and blind Helen Keller first grasps the meaningfulness of the fingerspelled word "water."

Although ASL was at one time compared to Native American "sign languages," the comparison is a faulty one. The truly manual communication systems of Native Americans did not replace spoken language, and as far as we know there were no silent tribes. Rather, Native American signs were used primarily to allow communication among different tribes having different spoken languages when they gathered for festive, political, or commercial purposes. Interestingly, some of those signs have nearly identical counterparts in ASL, including the three signs seen in Figure 3–3. Presumably, such commonalities are coincidental and appear to occur primarily for signs that are relatively *iconic* (see note 4; Tomkins, 1969).

Over the last 200 years, signed languages have become both more conventional and more rule-governed in their use by deaf people and more accepted by hearing educators. Until the mid-late 1960s, however, signing was still thought by many hearing people to be a relatively primitive communication system that lacked extensive vocabulary and the means to express subtle or abstract concepts. This impression remains in some

Figure 3–3. ASL signs for DRAW, COFFEE, BOAT, which were the same in early Native American sign systems

other countries, but in North America the language status of ASL and other signed languages has been well documented by linguists, psychologists, and educators. This linguistic revolution began in 1960 when William C. Stokoe, a linguist and head of the English Department at what was then Gallaudet College, first documented the fact that the signing used at Gallaudet had all of the defining features of a "true" language (Stokoe, 1960/

2005). It was another 10 years before the implications of American Sign Language for psychology and child development received much attention, but in the meantime the recognition of their languages empowered Deaf communities around the world and created a social-cultural revolution. As noted in the previous section, several alternatives to naturally occurring sign languages have been developed to foster literacy skills in deaf children, and natural blendings of sign languages and their spoken partners occur in most countries. These other forms of signed communication will be described after considering some of the mechanics of sign language. Those readers already familiar with the linguistic details of ASL might want to skip directly to the following section.

Components of Signs and Signed Languages

Fingerspelling   The availability of *fingerspelling* (the use of the manual alphabet for producing one letter at a time) within signed languages is sometimes misunderstood: It does not replace signing, but supplements it.[6] In part, fingerspelling fills the same function in sign language as it does in spoken language: We can spell words when they are new or when we do not know how to pronounce them. But, normally we do not use spelling in everyday spoken conversations, whereas it occurs relatively frequently in signed conversations (Padden, 2006). One use of fingerspelling is to communicate words for which there are no conventional signs or for which the sign is obscure or unknown, although in all of these cases the words have to be known. There is also a variety of words that are fingerspelled even when there are existing signs for the same concepts, although these *fingerspelled loan signs* may vary by region. The words "busy" and "easy," for example, are concepts that are frequently fingerspelled by ASL users, despite their having common signs as well. Fingerspelled loan signs also may have particular patterned movements, rather than all of the letters occurring in roughly the same place. S-A-L-E, for example, is made with a circular motion, whereas E-A-S-Y involves rotating the wrist while articulating the letters.

In some cases, fingerspelling is only used in particular situations (e.g., F-U-N indicates greater emphasis than the sign FUN). Alternatively, signs and fingerspelling may be used for different parts of speech: The signs LOVE and RENT may be used as verbs while L-O-V-E serves as a noun and R-E-N-T refers to a rental payment.[7] While such grammatical nuances in ASL fingerspelling are indicative of fluency, most signers are very flexible, and comprehension does not depend on them. A Deaf National Technical Institute for the Deaf (NTID) colleague tutoring me in ASL once told me that he could use 100 different sign languages—because he worked with 100 hearing people. Neither he nor most native users of ASL expect that newer hearing signers will know all the rules of fingerspelling, and as long as the fingerspelling is clear (many hearing people try to go too fast), the lack of fluency is not a problem.

We will look briefly at the acquisition of fingerspelling in chapter 5, but it is also worth noting that many signed languages also include a variety of *initialized signs.* Initialized signs typically involve a single sign made with various letter handshapes that give it several different but related meanings. Examples include a group of signs containing *S*-ITUATION, *C*-ONTEXT, *E*-NVIRONMENT, *C*-ULTURE and one containing *G*-ROUP, *C*-LASS, *D*-EPARTMENT, *T*-EAM. In true ASL, all four signs in each group are made with the same handshape, and the precise meaning must be derived from context. Many deaf people use initialized signs quite often, however, even if new signers are often taught that they are not really part of ASL. Quite separate from initialized signs, handshapes that correspond to letters in the one-handed manual alphabet are often contained in signs or *classifiers* (see below).

Modification and Inflection   A glance at any sign language book will reveal that signs can be described in terms of three primary characteristics: the *shape* of the hand or hands, the *place* at which the sign is made or where it begins, and the *movement(s)* involved in making a sign. Signs also can be distinguished by whether they are made with one or two hands, by the orientation of the hand(s) relative to the signer, and whether they involve a stable "base" hand or not. As can be seen in Figure 3–4, any one of the primary sign characteristics is sufficient to change the meaning of a sign (for example, EGG versus NAME, MOTHER versus FATHER) just as such small differences can change the meanings of words ("load" versus "toad," "beet" versus "beer"). Most signs, in fact, can be defined in terms of a combination of components from a set of 18 handshapes, 12 places of articulation, and 25 different movements. For comparison purposes, there are 44 different sounds and 26 letters that make up all English words.

Changes in the movement, place of articulation, or handshape of a particular sign also can be used to modify the number or tense of a sign, just as words in English can be *inflected,* or modified, by adding particular beginnings or endings: "dog" > "dogs," "jump" > "jumped," "important" > "unimportant," and so on. In these cases, the sign DOGS is made by the repeated signing of DOG, and JUMPED is made by adding a FINISH past-marker to JUMP or by letting context specify the past. Only the sign UNIMPORTANT is made by the addition of a simple NOT marker, although there are other ways to sign the concept as well. More extensive inflections also occur in ASL. For example, the movement in the sign COMPLAIN can change to communicate COMPLAIN CONSTANTLY or COMPLAIN VEHEMENTLY, and the sign CHAIR can be altered to mean COUCH or ROW OF CHAIRS. The ability to make such changes, in fact, represents one of the properties that distinguishes sign language from gesture. A true lan-

egg   name

mother   father

Figure 3–4. ASL signs EGG, NAME, MOTHER, FATHER

guage must have a mechanism for modifications of this sort in order to be efficient and allow a full range of communication. Similarly, new signs, like new words, are constantly being invented (within acceptable grammatical rules), and signs can be used in metaphorical ways or as puns.

Classifiers   One central component of signed languages is what is referred to as *classifiers* or, more recently, as *polycomponential signs*. Classifiers have now been found have been found in over 30 sign languages, and it has been suggested that all natural sign languages are likely to contain them. More generally—because it is not only sign languages that have classifiers—

classifiers are *morphemes* (linguistic units) that identify characteristics of their referents. Sign languages do this by shape, but there are classifier languages that are spoken (e.g., Thai, Japanese) that use inflections to accomplish the same thing. Within sign languages, most classifiers are particular handshapes that have meanings that are determined by the context in which they are used. In ASL, there are three distinct kinds of classifiers, each serving a different set of functions. *Entity classifiers* involve handshapes that represent individuals within a category (e.g., VEHICLES, ANIMALS) in the role of actor, receiver of an action, or an object and thus usually function as nouns, pronouns, or noun-verb combinations. *Handle classifiers* are those in which the hand is shaped as though manipulating an object (e.g., a baseball bat or a frying pan) and their handshapes thus reflect what is being handled and how the hand is handling it. *SASS classifiers,* for size-and-shape specifiers, represent the size, shape, or orientation of objects—their visual or physical (and sometimes metaphorical) features. Classifiers thus typically are described as indicating location, motion, manner of movement, distribution, extension, and shape.

There are specific rules within each sign language that specify how classifiers are used and combined, and they allow for a wide range of creative constructions. For example, rather than using the normal, literal signs in the context of a sentence, an upright 1-hand (see Figure 3–2) can be used to indicate a person; a bent, downward V-hand can be used to indicate an animal; and a rotated 3-hand (Figure 3–1) can be used to indicate a car or other vehicle. Classifiers typically first are assigned to a particular person or thing and then are used to indicate actions or directions taken within an episode. Figure 3–5 depicts two simple entity classifiers. In the left panel, the person classifier is used in the sign MEET, and in the right panel, the vehicle classifier is used in the sign PARK. More complex uses of classifiers also occur, and one can easily imagine classifiers used to describe a person (1-hand) who gets into a car (horizontal 3-hand) and weaves down a hill before hitting an animal (bent V-hand) which dies, with "feet" turned upward (two inverted, bent V-hands).

Among the most common SASS classifiers in ASL, functioning more like adjectives than nouns, are F-hands or C-hands (see Figure 3–2) moved vertically or horizontally to denote the size of cylindrical objects, and I-hands, which denote thin filaments or lines (the I-hand also is involved in signs like STRING and SPAGHETTI). Note that although these general classifiers and the more specific noun-like classifiers make use of alphabetic and numerical handshapes, their meanings are completely arbitrary and are not tied to the letter-meaning of the handshape.

As one might suspect by this point, sign languages have their own accents, dialects, and idiosyncratic signs. Signs can be limited to particular regions (Pittsburgh, Pennsylvania is notorious!), schools, or even individual families. *Home signs,* for example, are signs used in much the same

meet   **park**

Figure 3–5. ASL classifiers for PERSON and VEHICLE in MEET and PARK

way as some special words and names are used in hearing families. Both are most common in homes with small children, often originating from mispronunciations or mis-signs. Some such words seem to live on into adulthood, like the words *grabbers* (tongs) and *bazuter* (almost any small electrical device, but especially remote controllers) in my family. Dialectical differences in sign language, like some differences in spoken language, can make for some difficulty in communication.

Combining Signs   There are a variety of grammatical rules within sign languages, operating at several different levels, just as in spoken languages. Some of these are common to most sign languages while other vary language by language. The following descriptions thus refer primarily to ASL, recognizing that other languages will vary in some respects.

Languages vary in how strongly they require specific word ordering (e.g., the use of subject-verb-object ordering). In general, sign languages are not as rigid about word order as spoken languages like English or German, sometimes leading people to assume that it has no grammar. The difference is only relative, though, and the flexibility of sign languages like ASL is comparable to spoken languages like Italian or Japanese. ASL has other ordering rules as well, such as the Time-Agent-Action-Manner sequence used in narrating events (Emmorey, 2002).

In all sign languages, most signs must be made within the *signing space,* a roughly square area from the top of the head to the waist and about one foot to either side of the body. Signs made outside of this space might be seen as ungrammatical or as having some kind of special extended or metaphorical meaning. There are also rules about the positioning of "base" hands, the ways in which signs and classifiers are combined, and symmetry of movement. One example of the latter is the sign SIMULTANEOUS COMMUNICATION shown in the top of Figure 3–6. Because the two hands have the same movement but different handshape, the sign is technically ungrammatical even though it has been used for years. TIME-SAME-COMMUNICATION, in the bottom of Figure 3–6, thus has replaced the old sign for SIMULTANEOUS COMMUNICATION. As in English, however, some ungrammatical forms continue to stay in the language despite our best attempts to purge them (for example, nonwords like "alright," "irregardless," a whole "nother" issue). Soon after arriving at NTID, I took a sign language examination (on which my job depended!) in which I made sure that I used the sign TIME-SAME-COMMUNICATION to refer to Simultaneous Communication. But, when I used the same sign later that week in a meeting of deaf and hearing colleagues, one of the deaf people asked "huh??" Luckily, another deaf person interjected "Oh, he means SIMULTANEOUS COMMUNICATION," using the more common sign.

Using Space   One of the most salient grammatical characteristics of signed languages is their use of the signing space to communicate both time and location. ASL uses space to represent several different time lines. Most obvious is what is called the *deictic* (pointing) *time line.* In that one, time is indicated by positions moving from behind the signer (the PAST), through the here and NOW, and out in front of the signer (the FUTURE). The sign WEEK, for example, is normally made out in front of the body. When the basic sign is finished by moving the right hand backward toward the right shoulder, it means LAST-WEEK; finishing it with a forward arc means NEXT-WEEK. Signs for YEAR and MONTH can be similarly modified (see Marschark, 2005b, for a description).

The space in front of a signer also is used to establish the location of people, objects, and places that are part of an ongoing conversation. When first mentioning particular individuals in an event, usually via a *name-sign* or fingerspelled name, those people can be placed in different locations in the signing space, to the right, to the left or in front of the signer. Later, they can be referred to just by pointing at the location in which they were put, without having to rename them. The locations thus become pronouns, representing individuals or objects that have been placed in them. Sign language novices might have some difficulty keeping their sign spaces organized, but it is only a matter of practice before the utility of locating signs is appreciated, and both production and comprehension are made much easier. As with any language, regular use in many contexts is essential for the acquisition of the signs and rules of sign language. Being hearing does not make sign language any easier or harder to learn. You do not have to learn to read and write it, but most signers will tell you that pro-

simultaneous
communication

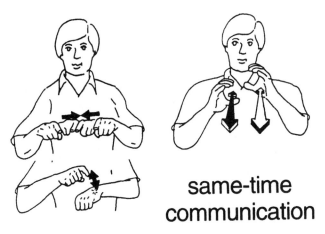

same-time
communication

Figure 3–6. ASL signs SIMULTANEOUS COMMUNICATION and SAME-TIME-COMMUNICATION

ducing clear fingerspelling and understanding it from a deaf person is a real challenge!

Beyond constraints on the form of individual signs, sign languages like ASL have rich varieties of rules for sign combination that had gone unnoticed until relatively recently. For example, although ASL has considerable flexibility in sign order, the subject-verb-object ordering of English is most frequently used, probably because of the immersion of ASL within a culture in which the "host language" is English. Still, the fact that all of the rules and structures of signed languages do not necessarily conform to those of their host languages should not be surprising. That lack of correspondence would only be worthy of wonder if signed languages mapped directly onto their host spoken languages, and we have already seen that this is not the case.

Alternative Forms of Sign Communication

In addition to ASL and Signed English, there are several sign systems[8] taught to deaf children in the United States. The majority of alternative sign systems are formally (versus naturally) developed combinations of signing and English. Collectively known as *manually coded English* or *English-based sign systems*, they present English on the hands rather than the lips. I have already noted that these hybrids are intended to help children learn to read and write. Because signed languages have different grammatical rules than their spoken partners, one cannot really be speaking a language like English and signing ASL. For use in *simultaneous communication* (SimCom) or on its own, however, the various forms of English-based signing can provide access to rules in English using a modality to which deaf children have full access. In theory, such combinations should offer support for literacy skills, although the evidence thus far is rather weak. One major problem appears to be that signed English most often occurs together with spoken English, and very few SimCom users are able to do so fluently. In the few studies that have included expert users of SimCom, deaf high school and college students have understood them just as well as users of ASL, but high quality research on the longer-term impact of English-based signing and SimCom is not available.

The systems described below have not caught on to the degree their developers expected, primarily because no one has provided any firm evidence about their effectiveness. Nonetheless, each has its proponents, and stories of successes of individual children with each system are not hard to find. This is not to say that one of these alternatives, or another yet to be invented, might not prove effective in facilitating the education of deaf children as a group or for a particular deaf child. They are not natural languages, however, and the lack of strong evidence for their effectiveness may well be tied to their artificiality. Meanwhile, there seems no reason why any one mode of language need be used in isolation, and various combined methods are possible. Most importantly, it is essential that deaf children begin to be exposed to language as early as possible and that parents and other family members be fully involved partners. If there is no one to communicate with outside of the classroom, language experience in any mode does little good. With this in mind, let us briefly survey some of the available alternative sign systems for deaf children.

Pidgin Signed English and Contact Sign

The term *Pidgin Signed English* (PSE) is often used synonymously with English-based signing, although it is really a misnomer. Pidgin languages, in general, are those that develop when different languages mix together, typically through the immigration of language groups into new locations. In this manner, English mixed together with French in Louisiana to produce Cajun, and English mixed with several African languages in South Carolina to produce Gullah. When a pidgin is passed on to a second generation as their first language, it evolves into a richer, more complex language called a *creole.*

Pidgins, by definition, are highly variable and have limited grammatical structures of their own, mixing those of the two merging languages. There is no single PSE, therefore, but rather it is an ad hoc mixture of ASL and English-based signing that varies from individual to individual. My first sign teacher was a hearing son of Deaf parents (or *CODA,* a child of deaf adults) who insisted that ASL could not be taught, only learned naturalistically. What he taught, therefore, was a hybrid signing that he called Pidgin Signed English. When I arrived at NTID, I discovered not only how much that system differed from ASL, but also that it was quite different than the English-based signing seen in NTID classrooms, where the mix of signing and oral deaf students often requires the use of SimCom.[9] The common use of signing with English word order by deaf and hearing individuals in a shared community is sometimes called *contact sign* in order to distinguish it from the more idiosyncratic PSE and more formalized created sign systems.

Signed English

Signed English was long a common form of signing taught to deaf children in the United States, although its popularity is waning in favor of ASL. It is unclear, however, how much of this change is attributable to the goal of providing deaf children with a natural language or to the fact that Signed English, like other systems before it, have not really proven effective for enhancing deaf children's literacy skills.

Like other forms of English-based signing, Signed English combines English grammar with the signs of ASL, but it goes beyond the use of initialized signs and English word order. Signed English includes a set of 14 markers that are combined with signs to communicate English structure. Consistent with its purpose of helping deaf children learn to read and write, these structural markers refer to important grammatical features of English. The 14 markers correspond to the following structures, all but one occurring at the end of a sign:

regular noun plural (duck**s**)
irregular noun plural (child**ren**)

possessive (Simon**'s**)
regular past tense verb (jump**ed**)
irregular past tense verb (w**ro**te)
third person singular (writ**ten**)
present progressive (jump**ing**)
past participle (**gone**)
adverbial -ly (slow**ly**)
adjectival -y (funn**y**)
comparative (funni**er**)
superlative (funni**est**)
agent (person or thing)
opposition: not, un-, im-, in- (**im**polite)

Although potentially an important aspect of language used in the classroom, the grammatical markers of Signed English are unnecessary when signing is in the hands of an expert.

Seeing Essential English (SEE1)

SEE1 was developed during the early 1960s as a way to express English literally using the hands. Every English word is supposed to have a basic (ASL) sign in SEE1, and signs are produced in English word order. Additional signs are used to represent English grammatical structures, as in Signed English, but SEE1 goes farther, using a different sign for each meaningful unit of English rather than for each concept. Thus, for example, while ASL and Signed English use single signs for compound English words that represent a single concept ("butterfly" or "sweetheart"), SEE1 uses two signs, one for each component unit. "Butterfly" is thus signed by combining the signs BUTTER and FLY, and "sweetheart" is signed by combining the signs SWEET and HEART—combinations that make spelling sense but not conceptual sense.

   SEE1 retains those ASL signs that conform to a "two-out-of-three rule." A single sign is used for an English word with two or more uses, as long as each pair shares two of the following: sound, meaning, or spelling. Thus "bow" as in "bow and arrow" can have the same sign as "bow" as in "tie a bow" or "violin bow" because they share sound and spelling. "Bow" as in "bow from the waist," however, would have to have a different sign because it shares only spelling with the previous two "bows."

Signing Exact English (SEE2)

SEE2 was a spin-off from SEE1, the consequence of a difference of opinions among the developers of SEE1 about their goals rather than any agreed-upon improvement in the system. SEE2 uses the same general rules as SEE1, but has a one-to-one correspondence between signs and meanings (it is more "exact"). In SEE2, therefore, the word "bow" has four different signs, and SEE2 thus has more signs than SEE1. SEE2 also makes considerable use of initialized signs.

Advocates of SEE1 and SEE2 (often referred to together, as just SEE) are as strongly committed to them as the supporters of Signed English and cued speech (see below) are to these systems. All of them believe that their system works, although their evidence comes primarily from relatively limited successes. In the case of SEE1 and SEE2, the research most often cited in their favor showed them to be superior for deaf children's literacy skills than PSE, but no better than ASL (Luetke-Stahlman, 1990). If English-based sign systems that have been developed to enhance the literacy skills of deaf children do not do so any better than natural signed languages, it is difficult to see a good reason for using them. Again, the theory behind English-based signing makes sense: to allow children to "see" English using an accessible mode of communication so as to improve literacy. But for a variety of reasons they have yet to be shown effective. This may be more a matter of implementation than some basic conceptual flaw, although linguists are quick to point out the artificiality of such systems that are neither sign language nor spoken language.

With regard to literacy, it seems that those systems that are likely to be most effective are those that combine as many sources of information as possible (see chapter 7). Indeed, this is precisely the philosophy behind simultaneous communication and total communication. Artificial sign systems, however, do not lead most deaf children to fluency in either sign language or in English. At present, it is unclear whether deaf children learning a hybrid sign system gain enough in English skills to offset their not being fluent in ASL, but my reading of the existing literature says that they do not. It may be that English-based systems are easier for hearing parents to learn than ASL, but that is not the rationale for using them, and the lack of parents' strength in ASL does not appear to undermine their children's eventual fluency. Until more work has been done, this issue will continue to be a problem.

Spoken Language

Up to now, this chapter has included relatively little discussion of spoken language. This is not to suggest that deaf children cannot learn to speak; surely some can. Rather, the point is that in the absence of hearing (especially during the critical stages of language learning), spoken communication traditionally has not been a viable primary means of communication for most deaf children. With extensive speech training, many deaf children reach the point where family members can understand their speech, but that does not mean that they will be understood by others outside the family or that they will be able to understand the speech of others. Recent figures suggest that only about a quarter of deaf children develop intelligible speech, a number that has not changed much in the last 20 years (Beattie, 2006). Because language development, speech reception, and speech production are related,[10] this number is higher among children with cochlear implants. Preliminary studies indicate that perhaps 60 to 65 percent of such children may develop intelligible speech, although it is still less fluent than that of their hearing peers.

And, of course there are exceptions. We have all seen deaf people on television or elsewhere, such as Heather Whitestone, Miss America 1994, who appear to have excellent, or at least pretty good, speech. In many cases, those are individuals with lesser hearing losses or people who had better hearing when they learned to speak and then experienced progressive or acute hearing losses. Others have improved their speech as children or as adults through intensive speech therapy. This shift may occur after using sign language early in life, at the point where an individual has the motivation and ability to benefit from spoken language methods. There are several schools and programs in this country offering education exclusively in spoken language and claiming varying degrees of success.[11] Still to be determined is whether the children who succeed in such programs are representative of all deaf children or whether they have particular characteristics that make them most likely to benefit from such exposure in the first place. In any case, even if it is understandably preferred by many hearing parents, the argument for exposure to spoken language only has never been supported in any broad sense and thus I believe that spoken language seems most likely to be effective when combined with ASL or some alternative (see Calderon & Greenberg, 1997). This seems an increasingly popular position among the "moderates" in deaf education, but is seen less favorably by those who I often refer to as being at the extreme left ("sign language is a deaf child's cultural heritage") or right ("all deaf children can learn to speak") in the language debate.

Speech Training and Speech Assessment

Speech training and speech assessment should be thought of as a whole, not as two different endeavors. Assessment of a child's skills and needs are essential for the effective teaching of spoken language, and the optimization of teaching requires regular assessments both of progress in speech skill acquisition and possible changes in young children's hearing. Both assessment and training therefore have to take into consideration the goals and capabilities of the children and their families, not just abstract principles about the importance of spoken language. Indeed, the intense adherence to the primacy of speech by some advocates of "oral approaches" has driven some deaf individuals away from its potential benefits.

The goal of speech and speechreading training should be to allow deaf children to take advantage of the most information possible and have access to the full range of opportunities offered to hearing children. In my view, that means adoption of a *total communication* approach, even if that is not the focus here. As indicated in the quote at the beginning of this chapter, the ultimate decision to use speech, sign, or some combination of them rests with the individual; parents and educators will find themselves—and their children—best positioned if they make all resources available to children until such time as the children themselves are able to make their own decisions.

As we will see in the next section, speech training can take on a variety of forms, depending on the needs of the individual child (or, more often, the philosophical approach of the speech therapist). Different programs focus on different "levels" of spoken language, from individual letter sounds, through syllables, to whole word pronunciation methods. Syllable methods, for example, involve repeated practice with single consonant-vowel pairs such as *pa, pa, pa* or sets of pairs that vary in their vowel "place of articulation" such as the set that would sound like *pee, pa, peh, po, pu,* where you can feel the tongue moving farther and farther back in the mouth. Examples like this are not visible on the mouth (just look in the mirror) and are extremely difficult for deaf children to learn; hence the potential usefulness of cued speech. Alternatively, speech training can focus on the pronunciation of whole words. This is often done with words in isolation, although their presentation within meaningful contexts can also contribute to reading as well as speechreading skill. Finally, what was long called the "natural method" of teaching speech to deaf children emphasizes its use in natural situations, with less reliance on practice drills.

Regardless of its level, speech training usually involves a child interacting one-on-one with a trained speech therapist, modeling their behaviors over numerous sessions. Parents are given exercises to work on at home with their child, but this is rarely sufficient. There are also a variety of technological tools available for professional and home use for speech training. For example, there is interactive computer software in which young children's productions of correct sounds lead to interesting visual events, such as a monkey climbing a tree. Older children might be shown speech patterns on the computer screen and work to match them with their own productions. One computer program, called Baldi, makes use of a life-like animated talking head, an *avatar,* to show children how the articulatory apparatus makes speech sounds, from both inside and outside of the mouth (Massaro, 2006). These and other methods serve to help coordinate motor movements of the tongue and mouth and appropriate inflow and outflow of air as well as establishing rapport and comfort between the child and the speech training enterprise.

As with speech training, speech assessment can take various forms. At the level of individual sounds, speech therapists evaluate vocal intensity, duration, and pitch, in addition to the correctness of the articulation. As individual speech sounds come into a child's repertoire, they have to be expanded, combined, and regularly maintained or they can degrade ("use it or lose it"). Some speech skills acquired at the level of individual sounds are not easily integrated into syllables and words, so that there must be a constant monitoring and correction of the full repertoire. Clearly, this relatively intense focus can be difficult for younger deaf children, and many will never master the basics well enough to engage in natural spoken conversation outside of the family. At the same time, because of positive responses from many hearing adults, spoken communication successes can add to a child's feelings of accomplishment, as well as facilitating their communication within the home and school.

To be most effective, speech training must be coupled with appropriate amplification, so that children can receive auditory feedback in addition to what they can see on the lips. If they have sufficient residual (aided) hearing and speechreading skills to also comprehend the spoken language of others, spoken language can be a valuable tool. There are several different approaches to enhancing spoken language by deaf children, however, and the apparent disagreements among their advocates are just as bewildering as those among advocates of different sign systems. Let us consider the primary methods individually.

Oral Methods

There are various methods intended to give deaf and hard-of-hearing children knowledge of and the ability to produce the sounds and structures of a given language[12] (see Beattie, 2006, for a review). Perhaps the most common and obvious of these is simple lipreading, or *speechreading,* but we have already seen that this is far more difficult and less helpful than is generally supposed. Other methods are more complex and, of course, each has its advocates. In general, however, formal approaches to teaching deaf children spoken language all include four characteristics deemed essential to their success:

- beginning diagnostic therapy as early as possible after identification of hearing loss
- early fitting of hearing aids, their consistent use, and careful supervision to ensure that they are in working order and used properly

- active involvement of parents and siblings to ensure consistent spoken language models and support for language use
- encouraging the child to participate—utilizing spoken language—in a variety of activities inside and outside of school.

Let us consider the two primary approaches, at least in North America: the *Auditory Verbal* and the *Auditory Oral* methods. In the United Kingdom, *Natural Oralism* (or *Natural Auralism*) and the *Maternal Reflective Method* are also popular, the former emphasizing the link between language and cognitive development, and the latter emphasizing the importance of writing (a return to "natural methods" popular in the 19th century).

The Auditory Verbal (AV) Method   The auditory verbal method (AV) is best known for its focus on enhancing deaf children's listening skills and limiting the use of speechreading. During therapy sessions, the therapist's mouth is usually covered, so that children cannot make use of visual cues to comprehension (clearly this method requires that the child have some usable hearing). Proponents of the auditory verbal method emphasize the importance of mainstream education, but couple it with intensive one-on-one, center-based speech therapy, especially for younger children. Regardless of whether children are using hearing aids or have cochlear implants, parents are trained to carefully monitor the equipment (it is amazing how often teachers find children coming to school with dead batteries in their hearing aids and implants) to ensure that their child maximizes use of their residual hearing. Therapists are seen as supporting parents, who are given the primary responsibility for their child's success.

The AV approach includes the notion of *integration,* at several levels. Most centrally, the emphasis of the approach on children's use of spoken language in a variety of social and family settings is intended to result in speech and hearing becoming a central part of the child's personality. Sound and speech are supposed to become rewarding, so that the child is motivated to utilize their residual hearing and speech skills.

The Auditory Oral (AO) Method   The auditory oral (AO) approach to spoken language development is similar to the AV method, with some different emphases. The primary differences between the two methods relate to their relative emphasis on audition and vision and differences in the kinds and location of therapy. Most prominently, the AO method allows children to make use of speechreading as well as residual hearing to support both comprehension and production of spoken language. The emphasis of most AO practitioners on the use of visual cues has been diminished, and while they still allow children to make use of speechreading and gesture, they no longer encourage their use.

AV and AO approaches also differ with regard to their philosophies concerning educational placement for deaf children. Unlike the AV emphasis on mainstream school placements, the AO approach includes supporting children in a variety of settings, from separate classrooms for deaf and hard-of-hearing children to reverse mainstream to full or partial mainstreaming in a regular classroom (see chapter 6). Students also may move from one kind of program to another, depending on their needs and preferences, throughout the school years. Finally, whereas the AV approach is, at its core, akin to the "natural method" mentioned above, AO therapy often includes more drill and practice.

Cued Speech

Cued speech is a supplement to spoken language, supporting it with a set of sound-related handshapes in particular positions. Each language for which a cuing system has been developed has its own cues (as with signing, deaf people who cue do not automatically have the ability to communicate internationally). The motivation for the invention of cued speech lay in the fact that many speech sounds look the same on the lips when they are pronounced, especially in English, making speechreading difficult. For example, if you look in the mirror, and pronounce the names of letters "c," "e," "g," and "z," they look very similar on the lips. Speechreading of some other languages, like Italian, is somewhat easier because of greater regularity in the way in which sounds are combined and their unambiguous correspondence to writing. More of the language therefore "can be seen on the lips," and one therefore might expect that deaf children in such countries would have relatively better speech skills, and perhaps reading skills, than deaf children in the United States. I believe that apparent differences in the success of cued speech in different countries supports this prediction.

It is worth noting that the developer of cued speech, the late Orin Cornett, did not intend or expect it to replace sign language. In his early writings, Cornett made it clear that he designed cued speech to help deaf children with the *phonological* (language sounds) system underlying spoken language and thus support their literacy skills. He fully expected that deaf children would continue to use ASL as a means of social communication and a mode of classroom instruction.

The idea behind cued speech is that if deaf children could be given cues sufficient to distinguish sounds that look alike on the lips in English, they would be better able to learn to lipread and reproduce those lip movements in spoken communication (LaSasso & Metzger, 1998). Cued speech today thus maintains an "oralist" approach to language, while providing a manual means of overcoming the limitations of oral ambiguity. Overall, it uses 36 different cues to clarify the 44 different sounds in English. Cues for vowel sounds are produced by placing the hand at one of 7 different locations on the face in the area of the mouth. Cues for consonant sounds are provided by making one of eight alternative handshapes and combining them with the vowel locations. The handshapes of cued speech thus play a very different role from the handshapes of ASL, which carry information about meaning rather than about sound. Accordingly, cued speech is not technically a language, but is a support for English—providing, of course, that everyone involved in a conversation knows how to read and produce the cues.

The body of research relating to cued speech is quite interesting. There is abundant evidence in the United States and elsewhere that cued speech can help deaf children to understand spoken language, although its impact on production is less clear (LaSasso & Metzger, 1998). The situation gets a little trickier with regard to the impact of cued speech on deaf children's literacy skills. Oliver Perrier, Jacqueline Leybaert, Jesus Alegria, and their colleagues in Belgium have shown that deaf children who are consistently exposed to cued French during the preschool years both at home and at school learn to read faster and show enhanced subskills in reading relative to deaf children exposed only to spoken language (see chapter 7; Leybaert & Alegria, 2003). On the basis of these findings, supporters of cued speech in the United States and Canada have advocated for its broader use. Despite 40 years of trying, however, there is still no evidence that cued speech enhances the literacy (or spoken language skills) of deaf children learning English. A variety of studies have been conducted, but few have been published and the findings of those are ambiguous or have not proven to be repeatable. This situation might arise because spoken French has much more regular spelling-to-sound correspondences than English (Alegria & Lechat, 2005), or there might be some other explanation. As a long-time supporter of cued speech (who learned to cue some years ago), I have to admit my disappointment with its apparent lack of utility for fostering English literacy.

We have not yet seen any evidence of how reading skills of children learning cued speech (even in French) compare to those of children learning both ASL and English or some hybrid, like Signed English. It also is not clear whether cued speech alone gives younger deaf children full access to spoken English. Some parents have found it effective to expose their children to ASL first, and then bring in cued speech during the school years. One former colleague of mine followed this route, teaching her son cued speech when he was about 8 years old. The problem, of course, is that if you are using your hands for vowel and consonant cues, you cannot be signing at the same time. Therefore, cued speech may be most effective in situations where a story or situation is first described in sign language and then, when it is fully understood, retold with cued speech. This combination may help to convey the link between speech and the printed word, but, for the time being, apparently only if you are learning French.

Final Comments

Language is an essential component of normal development. Because the vast majority of deaf children are born to nonsigning hearing parents, however, many of them will be denied access to many parts of the world until they have passed the most critical ages for language acquisition, the first 2 to 4 years. Although spoken language is often believed to be an essential component of a child's development, most available research indicates that for children with greater hearing losses, exposure only to spoken language is likely to fall short of giving children the linguistic tools they need for academic and social purposes. All of this is not to say that speech therapy is unimportant for deaf children, only to emphasize that only a minority of deaf children without cochlear implants will develop spoken language skills sufficient for the needs of day-to-day life. For most children with implants, an emphasis on spoken language is clearly appropriate because, after all, the whole reason for an implant is to improve hearing and speech. It is still unclear, however, what the minimum threshold is for the amount of spoken language a deaf child needs to experience for successful implant use. Most likely, that threshold will be somewhat different for each child, consistent with the considerable heterogeneity seen among deaf children. Spoken language skills also are likely to be useful even for children who will later depend more on sign language, although enmity between those on the left and the right in the debate often makes discussion of that possibility difficult.

Access to English may be essential for English literacy, but it is most important that deaf children, like hearing children, be able to communicate with their parents from the beginning. Following chapters will show the various ways that early communication affects social and cognitive development, and we will see that signed languages are as complete and rich as spoken languages and can fill all of the same roles in a child's development and education. This does not mean that children who grow up with signed versus spoken language will be the same, but for children who are not likely to acquire spoken language, sign language will offer them opportunities that are in many ways comparable. For these children, sign language will offer both advantages and disadvantages relative to hearing peers, but only advantages compared to deaf children who are not exposed to any effective language (see chapters 7–9).

True sign languages are characterized by the same kinds of features as spoken languages, including rules for formation, modification, and combination of units. Signs are generally characterized by several clearly defined characteristics such as handshape and movement. They are combined in grammatically defined ways using three-dimensional space and a variety of grammatical devices such as classifiers, used like pronouns, and linking movements. Like spoken words, most signs are arbitrary and combine with a manual alphabet, facial expression, and body movement to yield a full and natural language taught by deaf parents to their deaf children. Almost every country has its own sign language and some countries have more than one, corresponding to their multiple spoken languages. Consider, for example, American Sign Language, used in both the United States and English-speaking parts of Canada. Parts of ASL, and especially the grammar, originally came from France, but it differs dramatically from both the sign language used in Québec (La Langue des Signes Québécoise) and England (British Sign Language). Remnants of ASL's French past can be seen in the A-handshape used in the sign YEAR ("l'année" in French) and the B-hand used in GOOD ("bon" in French).

Various hybrid systems have been developed in an effort to provide deaf children with early access to language via signing, while simultaneously giving them access to English or another spoken language. Cued speech is a supplement to spoken language that uses handshapes in particular locations to disambiguate sounds (and hence words) that are made similarly on the lips. Other systems, such as Signed English and SEE, use signs with English word order, sometimes with additional grammatical markers. To date, however, these systems have not lived up to their raison d'être—facilitating deaf children's literacy development (see chapter 7). It may be that a combination of such a system combined with a natural sign language and/or spoken language might be successful, but attempts at such bilingual models are rare. Indeed, rather than providing deaf children with fluency in two languages, hybrid communication systems seem likely to leave them fluent in neither.

Regardless of the method—signed or spoken—deaf and hearing children need to have consistent access to a natural language if they are to have the tools necessary for becoming literate and getting a comprehensive education. Whatever system a deaf child might experience at school, language learning cannot stop there. Unless deaf children can bring language home with them and use it during play, to get help with schoolwork, and to communicate with their families, they cannot be expected to reach their full potentials. If educators of deaf students are not yet producing high school graduates who are fully competent (see chapters 6 and 8), the blame cannot be placed wholly on teachers and schools. The basic underpinnings of learning and education begin at home, years before the young deaf or hearing child goes off to school. We therefore now turn to consideration of deaf children's development from birth through adolescence. By this point, the reader should have some understanding of deafness with which to examine social, language, and cognitive development more closely. Thus armed, we will be able to see the implications of early hearing losses for growth throughout childhood and make some fairly good predictions about how and when we will need to compensate for those losses.

4

My son isn't handicapped. He just can't hear.
—Mother of a graduating college student

Early Interactions:
The Roots of Childhood

FOUR

Descriptions of deaf children written in the 1950s and 1960s often painted a bleak picture of them as living isolated and empty lives filled with emotional troubles and behavioral problems. Since then, investigations have provided a much better understanding of the psychological functioning of deaf children and deaf adults, and many of the earlier misconceptions and biases have been swept away. Newborn hearing screening and early intervention programs have been developed to provide young deaf children with a variety of social and educational experiences and to provide their parents with much needed information and support. Such programs now begin early and play a much more proactive role in preparing children for schooling, with particular emphasis on the importance of early exposure to language. Thanks in part to the Deaf community and to research into the psychological development of deaf children, many hearing people now have come to realize that once one gets beyond the appearances of sign language, deaf and hearing children are much the same, and in the end they grow up to have comparable roles and responsibilities in society.

These similarities notwithstanding, I used the word "comparable" rather than "identical." I think the difference is important. Deaf children's lives do not have to be identical to those of hearing children in order for them to be happy, intelligent, and successful. Deaf and hearing children have many of the same external forces acting on them, and they all respond more or less in the same ways. Most children therefore follow a similar course of development regardless of their hearing status. That course may be followed by different children at different rates, and it may have some rather different characteristics depending on the hearing status of the children and their parents. Such differences are not necessarily bad, however, and may reflect very good adjustments by children to various aspects of their family and social settings. What is essential is that the adults in a deaf child's world recognize the child's strengths and needs—to build on the former and to work to overcome the latter. All of this begins essentially at birth.

Origins of Social Relations

During the earliest stages of social development, mothers and children develop ways of interacting with each other through a variety of shared experiences. Eventually, their actions become intertwined in a way that both simplifies their day-to-day routines and teaches the child about successful (and unsuccessful) strategies for social interaction.

Consider a typical and almost universal routine: An infant cries or fusses, and his mother attends to him, touching and caressing him, talking to him, and perhaps picking him up. The infant temporarily ceases to fuss and looks at his mother, who is now speaking or smiling; he produces some vocal sounds and is "answered" by her with more sounds, more handling, and so on. Although relatively inexperienced at such things, the infant is clearly playing an important role in this interaction. Unwittingly, he is giving his mother cues that partially determine her behavior, including the passing of cues back to him for the next part of the interaction. Over time, both sides become better at this socialization game, developing better timing, more variety, and greater complexity. True conversation is still a long way off; but in the meantime, these back-and-forth interactions teach the child about taking turns both vocally and behaviorally (for example, by waving hands or smiling) and about being part of a social relationship.

Now consider the situation when the mother or the infant, or both, are deaf. A deaf mother may first be alerted to her child's fussing by a visual signaling device if she is in another room. From that point, the interaction is essentially just like that of a hearing mother with a hearing child, with gestures and signs replacing speech. Ultimately, sign language will provide a means for mother and child to interact at a distance, as long as they can still see each other, allowing both of them to turn their attention to other things while still maintaining contact.[1]

The situation is quite different in the case of deaf infants with hearing mothers, especially in the absence of newborn hearing screening, when the mother does not recognize or even imagine that her child is deaf. One potential source of difference stems from the possible medical causes for the child's hearing loss in the case of nonhereditary deafness. Even if there are no direct, health-related consequences beyond hearing loss, there may be indirect effects on mother and child, such as continuing maternal stress or differences in child temperament that could affect the frequency or the quality of their interactions (Calderon & Greenberg, 2003). Unless there is some reason to expect it, hearing loss often is not noticed early on by parents and pediatricians. For one thing, the loss might not be complete, so that deaf children may be able to hear some things—like the yelling of parents or siblings—but unable to hear normal speech. With greater hearing losses, deaf children will be sensitive to the vibration and pressure changes caused by loud noises, and reactions to clapping behind their heads or the slamming of doors might incorrectly be interpreted as signs of normal hearing.[2] Further, the multitude of mutual cues that mother and child have developed over the first weeks and months of life may give the impression that nothing is amiss. Sometimes, delays of more than a year in language development are overlooked as signals of hearing loss or, even worse, they are taken as indicators of mental retardation, autism, or incompetent parenting.

Early Interactions Have Far-Reaching Effects

To understand how the personalities and social relationships of deaf children develop, we need a feel for what happens between deaf infants and their parents during the first months at home. It is through their mothers, in particular, that infants have their first contact with the world, through feeding, cuddling, bathing, and, in most cases, hearing their mothers' voices. These earliest experiences do not determine the course of development, but they will have ever-widening implications for growth in learning, exploration, and social interactions. Humans are social creatures, and even diaper changing and bathing are social events for infants and mothers. What the infant learns from these experiences through behavioral interactions with caregivers will affect the building of more complex social relationships with others in the family and, eventually, with those beyond the family. Within these earliest experiences, language typically plays a central and ever-increasing role. Even before birth, it appears that sounds in a hearing child's environment may indirectly affect the course of development. During the last 3 months of pregnancy, the fetus usually rests with its head against the mother's pelvis. At this point in development, most fetuses have developed to the point where they can hear and even react to human speech. This means that for those mothers who speak and are carrying babies who can hear, the fetus can now hear its mother's voice, in addition to her heartbeat, as those sounds are conducted through her bones.

The fact that the fetus experiences its mother's voice before birth is not a matter of dispute among scientists, but the possible effects of that experience on later development are still unresolved. At the very least, we know that auditory experiences before birth can affect later learning and perception in both humans and animals, and they can play a role in the early bonding of mothers and infants. Working with humans, for example, Professor Anthony DeCasper and his colleagues have demonstrated that infants less than 3 days old can learn to suck on a nipple in a particular pattern (either faster or slower than their normal rate) in order to turn on a tape recorder that allows them to hear their mothers' voices. In one study, DeCasper found that 2-day-old babies were "willing and able" to adjust their sucking patterns in order to hear their mothers' voices rather than the voice of another woman, indicating that the newborns could tell the difference between the voices and that they had a clear preference (DeCasper & Spence, 1986). Perhaps most impressive of all were the results of a study in which mothers read a particular passage aloud (for example, from *The Cat in the Hat*), regularly, during the last 6 weeks of pregnancy. Later, their babies showed a preference for that passage over a different one within hours after they were born—due to the particular rhythmic structure of the sounds, not because they liked the story. Interestingly, fathers' voices, which cannot be heard by fetuses in the womb, do not show any sign of being especially attractive to newborns (sorry, dads!).

These results suggest that hearing mothers' speech both before birth and soon thereafter might play a role in early social interactions, by making the mother "familiar" to the newborn. But just as infants are likely to respond positively to the familiar sound of mothers' voices, so mothers are likely to respond positively, in turn, to an infant who smiles, gurgles, and looks at her mother's face in response to her voice. Building on this original relationship, mother and child gradually become more attuned to each other and expand on their early "conversations."

This typical scenario does not mean that early mother-infant relationships require vocal or spoken communication, and we already have seen that there are a variety of other forms of interaction between deaf babies and their mothers. Most obviously, there are visual, tactile, and other cues that serve to identify familiar people and objects to infants within the first few days of life. In the early relationships of infants and their parents, in fact, smiles and rhythmically patterned touching and stroking seem to be just as soothing as familiar voices. Maternal touch, in particular, has powerful effects on both deaf and hearing newborns (Koester, Brooks, & Traci, 2000). Deaf mothers tend to touch their infants more than do hearing mothers, but hearing mothers who are aware of their children's hearing losses also are likely to touch their infants more, to use more exaggerated facial expressions, and to try to keep objects and themselves within their infants' line of sight. Parents who have not yet discovered that their children are deaf also might unknowingly compensate for the lack of hearing with other means of communication, but there are as yet no data available on this possibility. Of course, this is because if parents are not yet aware of their child's hearing loss, there is no way to identify them for study. Nevertheless, it is clear that there are multiple, sometimes unnoticed cues involved in the early social interactions of parents and their deaf children, and that these cues will contribute to mother-child attachment and other relationships.

Unlike some animals, such as birds, which depend on maternal and sibling vocalizations to keep them safe, deaf children may not be at any particular disadvantage because they cannot recognize their mothers' voices at birth. As compared to hearing infants, deaf infants and their hearing mothers may simply begin their relationships interacting in somewhat different ways that have somewhat different consequences (or not). When we watch the interactions of deaf infants with deaf parents, they look very much like hearing infants with hearing parents. By the time they are a year old, both deaf children of deaf parents and hearing children of hearing parents can tell when others are happy, frightened, or sad, just by looking at their faces. At that age, deaf children show as much affection to their parents as hearing children, and they clearly know how to get attention by tapping people on the arm or waving to them rather than calling. Deaf infants and their deaf mothers thus have quite normal early relationships. The only way in which they look different is the use of signed rather than spoken communication.

Accepting Childhood Deafness

Discovering that one's child is deaf or handicapped in some way is not an easy situation for most parents to accept ("That's putting it mildly!" one mother recently told me). Pregnancy is an exciting but anxious time for parents-to-be. Still, most pregnancies are unplanned, and even those couples who want to have children are often nervous about whether the decision to do so at a particular time is a wise one. Parents-to-be wonder about how their child will be supported and cared for, about its impact on their lifestyle and their relationship, and about whether it will be healthy and happy. How must it feel to discover that your child cannot hear?

There are anecdotes about deaf parents hoping that their children will be deaf. Not surprisingly, this is a controversial issue, and a recent situation in the United States in which a Deaf female couple arranged for in-vitro fertilization to ensure they had a deaf baby made headlines around the world. Most Deaf parents report simply being far less concerned than hearing parents with the hearing status of their babies: deaf is fine, hearing is fine, too (but see Johnston, 2005). In the first edition of this book, for example, I recounted a story about my wife and I being out to dinner with some Deaf friends and encountering an acquaintance of theirs who came by the table with his wife and 3-month-old son. At the end of the introductions, the father introduced his young son, finishing with the proud statement "DEAF!" At the time, I congratulated him, thinking about how much different the situation was than it would be for hearing parents. When the fellow later read the story in the book, he recognized himself, but said that I had misunderstood him. He had not intended to express joy in having a deaf child (he said that it did not really matter to him, one way or the other). Rather, his announcement of DEAF! was intended as a comment about his son, not much different than saying "Isn't he handsome?" As I mentioned in chapter 1, viewing the Deaf community from outside has its dangers!

In the absence of newborn hearing screening, hearing losses in children of hearing parents typically are not diagnosed until the third or fourth year of life (age 2–3). The national average for age of diagnosis in the United States before legislation supporting screening was about 30 months. Delays of that magnitude are still the norm in states that do not have early screening programs and they are often much longer in other countries. Most deaf mothers of deaf children, in contrast, claim that they can recognize whether their children are deaf during the first few months of life, simply by the way their infants behave and react to them. Our acquaintances from the restaurant may have either figured out for themselves that their son was deaf, or they may have had him tested while still in the hospital. Hearing parents, of course, normally would wait much longer. By way of analogy, radiologists looking at x-rays of advanced changes in the body often can see their development in earlier x-rays that they previously had pronounced unexceptional. Similarly, hearing parents of deaf children, after hearing loss is discovered and confirmed, often are able to recollect having seen—but not recognized—some of the signs. When those early clues first appear, they are not so obvious. Sometimes, the fear of finding that something is in fact wrong can lead parents to convince themselves that they are overly concerned and just nervous with their status as new parents. It may be more comforting to believe grandmothers' and pediatricians' (correct) claims that some children are slow to talk, that some are louder criers and harder to soothe than others, and that some simply do not respond as warmly as parents might like. The fact that a baby sleeps through many loud noises and yet seems to respond to others when she is awake is perplexing, but at least it suggests that she is not *deaf,* and, perhaps, she really does have partial hearing. Suggestions from concerned friends and relatives about the possibility of early hearing loss thus are often shrugged off.

Eventually, the uneasy, troubled feelings win out. A deaf infant is not as quick as a hearing infant to notice people coming into a room; crying does not stop, or even pause, when mother calls to her baby; and gentle words do not seem to be very soothing. As the months go by, hearing parents come to realize that their child's behavior is varying more and more from what is considered normal. Hearing parents often report feeling rejected, guilty, or anxious about the apparent lack of a mutual relationship with their child. Some parents begin to think that their child might have some undetermined psychological problems. Others put "emotional distance" between themselves and their child. Ultimately, all parents of deaf children recognize that it is the child's hearing that needs to be evaluated. For those families lucky enough to be near a university or a medical center with an audiology clinic, an informed diagnosis then can be obtained relatively quickly. For those in more rural areas or without medical insurance, an audiologist or otolaryngologist (an ear, nose, and throat doctor) may be difficult to find.

Beyond blaming pediatricians for not recognizing their children's hearing losses earlier, perhaps the most common complaint of parents who receive a diagnosis of deafness in their child is the lack of informational support from professionals involved in their children's care. Hopefully, changes in public awareness about hearing loss and newborn hearing screening programs are making such complaints less common, but many people retain distorted and simply mistaken ideas about being deaf, sign language, and deaf education. In the case of parents who go through early screening with their babies, many later report that they had been given biased or incomplete information by the people conducting the screening. Otolaryngologists and implant surgeons I know all shudder when they hear such stories, but in most cases, they have no control over the individuals conducting hearing screening, and, as we have seen, this is an area in which opinions are strong and there are relatively few people who are disinterested enough to provide all sides of the story. Just as importantly perhaps, parents are often so upset at the screening when they learn of their child's hearing loss that they likely do not remember a lot of the information they received. For this reason, I have suggested that those initial meetings be videotaped, with one copy given to the parents and one kept by the audiologists. Parents can later use the tapes to recap the details of their child's situation and any relevant recommendations. The audiologist has a record of exactly what parents were told, just in case there is some disagreement later.

The Show Must Go On

Coupled with the need for more objective and accurate information is the need for sympathetic understanding for parents who are making the psychological adjustment to having a deaf child. The discovery that their child is deaf may be greeted by some parents with relief and the positive realization that "it wasn't anything worse." Other parents have a very difficult time adapting to the idea of having a child who is labeled "handicapped." In either case, there is likely to be a period of grieving that is both natural and helpful. Social, emotional, and practical support from family and friends is most important during this time—"helpful" advice from people unfamiliar with childhood deafness usually is not useful at all until parents are ready for it.

Parents' grieving after receiving a diagnosis that their child is deaf may not be so much over the loss of hearing, as over the loss of a "perfect" child and a "normal" life for the child and the whole family. Such grief has a natural course that serves a variety of psychological functions for us. Many hearing parents first shield themselves through *denial.* Especially in cases of profound hearing loss, parents may feel that the diagnosis must have been a mistake, that the error will be found, that the dream will end. Alternatively, hoping for "cures" that do not exist, parents may take their young deaf child from one specialist to another, or, as a last resort, visit quacks or faith-healers.[3] There can be pain and worry about the child's welfare and future, together with concerns about the stability of the marriage and of the family. These feelings are often accompanied by a period in which parents "negotiate"—with themselves, with fate, with God. Somehow, there is a feeling that by changing one's ways, by taking on a child's "suffering," his hearing will be miraculously restored.

But, most of the time, the situation does not correct itself. Parents' bargaining is often replaced by anger—again, toward themselves, toward fate, toward God. There may be a time of despair, when all hope seems lost, and it must be someone's fault! Although the anger is always misdirected (except perhaps for that aimed at fate) this emotional upheaval can make matters worse, as interactions within the family and especially with the innocent but offending child become more strained. Anger thus eventually gives way to guilt over one's own poor behavior toward the child and others in the family. It is not the mother's fault that a child is born deaf, and yet for a time she is willing to take the psychological blame and, for a time, the father (lagging behind emotionally as men often do) is willing to let her.

Only after a child's hearing loss is truly accepted can parents start to appreciate their child for who she is. Only then will they be able to begin a constructive rearrangement of their lives to accommodate their child's needs and their new status as parents of a deaf child. The adjustment of hearing families to the arrival of a deaf child will have a variety of practical, emotional, and financial ramifications, and the effects of such changes are felt by each member of the immediate and extended family. Although it might not seem possible to parents who are at their "low points," most families with a deaf child function quite normally after a period of adjustment. With relatively little disruption to regular family routines, life goes on quite naturally. Of course, there will be some changes involved in developing effective means of communication through signed or spoken language (using new methods consistently), and in the many trips to audiologists for children with cochlear implants. I do not mean to imply that "naturally" means "the same."

Some professionals suggest that such families nevertheless should be considered "at risk" as a result of having a continuous source of potential stress. Hearing parents of deaf children, in fact, generally do report more stress than do parents without deaf children. Perhaps the most significant factor in their adjustment is the amount of support they receive from others. When family and friends provide positive emotional and practical support, for example, helping with the added trips to doctors, schools, and clinics, parents adjust surprisingly quickly. Because mothers are the ones who typically take on most of the added responsibility, they are also the ones in greatest need of such support. In fact, social support of hearing mothers with deaf children has implications far beyond smoother family functioning. Mothers who have such support during the early months tend to have greater visual and tactile responsiveness to their infants and their infants appear better able to cope with stress factors. This provides added evidence of the importance and complexity of early mother-child interaction. At the same time, many mothers find this added responsibility a lot to handle, and it is important to remember that the number one job is just being a mother. There will be a time and place for explicit teaching later.

In our concern about parents' abilities to cope with the responsibilities of having a deaf child, we should not lose sight of the fact that their attitudes about their child's being deaf also will have important effects on later school success and social-emotional development. The home is the place where any young child should be able to feel safe, understood, and loved. It is the place that should provide deaf children with the emotional strength and resources to handle a world that is not entirely able to deal with them. Most deaf children will grow up to be just as emotionally well adjusted as hearing children, but they need the same kind of parenting and the same kinds of experiences as their hearing peers. To achieve this equivalence, parents will have to adjust the quantity and quality of interaction they have with their young deaf child. Let us therefore consider the nature of those relationships and the emotional bonds that develop between parents and children.

Attachment: Mother and Child Reunion

Attachment refers to the emotional bond that develops between young children and their mothers or other caregivers. Psychological attachment is not something that can be seen, but is inferred from what the infant does. In many mammals, including humans, youngsters initially attempt to stay close to their mothers and other companions. When separated from those significant others, toddlers of many species may wander around aimlessly, stop playing, or, in most species, indicate their distress through crying. This kind of behavior and the attachment it reflects are normal and important parts of early childhood.

In human infants, the early phases of attachment can be seen during the first months of life. They are reflected in the way in which children focus their attention and are most likely to interact comfortably with just one or two adults, usually either the parents or a parent and some other caregiver. By 8 months of age, infants obviously and intentionally attempt to stay close to their primary caregiver when confronted with new situations or new people. Although there are special laboratory techniques involved in scientific studies of attachment, there are also fairly regular behaviors that can be taken as signals of relatively stable or unstable attachments between mother and child. In particular, it is not unusual for children between 8 and 18 months of age to show some signs of distress if they are left either in a strange room or with a strange person (known as *separation anxiety* and *stranger anxiety,* respectively), although there is much variability in these phenomena both within and across children. When they are reunited, children who have warm and secure attachment bonds with their mothers generally will greet them and seek comfort from them. In contrast, children with less stable or secure attachments may not approach their mothers when they return, may begin to do so and then turn away, or may approach their mothers but refuse to be comforted, possibly throwing temper tantrums or reacting negatively in other ways.

In the case of young children of deaf mothers, we need to recognize at the outset that there may be cultural factors in the Deaf community relative to the hearing community that affect maternal attitudes toward mother-child interactions, just as hearing mothers' conceptions of "appropriate" attachment behaviors differ in various countries and cultures. Even in the absence of cultural factors, just being deaf—and perhaps the experience of growing up with a hearing mother—will make for some differences in mother-child interactions. For hearing mothers of deaf children, there is also the possibility that differences in the way they interact with their children, out of real or perceived necessity, may lead to erroneous conclusions about the nature of their emotional bonds with their children, when viewed from outside. Hearing mothers of deaf preschoolers, for example, frequently are seen to play a far more active role in their children's day-to-day behaviors than mothers of hearing children, often being described as intrusive or controlling (Henggeler, Watson, & Cooper, 1984; Musselman & Churchill, 1993). When a mother's attention to her deaf child is withdrawn, such as when she leaves the room, the change therefore may be greater from the child's perspective than in the case of a hearing child, and the child might appear more surprised or distraught than would a hearing child of the same age. Alternatively, less control might be welcomed by some children, who thus might appear less distraught than a hearing child in a similar situation.

Although we do not yet fully understand the dynamics of interactions between hearing mothers and their deaf children, it is sometimes claimed that deaf children generally are likely to be less securely attached to their mothers, as compared to hearing children of hearing parents. That characterization has not been supported by psychological research. What we do know is that those mothers who have good communication with their deaf children tend to have more stable and warm relationships with them, regardless of whether they themselves are hearing or deaf (Greenberg, Calderon, & Kusché, 1984; Meadow-Orlans, Spencer, & Koester, 2004). More effective communication between mothers and their deaf children also lead to better mental health outcomes, and neither spoken language nor sign language appears to have any advantage in that regard. Those mothers who have less efficient communication with their deaf children, in contrast, tend to have children who are less securely attached, who may exhibit unacceptable behaviors in school settings and at home, and be more prone to mental health difficulties through the teenage years (Wallis, 2006).

These differences, of course, are not entirely a function of communication fluency, even if communication is an essential ingredient for normal development. In situations where mothers lack the knowledge and communicative skill to deal competently with their children's behavior, they are more likely to have to depend on direct, physical means. This method might be effective in the short term, but it usually does little to teach children what is expected of them in the future. Those mothers who have established an effective channel of communication with their deaf children have less need for such control and are less likely than others to be overly directive or to use physical means of restraining their children. Thus, hearing parents of deaf children are more likely than hearing parents with hearing children or deaf parents with either deaf or hearing children to gain a child's attention by moving her head in the intended direction and more likely to use physical punishment. These differences are most pronounced when parents and children have not developed an effective system of communication. Apparently, when communication fails, punishment is a handy alternative.

Looking Beyond the Earliest Relationships

Let us now consider several components of early personality and emotional development in deaf children that relate to social interactions outside of the family (chapter 9 will discuss personality issues during the later school years). Keeping in mind the continuity in social development from the very earliest parent-child relationships, we should be able to gain some insight into links between those early interactions and later social functioning during the preschool years and beyond. In this context, it is important to note again that young children's social behavior with peers is not determined by the nature and quality of their attachment with mother or any other single aspect of the mother-child relationship.

Despite the lack of a strong *causal* relationship between security of attachment and subsequent social behavior, children who have better social relationships with their primary caregivers also tend to be those who develop good social relations with peers and higher self-esteem. Children who are good socializers probably have several personality characteristics that make them better able to get along with other children and hence more popular. Most of these qualities are acquired early in life through interactions within the family, but others may come as part of their natural temperament. Some deaf and hearing children, for example, simply are more sociable than others, a quality that is seen early by parents and appears to carry on through the school years. Some children are better at social problem solving, figuring out how to play successfully with other children and whom they can turn to for emotional or practical support. Part of this ability seems to lie in the fact that some children appear more sensitive to the social cues given off by other children and adults, and thus they are better at responding appropriately to both positive and negative overtures. Unfortunately, we have not figured out how to distill and bottle it.

It is not surprising that children's social behavior and their emotional stability are affected by the quality of parent-child relationships. For example, controlling or overprotective behaviors on the part of hearing mothers are likely to affect their deaf children's interactions with peers and other adults because they lead the children to "expect" those kinds of behaviors from others. Parents and teachers who are constantly "rescuing" deaf children from awkward situations will prevent them from developing their own strategies for solving problems. At the same time, we have to recognize that some maternal actions that might appear to be somewhat overbearing may be necessary in order to ensure their children's safety, cooperation, or obedience. What appears to be intrusiveness simply may be part of getting their children's attention, and some of their directiveness might reflect attempts to overcome communication barriers rather than any desire to control their children's behaviors (Lederberg & Mobley, 1990). We thus have to be sensitive to differences in behavior that can be interpreted in more than one way.

In considering the earliest parent-child relationships, we saw that parents and infants develop particular patterns of interactions. Hearing parents and their deaf children establish such mutual signals, even if it sometimes takes longer than in the cases of deaf children of deaf parents or hearing children of hearing parents. Given their hearing and speech intelligibility difficulties, deaf children may find that those signals do not work as well outside of the immediate family, unless they involve sign language and they are interacting with others who sign. Many of the skills involved in later child-child interactions are quite different from those involved in mother-child interactions. Young deaf children may initially approach peers in much the same way as young hearing children, but without a shared communication system they may not get or give as many social cues as hearing children. This situation is made more complex by the fact that, as compared to hearing age mates, young deaf children are likely to have had fewer other children and other adults with whom they have interacted socially.[4] The growth of early intervention programs have been particularly helpful in this regard, as deaf children are exposed to considerable diversity in social and communicative interactions in those settings.

Research conducted within early intervention settings has shown that the stability of friendships among deaf preschool children is similar to those of hearing children. Both groups, for example, show similar patterns of playmate preference. Although younger deaf children do not use much formal language in interactions with either deaf or hearing playmates, they do use a variety of nonlanguage communication in those interactions (Lederberg, 1991). Older deaf children appear to use more language and gestural communication with other deaf children than they do with hearing children. Their interactions with deaf playmates also tend to be more social and less object-centered than are their communications with hearing playmates. Finally, deaf children who have better language skills are more likely than children with poorer language skills to play with more than one child at a time, to interact with teachers, and to use language during play.

When one looks at children enrolled in early intervention programs involving both sign language and spoken language instruction, they also tend to show more cooperative play with peers than do children who receive spoken language instruction only. Children enrolled in speech-only programs have been found to be more disruptive and aggressive in their play than children in settings that include sign language (Cornelius & Hornett, 1990). These findings suggest that special programs for deaf children provide a variety of language and nonlanguage opportunities that would not be otherwise available. It seems likely that the availability of more diverse experiences enhances the ability of young deaf children to deal with later social interactions and the necessities of growing up in a largely hearing world. At the same time, early intervention provides support for parents who, as a result, are better able to accommodate their children's special needs.

It should now be clear that the emotional and academic lives of young deaf children are enhanced by parents who are sensitive enough to their needs to pursue early diagnosis of their children's hearing losses, intervention and education programs for themselves and their children, and communication instruction (Calderon & Greenberg, 1997). There is also strong support for a relation between early parent-child communication, attachment-related behaviors, and later social ability: Those children with stable and secure attachments early in life tend to be more socially competent during the school years than are children with less secure attachments.

At this time, there is no evidence to suggest that there is any benefit to the use of spoken language over sign language, or the reverse, in the establishment of early parent-child bonds, at least when parents and children share the same communication modality. Signing can fill all of the roles normally filled by parents' speech and is often indicated as the best route to follow with young deaf children until they are ready for the more arduous job of learning to speak. Still, some parents do not understand the importance of early communication and do not even consider sign language. Some of them view signing as a foreign and perhaps dangerous step that might impede the development of speech. Other parents are eager for their children to look and act as "normal" as possible, and sign language clearly does not fit that requirement. Little do they realize that early acquisition of sign language might be the best way to nurture a child who approaches their "normal" ideal and that the denial of that opportunity starts their child off at a distinct disadvantage relative to other children. Once again, this is not to suggest that sign language is "the only way," but it also is not a decision that can be delayed. Whether or not one agrees with my (or any other) perspective on the language question, there can be no doubt that early and effective communication is essential for normal development.

The Importance of Play

Playmate preferences of deaf children were alluded to above, but play really deserves more attention. Deaf and hearing children progress through similar stages of play behavior, stages that appear to parallel their language development (Meadow-Orlans, Spencer, & Koester, 2004). Children with lags in their language development, for example, show delays in the more complex aspects of play such as planning and object coordination, at least in part because they are unable to benefit from "advice" from their mothers. Although children with lesser language skills spend less time in higher levels of symbolic (pretend) play, the time spent in lower levels of play equals or exceeds that of children with more advanced language, which again suggests a link between play and language ability. Indeed, children with hearing loss but without delayed language development do not show reduced levels of play behavior (Spencer & Deyo, 1993).

More generally, one can view play as both a "window" and a "room" (Spencer & Hafer, 1998). The patterns of play behaviors observed in young children provide us with a "window" into their development. Beyond the use of language, children's progression through various stages of play (*representational, symbolic, dramatic,* and *imaginary*) reflect advancing cognitive development and growth in social skills. At the same time, play is the "room" in which children can explore, try out various roles, and test out the skills they are gaining in other domains. For parents of young deaf children, there is sometimes a concern that they should utilize as much time as possible in structured teaching situations so as to make up for or avoid lags in various domains. Not so! Play can always be used in a structured way to communicate particular concepts (e.g., the structure of categories or physical dimensions), but play itself serves an invaluable role in development of all children. In fact, at least with hearing children, it is the informal and unstructured communication interactions of parents and children that best support and predict later child language skills (Risley & Hart, 1995).

Coupled with findings indicating that children with age-appropriate language skills get along better with their peers in preschool settings, research on other aspects of play indicate that early-intervention preschool and kindergarten settings provide a variety of linguistic and nonlinguistic opportunities for interactions among deaf children (and between deaf and hearing children) that would not be otherwise available. Although comparisons of older children with and without preschool social experience still lie ahead, it seems likely that the availability of more diverse social, linguistic, and cognitive experiences can only enhance the flexibility of young deaf children in dealing with later social interactions and growing up in a largely hearing world.

Final Comments

Early childhood is a time of rapid learning for both deaf and hearing infants. In addition to learning about things and people in the environment, they also learn a lot about how to learn and how to interact both in language and in nonverbal ways. When mothers ask their month-old babies questions in "baby talk," they are not really expecting answers, except perhaps through smiles and other facial expression. When parents and infants share a language, either signed or spoken, those games can be important language-learning episodes. Those interactions teach infants about social interactions and support the development of a reciprocal emotional relationship between mother and child in which they each have their own roles. Eventually, an attachment bond will form, as children will seek out mother and other familiar figures and use them as "safe" bases for the exploration of places and other people.

Adjusting to having a deaf child is not an easy experience for many hearing parents. Periods of denial, grieving, depression, and guilt are normal and will eventually give way to concerted efforts to determine the needs and services available for their children—and for themselves. Mothers tend to take the greatest emotional and day-to-day responsibilities for deaf children, as they do for most children with special needs in most cultures, and they sometimes will feel overwhelmed. Those mothers and fathers who receive more social support from friends and family are the ones who are best at coping with their new situation, and the effects of that support are seen in better behavioral interactions and greater sensitivity to their children's communication needs.

Normally, language plays a continuing and expanding role in early social interaction, both through explicit communication and the child's noticing of relations between communication and behaviors of caregivers. As far as anyone can tell, signed and spoken communication are equivalent in their potential to supply all of the information and experience necessary for normal social development. That equivalence requires that parents be competent language users in whatever mode(s) is most accessible to their child. One way in which hearing parents can gain the language skills they need, as well as emotional and practical support for their needs, is through early intervention programs. Such programs, described more fully later, include communication instruction for both parents and children in sign language, spoken language, or both. They also expose children (and parents) to others who are similar to them. Together with explicit and implicit instruction within the home, such programs foster the early development of child-child social interactions. As deaf children move out of the home environment into the larger community, they gain much-needed diversity in their experience. Multiple social partners help both to offset the tendency of hearing mothers to be controlling and perhaps overprotective of their deaf children, and to contribute to cognitive and language development as well as to social development. Communication with those inside and outside of the home now takes on even greater importance, and we therefore turn to considering language development in some detail.

5

I knew how to sign because my grandparents and an uncle were deaf. But when my
son was born deaf, I was afraid that
signing would prevent him from learning
to speak. . . . It wasn't until Tim was 14
that we started signing at home. I can't
believe I waited so many years to get to
know my son! It's really sad.
—Kathy, a hearing mother of a deaf child

Language
Development

The basic question of this chapter is, "How do deaf children learn language?" or perhaps more specifically, "Do deaf children acquire language in the same ways as hearing children?" In order to answer either question, we have to look at both how children go about learning language and exactly what it is that they learn that allows them to communicate with others—that is, what they have to know in order to be able to use the language. As a starting point, let us consider the very beginnings of communication, when a child's spoken, signed, or gestural productions first begin to have what I call "communicative consequences" for mothers and fathers. This is the point, during the first year of life, when both deaf and hearing children are beginning to make regular vocal sounds and are using simple gestures.

Most researchers now believe that, with both hands and voices available to them, young children should be equally able to learn either a signed or a spoken language. Although both kinds of language require small but accurate muscle movements, such agility develops at different rates in different parts of the body. In particular, coordinated hand movements generally develop before coordinated mouth movements. This manual priority has been taken to indicate that children should be able to produce sign language earlier than they can produce spoken language, a possibility that we will consider later. At this point, it is sufficient to note that a biological "preference" for signed over spoken language is also consistent with the belief that in the history of humankind, manual communication was used before spoken communication (Armstrong, 1999).[1]

Most of the evidence concerning the development of spoken communication in humans, as a species, comes primarily from historical studies of brain development and anthropological findings concerning our distant ancestors. There are also some interesting newer studies of natural communication behaviors and physiological evidence from monkeys and other primates that draw inferences about the origins and evolution of language (Masataka, 2003). Closer to home, some relevant evidence comes from studies concerning the early use of signs and words by young hearing children of deaf parents and some hearing children of hearing parents who use sign language with their children for other reasons. These studies all indicate that sign languages can be acquired just as early as spoken languages, although the belief that they will appear significantly earlier has little support. In order to set the stage for discussions of the emergence of the first words and the first signs, let us consider what often seems—at least to parents—to be even earlier approximations to communication.

Do Deaf Babies Babble?

Babies come into the world with the potential to learn any human language. Not all languages, however, consist of the same basic elements. In Italian, for example, the pronunciation of a longer or shorter /s/ sound can make for two different words. I discovered this fact—to the delight of my Italian audience—when I once confused the verb for "to marry" (*sposare*) with the word for "to be worn out" (*spossare*) in describing my relationship with the woman who is now my wife. This difference is one that native English speakers do not hear without considerable practice, just as native Spanish speakers cannot easily hear the difference between *ship* and *sheep,* native Japanese speakers cannot easily hear the difference between *rice* and *lice,* and hearing students of American Sign Language (ASL) initially are unable to see the difference between I AM ALWAYS SICK and I FREQUENTLY GET SICK. It is only over time and exposure to many examples that children learn the range of elements, either sounds or sign components, in their native language. Meanwhile, they gradually lose the ability to discriminate and produce language elements with which they have no practice. This process may explain, in part, why it is easier to learn a second language in early childhood than in adulthood, regardless of whether that language is spoken or signed: Children's "language learning software" has not yet become exclusively tuned to the repertoire of only a single language.

Hearing infants appear to start homing in on the sounds relevant to their native language during the first few weeks or months of life, when they start producing the simple sounds we call *babbling.* There are at least two ways that the babbling of young infants might be related to later language acquisition. One possibility is that babbling actually is a direct precursor to language. From this perspective, when babies babble they are exercising their "language production equipment" (the diaphragm, tongue, lips, and so on) in preparation for language, even though they are not really "trying to talk." A second possibility is less concerned with the particular sounds or gestures that an infant might produce than with the effects of those productions on other people, and especially the parents. We will consider both of these possibilities in asking two related questions: "Do deaf babies vocally babble in ways similar to hearing babies?" and "Do deaf babies do anything with their hands that resembles the babbling that hearing babies do with their voices?"

Vocal Babbling by Deaf Infants

Although it might not seem that way to an untrained ear, hearing children's babbling actually follows a fairly regular course of development. During the first two months of life, for example, infants produce what appear to be simple vowel sounds: "ah," "ee," and "oo." From 2 to 3 months of age, these vowel-like sounds are joined by consonant-like sounds, made for the most part in the back of the mouth, producing sounds like "ka," "coo," and "goo." This stage is thus called the *cooing stage,* although it usually sounds more like a "gooing stage." Over the next 3 months or so, these vocal sounds are further expanded to include a variety of other sounds like grunts, growls, and squeals, as well as clearer vowels and consonant-vowel combinations. Typically, it is not until 7 to 11 months that hearing infants start to produce the well-formed syllables needed for babbling. This is the stage in which sounds are repeated to form the first vocalizations that excited parents might interpret as words: "mama," "dada," "kaka," and so on. This type of babbling is important for two reasons. On the technical side, such *repetitive babbling* is the first time that infants produce the syllables which will be the building blocks of words. On the social side, it is at this point that parents start responding to their children's apparent attempts at communication, leading to a new form of parent-child interaction and reciprocity.

In many books and articles written about deaf children, the question of whether deaf babies babble *vocally* appears very complicated. The confusion arises for the most part from informal observations of deaf babies made by parents and other untrained baby watchers. That is, it seems to make sense that deaf babies would babble early on, perhaps up to the point when hearing babies start to produce words, even if they cannot hear what they babble. This pattern of early vocalization would suggest that babbling is an innate, natural behavior that occurs regardless of a baby's early environment or hearing status. However, this sequence is *not* what generally occurs. When it comes to early vocalizations like crying, fussing, grunting and cooing, deaf babies really do sound much the same as hearing babies of hearing parents. Then, after the first few months, their vocal babbling usually shows a steady decrease both in how often it occurs and in the amount of variety in it. These declines contrast with the babbling of hearing babies, which increases steadily in both quantity and variability over the first year of life. Even when hearing losses are discovered early and children have received hearing aids and intensive early speech therapy, deaf children's vocal babbling diverges from that of hearing children. Repetitive babbling may still occur, but it appears later and less frequently than in hearing children (Oller, 2006). Some investigators also have reported vocal babbling in 2- to 5-year-old deaf children, but these vocalizations clearly differ from the babbling of hearing children who would have moved on to using words and phrases at that age. Further, recent studies concerning the relationship between early babbling and later spoken language skill in deaf children have been contradictory, so we clearly still lack sufficient information to be able to predict any long-term implications of reduced vocal babbling.

The lack of complex early babbling by deaf children likely does have some long-term implications, whether or not they are directly linked to language development. At the age when parents and siblings should be beginning to respond to their grunts and babbles, lack of such interactions would suggest that deaf babies already may be at a disadvantage both socially and communicatively relative to hearing children. Yet deaf infants' vocalizations at 12 months of age have been shown to be judged as having communicative intent just as often as those of hearing infants, so the interpretation of greater communicative consequences on the parents' side might help to offset less vocal engagement on the part of their deaf children. Further, as we will see in the next section, deaf and hearing children of deaf parents at this stage will be making and seeing signs and gestures that may function in the same ways as vocalizing and hearing do for hearing babies. For many deaf children, however, it is still too early for their hearing parents to suspect their hearing losses. The lack of spoken communication between hearing parents and their deaf children is thus a real and potentially important factor in development, with implications even at this early age for later cognitive and social development as well as for language development and day-to-day functioning.

There are, of course, other modes of communication used in hearing families with their deaf children even before hearing loss is identified. Hearing mothers and their deaf infants presumably have developed regular patterns of interaction through physical contact at this point, and they soon will begin to use gestures and "body language" to communicate just as deaf mothers do with their deaf and hearing infants. Often overlooked by hearing parents are the beginnings of nonvocal communication, beginnings at least as important as vocal babbling is for hearing infants. This topic has received far less attention than has vocal babbling, but it is an exciting one that may hold considerable promise for understanding and facilitating language development in deaf children.

Manual Babbling?

Whereas vocal babbling consists of the combined vowel and consonant sounds that make up language, there are various forms that manual babbling (what I call "mabbling") could take. One of these would be the simple production or repetition of components of signs, such as isolated handshapes or movements. Some of those movements actually will constitute complete signs that are made by repeating simple handshapes and movements. For example, the sign MILK is made by opening and closing the hand into a fist, as in milking a cow, and the sign MOTHER or MAMA is made by touching an open hand to the chin (see Figure 3–4). Mabbling of this sort is likely to have social consequences when seen by deaf parents, just as babbling by hearing infants ("mama") might get reactions from hearing parents. Another form of mabbling would resemble the combination of sounds seen in babbling. Young deaf children of both deaf and hearing parents, for example, produce individual and repeated sign components without any apparent attempt at communication. Since publication of the first edition, this form of mabbling has been documented in both deaf and hearing children, so it appears to be a more general phenomenon than was once believed, and not anything specific to deaf children.

There is a relatively small set of about a half-dozen hand configurations that frequently are seen in deaf infants who are learning sign language as a first language. These handshapes comprise the primary stuff of later signs and, like the basic vowel and consonant sounds in spoken language, are general enough to be found across all documented sign languages. Just as importantly, mabbling provides a motivation for deaf or signing-hearing parents to engage in "conversations" with their deaf infants in the same way that babbling prompts hearing parents to talk to their hearing infants. Eventually, the language-relevant parts of mabbling will become incorporated into communication and, along with meaningful gestures, deaf children will be well on the way to acquiring language. Mabbling is thus different from gesturing, because gestures are meaningful while mabbling is not. Nonetheless, early gestures play a vital role in early learning and communication and are worthy of consideration in their own right.

Gestures and Signs

The focus of most research on deaf children's early manual behavior has been on their use of meaningful gestures. My own research has shown that gestures accompany the signs of deaf children in much the same way as they accompany the speech of hearing children (Marschark, 1994). When hearing children use gestures, however, we can easily distinguish them from words. The distinction is somewhat harder to make when deaf children intermix gestures with their signs, because the two forms of communication share the same channel of communication—from hand to eye. Deaf children's gestures nonetheless may give us some insight into their language development and, later, into their cognitive development and the thoughts that underlie their behavior. We therefore need to look more closely at the relations among early gestures, early words or signs, and children's knowledge of the things to which they refer.

Observers and investigators of young children's early gestures generally assume that their use paves the way for hearing and deaf children's eventual use of words and signs, respectively (Bates, Benigni, Bretherton, Camaioni, & Volterra, 1977). When children are at the point of using only single words or signs (10–16 months) and also when they move to using combinations of two words or signs (16–24 months), gestures continue to play an important role in the language development of hearing children. In chapter 3, I suggested that this situation makes it odd and likely disruptive for language development to deny deaf children the opportunity to use gestures in interpersonal communication. Of course, we would not want deaf children to depend on gestures to the exclusion of signed or spoken communication, but there is no evidence that this ever occurs when a more regular form of communication is available. Rather, for both deaf and hearing individuals, gestures appear to be a natural component of communication from the first year of life through adulthood. The questions of interest are how deaf and hearing children use gestures and how they eventually come to be supplemented by language.

In fact, there appear to be several shifts in the frequency and purpose of gestures at various points of development. Among young deaf children of deaf parents, for example, there apparently is a noticeable change in use of pointing from its "immature" use as a gesture showing or requesting something to a "mature" form in the personal pronouns of ASL like ME, HER, and YOU (Petitto, 1987).[2] At around 9 months of age, both deaf and hearing children use pointing as a *showing* or *requesting* gesture. Then, at around 12 months, deaf children stop using pointing to refer to people, although it still can refer to things and places. Six to 12 months later, person-pointing comes back into use; but this time, those motions are used in the context of sign as personal pronouns. Such shifts indicate that gestures and signs are distinct, even if they look the same.

In terms of their form and frequency, most of the gestures of young deaf and hearing children appear to be the same until about age 2 (Volterra, Iverson, & Castrataro, 2006). During the school years, deaf children tend to use more gestures with their sign language than hearing children use with their speech, although this difference apparently disappears by the time they reach adulthood (Marschark, West, Nall, & Everhart, 1986). In terms of their function, it is during the earliest stages of parent-child communication that gestures are particularly important because of the role they play in social interactions. That is, both gesture and language initially develop in children largely because of the need to communicate their wants, needs, and desires. Even deaf children who do not have the benefits of early language input therefore show spontaneous and regular use of gestures to communicate with those around them.

First Signs, First Words

The ages at which deaf children first begin to use signs and words vary considerably. There have been occasional claims of deaf children using simple signs like MILK and MAMA as early as 5 or 6 months of age! One problem with such observations is that they almost always have been made by parents, who might read more into their child's behavior than would unbiased witnesses. Several investigators, meanwhile, have reported that deaf and hearing children who learn sign language naturally from their deaf parents produce their first recognizable signs at around 9–10 months of age. Hearing children, by contrast, tend to produce their first words around their first birthdays, regardless of whether they have hearing or deaf parents and regardless of whether they are already using some simple signs.

So, while it is clear that signs do *not* slow the emergence of speech, some researchers have argued that it may facilitate language development. At present, however, this belief is in some doubt. Much of the confusion appears to have been caused by different criteria for determining children's first signs. When gestures are clearly distinguished from signs, deaf children of deaf parents and hearing children of hearing parents appear to produce language at essentially the same age—although that age varies considerably across children (Anderson & Reilly, 2002).

In fact, deciding when the first words occur has never been easy, even with hearing children. Between 9 and 12 months of age, hearing children make some sounds that are similar to adult words. These *proto-words* ("almost words") often, but not always, are produced in the correct context and so they tend to sound like real words, at least to their parents' ears. At the same time, the fact that proto-words are also produced in contexts that are not correct, and thus are less likely to be noticed by parents, suggests that the child does not understand the "language" they are producing. Proto-words simply may be attempts to imitate sounds made by adults and may have no more meaning for the child than babbling.

In the context of dealing with a young child at home, as opposed to in a research study, it probably is not too important to decide which early sounds are proto-words and which are true words. What is important is that whatever they are, these vocalizations lead to responses from listeners. As a result, proto-words either get used more often and more correctly, gradually becoming or being replaced by real words, or they drop out of a child's vocabulary. For this to occur, it does not matter whether the "words" are real, baby talk, or even babbles, as long as there is some kind of social agreement between the child and her listeners that particular utterances have particular meanings. Some of these "baby words" will remain with children if they continue to be used in the family.[3] As described in chapter 3, such *home words* are paralleled by *home signs* in families with deaf children and/or deaf parents.

A parallel scenario presumably develops for deaf children who are "ready" to produce their first signs. As with the appearance of the first words, it is difficult to know how seriously to take reports by parents of signs being made as early as 6 months of age. Like the "first words," "first signs" tend to be rather simple approximations that, at least initially, could be entirely unintended by the child. The sign MILK is a good example, here. Is it because milk is so important for infants (from whose point of view?) that MILK is most frequently reported as children's first sign? Or is it because the sign is so simple, being made by the simple opening and closing of a 5-hand? Flexing of the unformed hand occurs frequently in both deaf and hearing infants, and it seems only a matter of time before it is produced in an appropriate context and interpreted as a sign by enthusiastic parents. Similarly, the signs MAMA and DADA or some simplified version of them (see Figure 3–4) seem likely to occur occasionally just by chance. As it happens, MAMA generally occurs earlier and more frequently than DADA. Is this because mama is "more important" to the child than dada? Is it because mama is more likely to be around and *see* early MAMA signs? Or is it because DADA is made on the forehead, outside of the infant's line-of-sight, and thus is more difficult to repeat correctly once it has been seen by an excited father? It could be a combination of all of these factors.

Examples of this sort suggest some caution in attributing intention or meaning to the very early signs produced by young deaf children. Nevertheless, the social implications of those early signs and proto-signs are exactly the same as those created by hearing children's first words and proto-words. So, once again, it seems that deciding exactly when early spoken or signed productions should be considered language may be less important than identifying their roles in social communication. That is, even if it now appears that deaf children generally do not display an *early sign advantage,* it may be that because gestures and signs share the visual mode, there is a smoother transition between them than between gestures and spoken language. Moreover, language in the visual mode may allow more room for interpretation (even if only because it is less familiar). Parents may thus believe they are having earlier conversations with deaf than hearing children and, indeed, it appears that the early gestures of hearing children are less likely to be seen as examples of "real communication" than are those of deaf children (Volterra et al., 2006). Whether or not this situation gives deaf children who sign any long-term edge over nonsigning deaf or hearing peers remains to be determined.

Growing Vocabularies

Consider now the relation between the number of words a young hearing child knows at any particular age and the number of signs that a young deaf child knows at the same age. Some children learning to sign have been reported to have larger vocabularies during the first year or two than hearing children learning spoken language only. This finding could be taken as support for the suggestion that signed languages can be acquired earlier than spoken languages, but in almost all cases where such advantages have been documented, the children have been hearing rather than deaf. Hearing children of deaf parents who use a natural sign language are able to benefit from a much wider range of language experience than deaf or hearing children who have only spoken language available to them. In a bilingual preschool program (see chapter 6) for deaf and hearing children at the Royal Institute for Deaf and Blind Children in Sydney, Australia, it is hearing children who are learning sign language (Auslan) most rapidly, regardless of the hearing status of their parents. Evidently, that advantage stems from the fact that they already have a strong language base (English) from their parents on which to base learning of a second language. It thus is unclear whether the advantage seen in early vocabulary of hearing children of deaf parents should be attributed to the *language* or to the *context* in which those bilingual children are learning language (though, at this point, the latter seems more likely).

In any case, small differences in early vocabulary size do not last long. Typically, any sign language advantage disappears by age 2, when the ability to combine signs and words becomes important in the two-word, *telegraphic speech* stage (e.g., "want milk"; Meier & Newport, 1990). In other words, when we remove the small head start that signing (deaf or hearing) children may have over speaking (hearing) children, signs and words ultimately appear to be learned at about the same rate. Note, however, that I hedged by suggesting that *ultimately* signs and words are learned at the same rate. That is because recent evidence suggests that the pattern of early vocabulary development is different for deaf children of deaf parents and hearing children of hearing parents, the two groups most appropriate for a comparison.

Early vocabulary growth in hearing children has long been known to go through three distinct stages. In the first, the *slow word learning* stage (up to 12–14 months), a word (or sign) will have to be repeated numerous times before it appears to be linked to its referent (person, object, or event), understood by the child, and used spontaneously. At that point, child language investigators say that the word is part of the child's *repertoire.* In the second, the *fast word learning* stage, a word might only have to be encountered once or twice (in context) to become part of the child's repertoire. Finally, at about 18 months of age, vocabulary learning undergoes another, more dramatic change. With the beginning of *cognitively mediated word learning,* children can make use of what they know to figure out the meanings of new words at an amazing rate. As an example, assume that a child already has "duck" and "teddy" in her vocabulary repertoire. If she is then presented with a toy duck, a teddy bear, and a cup and asked "Where is the cup?" by process of elimination (that is, cognitively mediated word learning), she knows that the third item must be the cup. This efficient, knowledge-based strategy for word learning results in a very rapid increase in the rate of vocabulary growth, at least in hearing children, usually referred to as the *vocabulary spurt.*

A recent study involving a large number of deaf children of deaf parents, in contrast, showed that essentially none of them demonstrated a vocabulary spurt. At 3 years of age, many of the children were in the range of vocabulary size typically seen in hearing children, but they arrived there through a more gradual increase in their sign repertoires, without any indication of using cognitively mediated word learning (Anderson & Reilly, 2002). This does not mean that they do not have or use that strategy. Other investigators have demonstrated use of the strategy in deaf children, but found it to emerge up to three years later than in hearing children (Lederberg, Prezbindowski, & Spencer, 2000). While the long-term implications of this difference in one mechanism of vocabulary learning are still unclear (see Marschark, Convertino, and LaRock, 2006, for several possibilities), such findings indicate that even deaf children of deaf parents may follow somewhat different paths of language development than hearing children, and it would be a mistake to take comparisons of the two groups too seriously.

In short, the situation seems to be that learning to sign does not confer any special advantage on deaf children's vocabulary development relative to hearing children, even if early signing provides broad support for later language learning in general, both signed and spoken. As far as I can tell, the spectacular exceptions with regard to vocabulary growth—that is, children who have been reported to have sign vocabularies that increase much faster than normal—have been not only hearing children, but also children of university professors who are fluent in ASL and specialists in language development. This is why they are studying their children in the first place! This observation suggests that under special circumstances signs *can* be acquired at a faster rate than words, but this does not seem to be the case under more natural circumstances.

Hearing children of hearing parents generally use about 10 different words when they are 15 months of age, 50 words at 20 months, and about 10 phrases also around 20 months. Of course, these numbers are rough averages, and particular children may be faster or slower in their rates of vocabulary growth. Those averages, however, also appear to hold for the sign vocabularies of deaf children with deaf parents learning ASL in the United States and Canada as well as those learning La Langue des Signes Québécoise in French-speaking Canada. Children learning to sign and those learning to speak also seem to have a lot of overlap in the particular words and signs that they use. This consistency makes some intuitive sense, as we would expect that regardless of their language, deaf and hearing children likely would have similar things to talk about.

One aspect of signed languages that people expect to affect early learning is the fact that some signs look like what they mean. In fact, signs actually fall along a continuum, from looking very much like what they mean (GOLF, BOWL), to having some obvious association with what they mean (BOY, DOG), to appearing fairly arbitrary (CABBAGE, CHURCH).[4] It would not be surprising to find that the earliest-acquired signs are those falling toward the "obvious" end of the continuum, and naive observers, including both parents and scientists who are unfamiliar with sign language, often claim that this is the case. But those observers are wrong! Such claims frequently are based on the incorrect interpretation of signs: The observer thinks that a sign means "what it looks like," when it actually means something quite different. Alternatively, the observer may only notice the few obvious signs that occur in a signed conversation and assume that most of the language is like that.

More important than the fact that there are not really very many "transparent" or *iconic* signs, is the fact that the obviousness of a sign actually has no effect on how likely it is to be learned by young children (Orlansky & Bonvillian, 1984). Transparent signs may be easier for hearing adults to remember when they take sign language classes, but that is a function of experience and learning strategies that young children do not yet have. Either deaf children do not understand the "obvious" bases of such signs (any more than they understand words like "submarine" or "antiseptic" from analyzing their component parts) or they may have less use for them. Looking at any beginning sign language book, it should be apparent that most of the signs likely to be important for young deaf children bear little resemblance to their meanings.

Before moving on to more complex language, a note seems in order concerning the early language of deaf children in programs that emphasize spoken language. Regardless of the rate of early sign acquisition by young deaf children in sign language settings and hearing children in spoken language settings, there is little doubt of the contrast they provide with the rates of language learning by deaf children exposed to only spoken language. Among children with severe to profound hearing losses, even the best pupils of the best spoken language programs have extremely limited early vocabularies. The language of deaf preschoolers in speech-only programs generally is at least 2 to 3 years behind the language of hearing children, even after more than a year of intensive speech therapy as part of early intervention programs, and lags of up to 4 years are still present by high school age (Geers, 2006). We expect that newborn hearing screening, early intervention, and cochlear implants will make a difference in such statistics, but even when deaf children compare favorably to others without these advantages, they still lag behind hearing peers (Yoshinaga-Itano, 2006).

Beyond the extent of their hearing losses, part of the difference in language development by deaf children in speech- and sign-oriented programs may be related to differences in the ages at which their parents become aware of those losses. Prior to newborn hearing screening, surveys indicated that children who attend speech-oriented programs, on average, had their hearing losses discovered later than children who attend sign-oriented programs. Further, parents who notice their children's hearing losses very early may be, in some sense, more sensitive to their children's language needs or might have less time and emotion invested in attempting exclusively spoken language instruction before trying the route of sign language or total communication. Whatever the reasons, on average, severely to profoundly deaf children who receive early exposure to sign language (with or without spoken language) tend to be more competent in their early language development than those children who receive only exposure to spoken language, even when the latter have mild to moderate hearing losses (Calderon & Greenberg, 1997).

Learning to Fingerspell

Although fingerspelling is typically acquired somewhat later than the first signs, it is not as much later as one might expect. That is because for native signers, fingerspelling in not just a combination of letters; a fingerspelled word is a complete unit. This is most obvious in the case of *fingerspelled loan signs* (see chapter 3), in which both patterned movements and the letters provide information about their identity. Even without unique movements, however, deaf children of deaf parents learn many fingerspelled words "as wholes," rather than as a sequence of individual letters. Indeed, when learning a sign language as a second language, most adults are taught not to focus on individual letters and try to identify each one, but to see common letter combinations in words (e.g., I-N-G or A-B-L-E) and to try to see the pattern of the whole word. In part, this "defocusing" allows the receiver to take advantage of information on the lips or face of the signer, but in the hands of a skilled signer, individual letters in fingerspelling may be too fast for us mere hearing mortals to see anyway.

On the positive side, deaf children seeing fingerspelled words as wholes have a means of acquiring labels for concepts for which there may be no signs (including names), and they get practice with an important grammatical component of the language. On the negative side, hearing parents might expect that a child (or adult) who fingerspells also has a one-to-one correspondence between fingerspelling and spelling in written language. Given the nature of fingerspelling, this usually is not the case, and many deaf adults who use fingerspelling often will omit various letters when they do (note again the role of holistic patterns and possible patterned movements in allowing comprehension in these cases) as well as in their writing. Rather, it has been suggested that deaf children essentially learn to fingerspell twice, once holistically and once via spelling (Padden, 2006). This likely is not much different than hearing children who, for example, learn to use the past tense of both regular and irregular nouns and verbs (*dogs, children, chased, ran*) quite easily, without recognizing them as combinations of *stems* and *inflections*. This situation makes itself clear later, when they learn the rules, and *children* becomes *childrens* and *ran* becomes *runned*.

Studies have suggested that deaf parents frequently fingerspell to their children when they are 2–3 years old (considerably before the children are reading), but fingerspelling has been observed in parents' signing to infants as early as two months of age. Fingerspelling starts to appear in the language of both deaf and hearing children of deaf parents also at around

2–3 years of age, and parents are quite vigilant about ensuring that their children's fingerspelling is correct. Although no one has done the study yet, I expect that deaf parents are far more careful about the accuracy of their fingerspelling in communicating with their children than with other adults.

Does Learning to Sign Affect Learning to Speak?

We have seen that research over the past 30 years has shown that signing can fill all of the requirements for development and education. For more than 130 years, however, there has been a debate within deaf education about whether teaching young deaf children sign language will impair their ability or motivation to acquire spoken language.[5] As I indicated earlier,

there is no evidence to support the claim that signing interferes with learning to speak. Although it has been observed that ASL grammar sometimes intrudes into young deaf children's speech and writing, this phenomenon is common among children and adults learning a second language or more than one language at a time, and it has nothing at all to do with sign language per se. Over time, deaf children will come to separate signed and spoken languages just as children in Switzerland come to separate their use of German, Italian, and French. In fact, the intrusion of ASL or other sign language constructions into writing may offer opportunities to foster a deaf child's literacy skills by pointing out the difference between signed and written/spoken language (see chapter 7).

Intrusions from sign language into deaf children's spoken language appear to be relatively rare.[6] Hearing children and adults actually use ungrammatical language quite often (if not most of the time), even if it is not as noticeable as it would be in a deaf child with hypervigilant parents. No, the primary questions that have appeared in deafness-related journals for the past 150 years—and the ones still asked by many parents—are more basic: *Does the ease of learning to sign, relative to the acknowledged difficulty of learning to speak, make a deaf child lazy and unwilling to expend the effort to acquire spoken language? How can a deaf child function in society if he cannot speak? Does learning to sign rather than to speak create difficulties for learning in school?* The answers to these questions are not simple, and each could consume an entire chapter if not an entire book, but let me try to address each one very briefly.

Does Signing Remove a Deaf Child's Motivation to Speak?

No.

The issue here is not one of hearing loss or sign language, but one of individual differences among children. Children vary widely in their temperaments and abilities, and some children are faster language learners than others. If a child baulks at learning to speak, it is because of the difficulty of the task, not because there is an "easier way out." The child who does not learn to speak is not being difficult or demonstrating lesser intelligence; it is just an indication that it is a talent she does not have, not much different than my own inability to carry a tune or some people's lack of coordination in sports. It has always been a minority of deaf children who acquire fluent spoken language. This is not an issue of debate, as the data are very clear (Cole & Paterson, 1984; Geers, 2006). Notice that oral programs for deaf children do not advertise "We can teach any deaf child to speak!" They cannot, they know they cannot, and that is simply the reality of the situation. As noted earlier, most such programs screen prospective students and admit only those who show some aptitude for spoken language. That is not an admission of defeat, but a realistic approach to the issue—and a very "humane" one in my opinion. However, it means that parents have to be careful when considering alternative placements for their deaf child: Just because all of the children in a particular program appear to have good speech does not mean that their child will succeed in it. Not only are children unlikely to succeed discouraged from enrolling, but those children who are unsuccessful in acquiring spoken language will eventually move to a different kind of program (hopefully sooner rather than later).

The task of learning to speak may be easier for those children with lesser hearing losses, but for those with greater hearing losses (especially profound losses), acquiring speech that can be understood by others is difficult and frustrating. It is also noteworthy that some deaf adults do not use spoken language, despite having excellent speech skills, simply because of the way that spoken language training was forced upon them as children. In their view, that frustrating experience impaired their ability to establish positive self-images and deprived them of alternatives that would have allowed them to have a more normal childhood. That makes a profound statement, and one that brings us to the second question.

How Can Deaf Children Function in Society If They Cannot Speak?

Not as easily as if they can.

As indicated in the previous section, this is not really the question. Certainly, there are challenges associated with being deaf; no one said otherwise. Difficulty in having people understand your speech is definitely one of those challenges, but it is the lack of hearing that is the major hurdle. Most deaf adults have adjusted to their hearing losses (unless they became deaf as adults, but that is another book), usually as either Deaf adults who sign or oral deaf adults who do not (see chapter 1). Some enjoy both worlds. Members of the Deaf community, who identify with each other through their use of sign language, may embrace that language and the community membership and be perfectly content with who they are. Nevertheless, I have yet to meet someone who, if magically given a choice at the outset, would have chosen to be deaf (see Johnston, 2005, for a excellent discussion of this issue). Deaf parents who hope their newborn child will be able to hear are surely far more common than those who say they want a deaf child, but they would never capture headlines. Note that these are not topics often discussed publicly, and when they are, it usually gets heated and emotional.

When it comes to making oneself understood, almost all deaf people are aware of how good their speech skills are and under what conditions they can be understood. If they know their speech is difficult to understand, they will write, use interpreters, or employ technological alternatives. Deaf children also learn quickly who understands them and how well, and they adjust accordingly. Children who have both speech and sign skills will *code-switch*, that is, shift between the two in order to match their communication partner. It is in situations where children become frustrated at not being able to communicate that even the most ardent supporter of unimodal language training for deaf children has to realize the need for an array of alternatives. Deaf children should be allowed to use whatever means of communication is most effective, regardless of whether it suits someone else's philosophical perspective. For those deaf individuals who sign, and especially for those who had the opportunity to learn sign language early, that is the normal state of affairs. It may be a bit more complex than being left-handed or of short stature, but it is just the way it is. You go to school, you take advantage of support services and technologies, and you live a life of work, family, and friends. It may look different from the outside, but that is why it is called "outside."

How Does Not Being Able to Speak Affect Learning in School?

It would be nice if I could give the short answer, "It doesn't." Unfortunately, the situation is not quite that simple. Indeed, in the years since the first edition of this book, I have become much more aware of how complex the question really is, in part due to my own research and in part to being more broadly involved in deaf education at all levels. The immediate difficulty is distinguishing issues related to the ability to speak (or not) from those related to hearing loss and schooling, which are dealt with in chapter 7. Although the two are tightly intertwined, there are at least three implications of not being able to speak in school. One of these, of course, relates to social development and interactions with peers. For those children who sign and are with signing peers, this is not an issue. But children are children, and it would be both dishonest and unrealistic to suggest that deaf children (or even hearing children) with atypical speech will blend in with normally hearing-speaking peers in mainstream programs. In many countries, being "different" in school is less an issue than it is in much of North America, although it appears that Americans are making progress in that regard. In any case, there is considerable evidence that deaf children in mainstream settings tend to feel isolated and uncomfortable, and it is likely due in large part to speech as well as hearing difficulties (Antia, Stinson, & Gaustad, 2002; Stinson, Whitmire, & Kluwin, 1996; see chapter 6). Insofar as a large part of learning during the school years comes from peers, lack of peer interactions in curricular and co-curricular activities also seems destined to slow academic progress.

With regard to classroom learning, most of the educationally relevant differences observed between deaf and hearing children appear to derive from their hearing losses rather than their lack of spoken language skill. Still, difficulty in asking questions in class and participating fully with hearing teachers and classmates clearly will affect the quality and quantity of learning. Optimal learning for any child requires active participation, and the normal give and take of classroom discussions teaches far more than just the subject matter. Through such interactions, children acquire problem solving skills (both social and academic), acquire new vocabulary, learn that there are alternative perspectives and opinions, and so on (Marschark, 1993a). Speaking is also part of how people present themselves, and I know deaf adults with good speech skills who speak on the telephone, while having an interpreter hold a receiver and sign what the other person on the line is saying. Recent advances in telecommunications and changes in our telecommunication habits are changing this situation, as e-mail and instant messaging have come to play a more prominent role in day-to-day communication. How these technologies will be incorporated into classrooms in the future remains to be seen, but it seems likely that deaf people and those involved in their education will be pushing the boundaries (Power, Power, & Horstmanshof, 2007).

Finally, there likely are some aspects of learning that directly relate to spoken language skill, although I am not aware of any research on them. For example, a former graduate student (now a teacher of deaf children) working with me was interested in whether deaf children (and adults) have any equivalent to the many rhymes that hearing people use as learning or memory aids (e.g., "Thirty days has September . . . "). There may be alternative strategies used by deaf individuals who do not use spoken language (e.g., relative lengths of the months also can be determined by examining your knuckles), and some such rhymes may be adaptable to sign language. At a more subtle level, there are some cognitive processes, such as the capacity of *working* (short-term) *memory,* that are related to deaf individuals' use of spoken or signed language. In part these differences are related to the relative efficiency or time required of spoken language or sign language "in the head," but they may also be related—either as cause or effect—to differences in brain development in deaf and hearing children and the nature of our auditory versus visual systems. These issues are discussed further in chapter 8.

In summary, there is no evidence that learning to sign interferes with learning to speak. Rather, early expressive language—either signed or spoken—is a good predictor of future spoken language ability (Yoshinaga-Itano, 2006). Early success in communication also may enhance the desire of young deaf children to acquire social language skills. What seems to be neglected in most pro-speech arguments is the importance of early linguistic stimulation of children, in *any* mode. What seems to be neglected in most pro-sign arguments is the need for a bridge from signing to English literacy skills. Regardless of how language acquisition occurs, it requires regular input and feedback during the first 2 to 3 years of life. Spoken language communication simply does not work as well for very young deaf children, because they lack the attention span and cognitive abilities of older children and adults, not because spoken language is in any way inferior to sign language. Later, some deaf children will develop speech that is well-enough understood by others and sufficient for the practical purposes of day-to-day life. Other children will not reach those levels of proficiency. Importantly, speech ability does not confer any advantage on the receptive part of language—speech and speechreading are not the same skill. Sign language is not a cure-all, but the consistency of the available evidence clearly tells us that it is potentially an important tool in childhood as well as later.

Signs and Words in the Same Child

During the first 2 years of life, young hearing children, as a group, tend to have considerable overlap in the ideas that they express, although some children communicate them via gesture and others via words. Looking at individual children, however, we see that any particular child generally has *either* a gesture or a word for a thing, but not both. Similarly, it appears that deaf children either have a gesture or a sign for a thing, but not both, even though their gestures and signs are in the same modality. One family I know, for example, includes a mother who is deaf and a father and one child who both have normal hearing. As in many such families, the daughter has grown up a bilingual, using both spoken English and ASL (neither the parents nor the girl use simultaneous communication). This girl started signing before she started talking, although the precise ages of each are not clear. During her early childhood, when her parents kept careful records of her language progress, the girl acquired signs and words at about the same rate. In this natural setting, well over three quarters of all of the signs and words she used occurred in only one of her two languages. That is, she had either a sign or word for a concept, but not both. Only about 15 percent of the concepts in her vocabulary were expressed in both signs and words (although not necessarily at the same time).

Beyond this frequently reported tendency to have a label for a thing in only one language at a time, there is also an inclination in later childhood to use only one mode of communication at a time, that is, *not* to use simultaneous communication. Deaf preschoolers, for example, tend to prefer signed communication over spoken communication even when both languages are available. This preference results from the simple fact that signed communication is more likely than spoken communication to be successful for those children. In both later childhood and adulthood, some deaf individuals are more comfortable with spoken language than others, and some are more comfortably and competently bilingual than others. Deaf children's *bilingual balance,* that is, their relative fluencies in the two languages, will depend in part on the age of onset and the degree of their hearing losses. Other factors, such as parental language abilities (signing by hearing parents, speech and signing by deaf parents) and the quality of early education and exposure to language also will make a difference.

Finally, for children who are initially exposed only to spoken language, later learning of sign language does not affect how often they use their voices, and parental concerns that sign language will replace early speech are unfounded. Rather, speech and sign skills may become increasingly intertwined in those children, improving both speech production and comprehension. This combination also seems to have advantages for children with cochlear implants (Spencer, Gantz, & Knutson, 2004). Nevertheless, there are large differences in the ease with parents, teachers, and implant surgeons find this acceptable.

Putting It All Together

The preceding sections have focused on young children's use of single signs, words, and gestures. We now move beyond those early vocabularies to the ways in which signs and words are put together into what really looks like, and is, language. In considering the learning of sign language and spoken language, we need to recognize that languages vary in the ways that particular ideas are expressed, and one cannot always translate word for word from one spoken language to another even though we can translate the meaning of what is said. This situation also holds when it comes to ASL and English, and that is why ASL and Signed English are not identical.

The ability to translate meaning fully between signed and spoken languages is important to note because some observers of deaf children's early language learning have claimed that the children's signing tends to be more concrete and more tied to the "here and now" than the speech of hearing age-mates. We have seen that deaf and hearing children follow essentially the same course of early language learning in terms of their ability to express various meanings, but this claim concerns *what* young deaf and hearing children talk about. For example, the vocabularies of deaf children of hearing parents generally have a greater percentage of words that refer to people, places, and things as compared to hearing children of hearing parents or deaf children of deaf parents. At the same time, their vocabularies have fewer signs or words that allow them to refer to more abstract concepts like time or the existence of things. A major contributor to this difference is undoubtedly that their parents differ in what *they* talk about. The majority of deaf children learn to sign from hearing parents who themselves are only beginning signers and thus are less able to communicate at a complex or abstract level.

To make this more apparent, we need only think back to the ways in which we were taught foreign language in school. Generally, we learned about practical things, about going to a restaurant or to the doctor, about traveling on a train, and about visiting museums or other historical places. I, for one, do not ever recall having learned how to talk about abstract things like religion, politics, or the meaning of life in my Russian, French, Italian, or ASL classes. If parents are able to sign or speak only about food, toys, and simple social situations, their children are likely to have similar limitations, at least early on. At the same time, chapter 3 pointed out that parents' imperfect use of ASL is not an impediment to their children's eventual ASL fluency.

To the extent that slow growth in deaf children's vocabularies is a consequence of the context of their early language learning, we would not attribute the observed lags to anything inherent in the children. After all, deaf children of deaf parents have no trouble becoming fluent in ASL. Rather, parents' shortcomings in the language domain are often "passed on" to their children, who may not yet have sufficient vocabulary to function in social and academic settings. Unless deaf children *and* their hearing parents receive additional language instruction, those children will continue to fall behind hearing age-mates. That is why deaf children of hearing parents often enter school already at a language disadvantage relative to hearing age-mates—and some never overcome that lag.

As deaf children move into preschool and other settings outside of the home, they usually have more varied language experiences with more partners, and the language learning context becomes more complex. One interesting aspect of this situation is that young deaf children who sign often learn sign language at a faster rate than their hearing parents. There are at least two factors that contribute to this situation. One of these is the fact that once they enter a preschool program, those youngsters are exposed to far more sign language, and more natural sign language, than are their parents. It would be the rare parent, indeed, who had the time to spend 4 to 6 hours a day in a room where signing was the primary means of communication.

A second factor affecting the rate of sign language learning is that deaf children are far more dependent on signing than are their parents. For many deaf children, sign communication is essentially the only way to express their needs, desires, curiosity, and creativity. Their parents, in contrast, have a full range of spoken language at their disposal. This situation is unfortunate in some ways, because parents and teachers of deaf children often do not realize that they may be saying far more in their speech than in their signing. The problem is not that the signs cannot express the same information, it is just that greater fluency in speaking seems to overpower one's signing ability. It therefore is not at all unusual to see people who think that they are using simultaneous communication omitting signs from over half of their sentences. Language ability varies, of course, and the same is true of peoples' skills with simultaneous communication. Some investigators have argued that up to half of what is spoken during simultaneous communication is missing from the hands (e.g., Marmor & Petitto, 1979). The few studies that appear to support that claim, however, involved observations of relatively few parents and teachers, none of whom appear to have been particularly skilled signers. More recent research, in contrast, has shown that in the hands of a competent user, simultaneous communication can be just as effective as any other form of signing (Cokely, 1990; Power & Hyde, 1997). Nevertheless, those of us involved in deaf education have certainly seen colleagues sign poorly regardless of whether they are using their voices. Perhaps it is only more obvious—and more troubling—when they say one thing and either omit signs or incorrectly sign something else. The latter case is especially troubling when a child is involved, because not only is there no real communication in that case, but the child is faced with erroneous information about which signs mean what. Many deaf children thus not only start learning language later than peers who share a language with their parents, but they are confronted with less consistent and less useful language experience when they do start. Is it any wonder that they often lag behind those other children in the quality and complexity of their language skills?

Learning to Use Sign Efficiently

During the preschool years, ages 2 to 5, deaf children who are naturally exposed to signing in the home rapidly increase the frequency with which they use conventional signs to communicate about objects and actions. When signs begin to fill out the vocabulary, we have seen that they do not necessarily replace gestures. As with the words of hearing children, they often fill other roles in communication instead. In addition to the accumulation of new signs, modifications of existing signs also enhance the preschooler's ability to communicate with others. Deaf 2-year-olds exposed to ASL, for example, appear to understand conventional sign modifications, such as verb inflections (see chapter 3), and by age 3 they are modifying signs themselves. The early modifications produced by those children generally do not conform fully to the rules of ASL until they are closer to 5 years old. Nevertheless, deaf 3- and 4-year-olds clearly know that signs can be altered to modify their meanings. Most of their invented modifications make sense, and, like the spoken modifications of words produced by hearing children, there is remarkable consistency across children (Schick, 2006).

One common example of such approximations to ASL occurs with *directional signs.* Directional signs (SEE, GIVE, INFORM, and so on) are those signs that include a movement component that indicates the "from" and "to" of the action, as shown in Figure 5–1. Prior to their understanding of the directional quality of signs, deaf children often use sequences of several signs linked together to communicate the same information. For example, an older child can sign YOU-GIVE-ME as a single sign, as shown in Figure 5–1. Two-year-olds, in contrast, are more likely to use the three-sign sequence YOU GIVE ME containing two personal pronouns and a verb. From about 2½ to 4 years of age, pointing and other gestures are used together with signs instead of using more grammatically complex, if formationally simpler, verb inflections. These replacements are most common during the latter half of that period, although many deaf children continue to use them occasionally until they are near 5 years old. Interestingly, this seems to be a common phenomenon in language learning, and I still find myself doing exactly the same thing in Italian, even though I have all of the pronoun forms in my repertoire (and I do not use the child forms in ASL).

During the second half of their fourth year, when deaf 3-year-olds begin to modify verb signs, they tend to use them first to communicate directions and locations. They begin to include additional information in their signs, indicating how big, how good, how bad, or how fast something is.

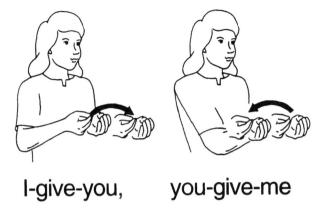

I-give-you,   you-give-me

Figure 5-1. The sign GIVE (left panel) is a directional sign that can be inflected to mean I-GIVE-YOU (center panel), YOU-GIVE-ME (right panel), and so on.

They also modify signs and their meanings through conventional ASL facial expression to indicate subjective meaning. For example, I WANT THAT becomes I REALLY WANT THAT A LOT! when signed with vigor and appropriate expression, and THERE'S A WORM similarly becomes THERE'S A YUKKY WORM! with correct changes to the face and orientation of the head. By the time they are 4, deaf children exposed to fluent sign language are able to express how things occur, why things occur, and their intentions.

As with hearing children, deaf 3- and 4-year-olds also use some signs incorrectly, in what are called *overgeneralizations.* Hearing children of this age frequently overgeneralize irregular verbs and nouns that they previously used correctly. Thus, *fell* becomes *falled,* presumably because they have learned the general rule (for the past tense in this example) and attempt to make all similar words conform to that rule. Deaf children similarly are seen to overgeneralize, for example, by adding direction to nondirectional verbs such as TOUCH or DRINK, giving them understandable points of origin and conclusion. Overgeneralizations of this sort are as well understood by others when they occur in deaf children's signing as when they occur in hearing children's speech and may be laughed at, responded to, or corrected by others around them. Whatever their reaction, parents and teachers should recognize the importance of such "errors." They indicate that the child is making sophisticated guesses about the grammar of the language and acquiring its component rules.

In deaf 3-year-olds, we also see the beginnings of demonstrative pronouns such as THAT, THERE, and THIS, and possessive pronouns such as YOUR, MINE, and OUR. Both types of pronouns appear to occur somewhat later in deaf children than in hearing children, who begin to use them by the middle of their third year (age 2½), but there is very little evidence on this subject. In fact, there is surprisingly little research on the development of sign language in deaf children between the ages 3 and 6 years, regardless of whether they have deaf or hearing parents. We know that the order in which new aspects of language are learned by deaf children of hearing parents is consistent with that of hearing children of hearing parents and deaf children of deaf parents, even if it tends to lag some months behind. Beyond that general conclusion, however, there is not much information available to parents, teachers, or researchers, as most of the available research has focused on younger or older children.

Deaf Children's Exposure to Social Language

In general, deaf parents appear to show greater awareness of the communication needs of deaf children than do hearing parents. This awareness results in part from their own experiences, but they also are likely to be more sensitive to visual signals from their children and more able to use visual strategies to gain attention and foster communication (Mohay et al., 1998; see Table 5–1). Deaf parents also will have a more efficient and effective means of communicating with their children via sign language. Some hearing parents also are very aware of cues from their young deaf children about the success or failure of communication. Many, however, lack competence or confidence in their signing and other visual communication skills, and this can make it more difficult for them to adapt to the needs of their children.

A moment of reflection or observation will reveal that the language that adults use with children frequently is modified to be appropriate for the presumed language capabilities of the young listener. Sometimes called *motherese,* such modifications are seen regardless of whether a child is hearing or deaf and regardless of whether signed or spoken language is used. When directed to young children by either deaf or hearing mothers, language tends to be slower, simpler, and more likely to include shortened versions of words or signs than the language directed to older children or adults. Because language development in deaf children of deaf parents occurs in a natural manner, we would expect that deaf mothers' use of motherese in communicating with their young children would begin just as early as it does in hearing mothers of hearing children, and this turns out to be the case. When their babies are as young as 3 months of age, deaf mothers use primarily single signs with their babies, frequently with the same kinds of repetition as we see in hearing mothers speaking to their hearing babies. Deaf mothers' signing also tends to be accompanied by smiles and numerous mouth movements, and they use exaggerated facial expressions with their babies even more than hearing mothers. "Baby talk" thus clearly occurs in signing as well as speech.

Table 5-1   Helping to Ensure Communication With Young Deaf Children

To get and keep a young deaf child's attention:

Use facial expressions and body language to appear "interesting" to the child

Use hand and body movements within their line of sight (to "break" their gaze)

Touch the child gently to interrupt other behaviors

Point to interesting things (and look at them yourself)

To facilitate communication:

Point to things and then say what they are (and perhaps point again)

Wait until the child is looking before communicating

Slow down the rate of communication

Don't make the child continually have to shift attention away from something interesting

Use short utterances

Position yourself and objects with the child's visual field

Ensure that your hands (if signing) or face (if speaking) is in the child's visual field

Put important information (e.g., the topic) at the beginning *and* the end of utterances

When referring to things, make signs or gestures with the hands on or near the objects

Exaggerate, repeat, and prolong signs to make sure they are seen and recognized

Allow more time for children to understand messages

(Adapted from Mohay, Milton, Hindmarsh, & Ganley, 1998)

Speech makes language available to hearing children regardless of whether they are looking in the right direction. When it appears that a deaf infant or toddler is not watching his mother, many hearing mothers are reluctant to sign. Deaf mothers also sometimes report they resist signing to their children unless they have made eye contact, but they commonly move their hands out in front of their babies, rather than moving a child's head or physically changing his position, so that the children will see their signs (Meadow-Orlans, Spencer, & Koester, 2004). Over time, this strategy teaches infants to attend visually to cues in the environment and deaf babies seem remarkably good at picking up on mothers' visual cues across a much wider range of positions than one would expect from a hearing child. In fact, there is now evidence that deaf children actually are better at detecting movement in the periphery of their vision than are hearing children (see Proksch & Bavelier, 2002, for discussion). This ability does not result from their being deaf, but from the fact that for them, there *are* important things happening on the edges of their visual range. Their eyes and brains adjust accordingly, with important implications for social and language development. To some extent, the same phenomenon is seen in hearing children of deaf parents, because the same behavioral contingencies occur during their development.

The ways in which parents accommodate the language needs of their deaf babies as well as their hearing babies seem to play an important role in determining the effectiveness and interest in communication on both sides of the "conversation." It therefore would not be surprising if a lack of effective visual communication between hearing parents and their deaf children were to reduce the quality of their social and educational interactions. In fact, when they are either signing or speaking to their deaf children about a common object of attention, hearing mothers often tend to *over*simplify and end up producing language that carries far less information than the language they use with hearing children in similar situations. Similarly, parents often oversimplify language for younger hearing children, using constructions well below their comprehension levels. Such limitations are not unexpected given that most hearing mothers have little more than beginning competence in sign language, and young hearing children's receptive skills for spoken language are quite limited. Their implications for subsequent development nevertheless appear considerable, and should give everyone who is involved with deaf children pause for thought.

Final Comments

This chapter explored the contexts, capabilities, and components of language learning by deaf children. From vocal and manual babbling, to first words and signs, to more complex language, we have seen that normal language development depends on frequent and regular communication interactions between deaf children and those around them, regardless of whether it is signed or spoken. Deaf children initially babble like hearing children, making sounds that may be responded to by excited parents, even if they bear no relation to later language ability. Unlike hearing children, however, their vocal babbling decreases in quantity and variety over the first year of life. Manual babbling also seems to occur in deaf children, although its function and characteristics are not well understood. In any case, babies' vocal and manual babbling appear to have important social roles for hearing and deaf parents, respectively, and lead to "conversations" that contribute to social and cognitive development as well as language learning.

In young deaf and hearing children, gestures serve practical functions of identifying, requesting, or showing things in social situations. In the case of hearing children, those gestures are obvious and distinct from ongoing spoken language. In the case of deaf children, the fact that gestures and sign language use the same modality (hand to eye) makes the two difficult to distinguish. Actually, the gestures used by deaf and hearing children are remarkably similar. Deaf children use more of them than hearing children, but that difference disappears by the time they are adults. As both deaf and hearing children develop, their vocabularies grow and their gestures are replaced with conventional language. This and other evidence suggests that although gestures may have a special role within American Sign Language, they are natural and normal for both deaf and hearing children. There is no evidence that preventing their use by deaf children has any positive impact on their spoken language skills, and it may even work to their disadvantage.

There also is no evidence that early sign language learning impedes or prevents spoken language learning. Sign language may provide a bridge to spoken and written English (Mayer & Akamatsu, 2003; see chapter 7), and different children will excel in and prefer different modes of communication. Overall, exposure exclusively to spoken language tends not to be as successful as signing (or signing plus speaking) for language learning in young deaf children without cochlear implants. There are certainly exceptions, and the extent to which speech instruction, or any language instruction, will be successful depends on a variety of factors within the child (e.g., extent of hearing loss), within the parents (e.g., acceptance of the child), and within the language-learning context. My concern is that many deaf children spend years in intensive speech therapy—often to the exclusion of sign language—while missing the critical first years of language learning. This and the previous chapter therefore have raised a variety of issues that need to be taken into consideration before any decision about "the language of choice" is made by parents.

For parents who learn that their infant has a significant hearing loss, early intervention programs provide instruction about spoken language, sign language, and other visual communication strategies. Research has shown that spoken language has a significant visual component as well, and how the mouth moves during speech provides important cues even for hearing individuals. "Visual communication" as used here, however, refers to gestures, signs, and other nonvocal productions. Visual strategies for gaining and keeping attention, as well as supporting communication, are an important part of the early parent-child interactions regardless of whether a child will eventually be encouraged to use sign language or spoken language. Early skills in either mode are predictive of later spoken language skills, and given that it is easier for younger children to acquire sign language than spoken language, there is no reason why they should not be exposed to both.

A variety of investigations have suggested that children learning sign language might even have an advantage over children learning spoken language as a result of differences in the maturation rate of the fingers, hands, and arms relative to tongues, mouths, and vocal tracts. This benefit appears to maintain only through the one-word/one-sign stage; as children start combining words into longer strings, the difference disappears. Increasing complexity and skill in signed and spoken language subsequently follow the same course in deaf and hearing children, even if a lack of early language experience creates a lag in development for some deaf children. If normal language development, whatever its form, requires early and consistent input, many hearing parents of young deaf children will find it useful and important to learn sign language. If their skill remains limited and their vocabularies concrete, they should not be surprised to see that reflected in their children's language skills, at least temporarily, until the children are exposed to more and better language models. Those children with full access to natural languages such as ASL or English will eventually gain fluency; the same cannot be said for artificial languages such as SEE1 or Esperanto. Most importantly, parents and professionals have to address the needs of each child, as an individual, in the context of the family and educational system.

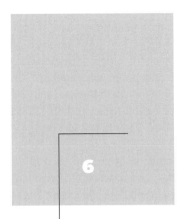

In the dormitories [of residential schools], away from the structured control of the classroom, deaf children are introduced to the social life of Deaf people. In the informal dormitory environment children learn not only sign language but the content of the culture. In this way, the schools become hubs of the communities that surround them, preserving for the next generation the culture of earlier generations.
—Carol Padden and Tom Humphries, in *Deaf in America* (1988)

6

SIX

Going to School

After deciding which language they want their deaf child exposed to during the preschool years, deciding on what kind of school they want for their child to attend is perhaps the most difficult decision parents have to make. As this chapter will make clear, the choice of schools may "lock in" the language decision until children are either able to learn a second language or until parents abandon one system that does not fully meet their child's needs and attempt to "start over" with another. This is not to say that it has to be this way, just that it is.

As at other critical milestones, some parents of deaf children find the information available to them in making "the school decision" confusing and contradictory. Federal legislation in the United States has been aimed at making access to education easier for deaf children and their families, but, as is often the case, the laws have been interpreted in so many different ways that the results are often more rather than less baffling. The present chapter, therefore, will try to make some sense of this issue, while avoiding any a priori judgments about what is best. Looking ahead, there will not be a single answer to the question, "What kind of school is best for my deaf child?" Rather, different children will have different needs, and different programs, as well as different kinds of programs, will be better suited to them. The two conclusions of which we can be sure are that there must be a broad range of educational options available to deaf children and their parents and that the choice of a school program will have long-term implications for personal and career goals as well as academic achievement. In order to help the reader wade through the many relevant issues, we therefore will first examine the kinds of educational options available for deaf children, and then look at the academic and psychological implications of them.

Educating Deaf Children

Over the past 100 years or so, the education of deaf children has changed dramatically both in the number of children it reaches and in its content. From 1850 to 1950, for example, enrollment in residential schools for the deaf and other special programs rose from just over 1100 to over 20,000. By the early 1970s, that number had more than tripled, largely due to the rubella epidemic of 1962–1965. By the mid-1970s, over a third of all deaf children attended residential schools, and another third attended special school programs.

More recently, the number of deaf children in residential schools has been decreasing, especially at the elementary school level. According to the Gallaudet Research Institute 2003 Annual Survey of Deaf and Hard-of-Hearing Children and Youth, which includes just over 40,000 children in the United States, 27 percent of those children identified attended a special school or center, compared to 46 percent who were fully mainstreamed in regular public schools. The latter is likely to be an underestimate, however, as many of the children who were not identified by the survey would likely be those who are in mainstream classrooms, where they might be the only deaf or hard-of-hearing child. Indeed, 2004 data from the United States Office of Special Education Programs indicated that of all students ages 6 to 21 years and being under IDEA due to hearing loss, over 85 percent attended regular public schools for all or part of the school day. Such changes from the 1970s to today are largely the result of federal and state laws mandating the education of handicapped children in the "least restrictive environment," and the emergence of *mainstreaming* and *inclusion* movements. Similar changes have occurred in other countries. Several issues involved in these movements are far more complicated than many people have assumed, and so I will deal with them in some depth below.

Perhaps the two most dramatic changes in the education of deaf children have been the introduction of sign language into the learning environment and the movement away from largely vocational training to a more academic curriculum, comparable to that offered to hearing children. At the same time, the greater involvement of the federal government in ensuring appropriate educational opportunities for children with disabilities has had a profound impact on deaf education, primarily through a series of laws passed in the United States between 1973 and 1990. These laws are often misinterpreted or, perhaps better said, interpreted in a variety of ways that often leave parents and educators frustrated. Before considering the variety of school programs available for deaf children, it therefore will be worth a brief overview of the primary legal issues.

Legal Issues Confronting the Education of Deaf Children

The powerful role played by the United States Congress in changing the face of education for deaf students (and those with other disabilities) started with the Rehabilitation Act of 1973 (PL 93-112), especially its Section 504, and the 1975 Education for All Handicapped Children Act (PL 94-142). These laws combined to assure free and appropriate public education (FAPE) for children with disabilities. PL 94-142 was amended by the Education of the Handicapped Amendments of 1986 (PL 99-457) and the 1990 Individuals with Disabilities Education Act (PL 101-476), known as IDEA. IDEA has now come to be used to refer to the entire PL 94-142 package. Among other requirements, these laws mandated early identification of hearing losses in school-age children as well as appropriate and unbiased evaluation of deaf children using a variety of alternative communication methods, including sign language.

This extraordinary congressional action resulted from the realization that only about 50 percent of children with disabilities attending public schools were receiving the support necessary for academic success, and that over 1 million disabled students were excluded from public school classrooms. Although the laws did not specify the nature of the education that school boards would have to supply, they did require (1) that all children from age 3 to 21 years be educated "in the least restrictive environment" (LRE) as close as possible to a child's home, (2) the availability of a continuum of placements from hospitals to regular classes, and (3) the development of individualized education programs (IEPs) for each child requiring special educational programming. For the first time, they also included parents in decision making about educational decisions affecting disabled children. This opportunity for broader family participation in educational planning has affected several factors contributing to deaf children's development, including children's exposure to deaf adults (now a required IEP consideration in some states), interactions with deaf and hearing peers, and the level of parent and teacher expectations for deaf children.

The confusion surrounding IDEA primarily concerns the definition of "least restrictive environment" and the intent of the law's requirement that disabled children should be educated with nondisabled children to the maximum extent possible. Perhaps more than anything else, it was this language that led to the mainstreaming and inclusion movements. The primary goal of the law was to eliminate discrimination in education by preventing the exclusion of children with disabilities from programs in which they could favorably compete with nondisabled peers. Unfortunately, the lack of detail in the law and the fact that it was an "unfunded mandate" led to conflict at state and local levels. IDEA clearly intended children with disabilities to be integrated into public school classrooms whenever appropriate, but the law was not clear on whether putting children into mainstream environments was a requirement or an option. Nor was it clear how deaf children and other students with special needs were to obtain access to the support services necessary for their educational success (Aldersley, 2002; Siegel, 2002).

This issue has become all the more important since passage of the No Child Left Behind Act (NCLB) (PL 107-110), which mandates greater accountability on the part of academic programs to ensure adequate yearly progress of their students. One interesting and unexpected consequence of NCLB is that some deaf children who have not done well in public schools are now being shifted to schools for the deaf. Unfortunately, those transfers often seem designed for the benefit of the public schools rather than the children, so deaf students who are lagging behind will not pull down school test scores. While the public schools have higher average test scores as a result such transfers, the schools for the deaf receiving such children will have lower average test scores. Parents and state education officials thus should use caution in interpreting the test scores of schools for the deaf, low test scores may be partly the fault of public schools which may appear to be doing a better job than they really are.

Both proponents and opponents of PL 94-142 applauded the outlawing of educational discrimination against deaf children and others, just as the greater school accountability required by NCLB would appear to be an important step forward. How could anyone be against greater educational opportunities for children with disabilities? People who are referred to as "opponents" of IDEA fall into two categories. Some parents have complained that the presence of disabled children in the public school classroom—especially those with behavioral problems—infringe on their "normal" children's opportunities for academic success.[1] Many such situations result from overly broad interpretations of the law itself, placing some students in inappropriate contexts in the interests of satisfying vague legal jargon. Other complaints reflect the kinds of continuing discrimination that the law was intended to eliminate. A second category of opponents to PL 94-142 includes parents—including parents of deaf children—who argue that the law requires mainstream classrooms as an available educational option, not as the only option. For those parents and many educators of deaf children, it is important to maintain a variety of educational alternatives for deaf children that allow for optimization of their potentials.

One aspect of this position involves the potential recognition of deaf children as a linguistic minority with the right to receive their education via sign language in either their local public schools or separate school settings. Consistent with this argument, the Bilingual Education Act of 1988 provided legal definitions for the terms "native language" and "limited English proficiency" frequently used in educational legislation, and it included deaf students and sign language under bilingual terminology for the first time. In 1992, a "Notice of Policy Guidance on Deaf Students' Educational Services" was published by the Department of Education emphasizing that determination of the most appropriate and least restrictive educational environment for a deaf child must be made on an individual basis in order to ensure FAPE (see Office for Civil Rights, 2006). Moreover, it listed five considerations that local and state education agencies were supposed to take into account in determining educational placements and IEPs for deaf children (these became mandates under reauthorizations of the IDEA in 1997, PL 105-17, and 2004, PL 108-446):

- Linguistic needs
- Severity of hearing loss and potential for using residual hearing with or without amplification devices
- Academic level
- Social, emotional, and cultural needs, including opportunities for interactions and communication with peers

- Communication needs including the child's and family's preferred mode of communication

Secretary of Education, Richard W. Riley later re-emphasized this point in a statement published in the newsletter of the American Society for Deaf Children when he noted,

> We do not advocate a "one size fits all" approach in making decisions about how students should be educated. Educational placement decisions for students with disabilities are made at the local level and should be based on individual student needs and address the issue of adequate resources for both students and teachers.

Questions remain, however, about how best to ensure that deaf children and school systems have the resources necessary for educational success and how teaching in a mainstream classroom can be adapted to meet the strengths and needs of deaf children. Recent research also has indicated that deaf children do not always learn in the same ways as hearing children, and therefore the methods and structure of the mainstream classroom may not be to their greatest advantage (Marschark, Convertino, & LaRock, 2006).

Coupled with the Americans with Disabilities Act (ADA, PL 101-336), laws aimed at preventing educational discrimination against deaf children promised to improve their access to diverse educational options and a slice of the budgetary pie. More recently, with shrinking local, state, and federal dollars, unfunded mandates like IDEA and NCLB offer a glimpse of educational opportunities, but they often leave deaf children, their parents, and schools without any real way to achieve them. Bickering among various groups about the "right" answer to these problems does not help the situation, even if it is understandable given the diverse and often contradictory arguments confronting them.

Educational Program Alternatives

Legal questions are not the only issue that confront parents trying to find the best educational placement for their children. Concerns about facilitating social development, academic achievement, and giving deaf children equal access to all of society clearly enter into the decision when seeking the best school for a deaf child. In order to fully understand the dynamics and consequences of changing education opportunities for deaf children, we therefore need to consider the several kinds of programs available.

Preschool Programs

Previous chapters have touched on the importance of preschool intervention programs for deaf children and their parents. Like other preschool programs, early intervention programs for deaf children are intended to give them the skills necessary to succeed when they enter formal schooling, usually kindergarten. In the case of deaf children, they usually are designed to accommodate youngsters from birth to 4 years and are sometimes divided into parent-infant (early intervention) and preschool (academic) categories. Such programs are run by public school systems, state health and human services departments, schools for the deaf, and some private organizations. Many school systems also offer the opportunity of home-based early intervention and preschool education in which itinerant teachers work with parents, children, siblings, and other family members. In providing services for parents as well as children, preschool programs focus on language development; parent-child communication; social skills; and appropriate support for any residual hearing children might have, through testing and possible fitting for hearing aids. Early interventionists and teachers generally provide parents with strategies for enhancing their children's development, including instruction in sign language, speech training, or both, depending on the particular program and children's needs. Because of the small numbers of children in each class and the number and variety of programs available, these programs are readily available for children in both metropolitan and rural areas.

The educational impact of various kinds of preschool programs has not been fully investigated, but there is broad agreement that they serve to foster social functioning, both in later school settings and within the family. In chapter 4, it was noted that friendships and playmate preferences among deaf preschool children are just as stable as those among hearing children, and these children tend to initiate more interpersonal interactions than children who do not attend such programs. At least one study also has shown a strong relation between social functioning and the kind of preschool program that deaf children attend. In that investigation, children who were exposed to simultaneous communication showed higher levels of social play and more frequent dramatic play (usually taken as an indicator of cognitive development) than children in speech-only preschool settings. The speech-only children, meanwhile, were found to be far more disruptive in their play, exhibiting many more aggressive acts like pushing and hitting (Cornelius & Hornett, 1990).

While it is difficult to unravel the many factors that might make for such differences, there seems to be fairly consistent evidence that early exposure to sign communication facilitates deaf children's social interactions with peers as well as with their parents (Calderon & Greenberg, 1997). Although studies involving older deaf children with and without preschool experience still lie ahead, it seems likely that the availability of more diverse social, language, and educational experiences can only enhance the flexibility of young deaf children in dealing with later social interactions with hearing peers. We also would expect that such programs would have beneficial long-term effects on academic achievement, although reports thus far have tended to be anecdotal and testimonial, rather than supported by hard data.

Schools for the Deaf, Residential Schools, and Separate School Programs

The term "residential school for the deaf" elicits a variety of reactions in hearing people. People who have never visited one should forget the old exaggerated image of an institution with green walls, stark rooms, and "lost" children. Residential schools have a long and venerable history in this country, even though they may be rejected by people who are opposed to either the teaching of sign language or to any kind of special education programs for deaf children. They also are rejected by those parents who simply want their child living at home. Residential schools, both public and private, are at the heart of the Deaf community. They are places where life-long friendships are formed, language and culture are learned, and where teaching can occur directly without the need for intermediaries such as interpreters. Many schools for the deaf actively seek collaborations with their mainstream neighbors in order to best to accommodate the educational needs of deaf children and the educational preferences of their parents (e.g., through partial mainstreaming).

As the quotation at the top of this chapter indicates, in the dormitories and after-school activities at schools for the deaf, deaf children can acquire the knowledge and skills that make them feel a part of Deaf society, or any society. Looking up to older, fluently signing and socially competent deaf children, younger deaf children discover role models and an environment in which they are on an equal footing with their peers. Schools for the deaf traditionally have drawn children from all parts of every state into settings specially designed to fit their needs. They serve deaf children of both hearing parents and deaf parents, the latter group traditionally having a strong preference for that setting for their children. During the 1970s and 1980s, as a result of the rubella epidemic, these schools multiplied and expanded. With the more recent decline in the population of deaf children since the development of a rubella vaccine and the increasing popularity of mainstreaming/inclusion, some schools for the deaf have closed, and those that remain typically have more commuting students than residential students. Some day school children eventually spend some time living in school dormitories, gaining a social and co-curricular life usually not available to individual deaf children who live at home.

Different kinds of school programs are likely to be more or less beneficial for children with different strengths and needs. Adding to arguments about the appropriateness of placement in schools for the deaf versus local public schools, there is conflicting evidence supporting each as leading to better educational outcomes for deaf children. A variety of reports through the years, for example, have called for more deaf teachers and more hearing teachers who are fluent signers at schools for the deaf, as well as more teachers who are certified in the content areas they teach (see Marschark, Lang, & Albertini, 2002). At the same time, there is considerable evidence of a lack of access to classroom information in public school settings encountered by deaf children who rely on sign language. Even when public schools offer interpreting services, interpreters are in short supply and often underqualified (Jones, 2005; Schick, Williams, & Bolster, 1999).

Educators and parents who advocate for the option of a school for the deaf point out that the presence of deaf adults who are well educated and fluent in sign language has a significant, long-term impact on young deaf children's educational and personal well-being. Deaf adults also can serve as models for the development of appropriate social behavior, sex roles, and moral reasoning in deaf children. Consistent with this argument, deaf children who attend schools for the deaf tend to be better adjusted and more emotionally mature than deaf children enrolled in public schools programs, as will be discussed in a section later in this chapter. In the absence of such models, deaf children from hearing families occasionally have been reported to believe that they will either regain their hearing when they get older or die as children. After all, they never see any adults who are deaf!

The maintenance of the cultural hub of the Deaf community is not an insignificant part of the argument to preserve residential schools, but it is separate from the consideration of their educational impact. A variety of factors related to initial school placement—degree of hearing loss, early intervention experience, parental factors, and so on—make any general conclusions about the utility of residential versus public school programs difficult to make. There are, nevertheless, several domains in which consequences of school placement appear fairly clear, and these will be discussed at various places in this and subsequent chapters. In any case, the primary goal should be to identify the educational strengths and needs of each child before choosing the appropriate educational environment. Then, there must be alternatives available that provide different kinds of programming.

Not all separate school programs for deaf children are housed in schools for the deaf. Special school programs also are offered in public schools and other educational centers. These programs typically employ some deaf teachers and teachers' aides and expose deaf children to others who are deaf or hard of hearing. Most importantly, they have teachers and staff who are specially trained in educational methods designed to optimize educational opportunities for deaf children. When parents are involved in their child's language learning, take the time to work with their children after school hours, and participate in extra-curricular activities, such programs can be an excellent compromise between schools for the deaf and full inclusion. We have already seen that parental involvement is an essential component in deaf children's academic success (see also chapter 8), and day school programs can provide very effective environments for deaf children, meshing home-based and school-based support.

Public School Mainstreaming and Inclusion

Mainstreaming and inclusion are the dominant educational placement for deaf students today and the primary alternative to deaf children's attending schools for the deaf. Both *mainstreaming* and *inclusion* involve placing deaf students or others with special needs in regular public schools rather than separate programs. The primary difference is that mainstreaming typically involves attendance of some special classes (taught by a teacher of the deaf) and some regular classes, whereas inclusion entails students being "fully included" in all aspects of public school setting with any additional services provided in the classroom setting rather than on a "pull-out" basis. Mainstream programs also may involve the availability of a special resource room with appropriately trained teachers and/or aides, whereas inclusion explicitly does not. In some cases, a child's IEP calls for partial mainstreaming, where the child spends part of the day in a separate school setting (perhaps a school for the deaf) and part of the day in a local public school classroom.

One common complaint about mainstream programs is that they do not provide the quality, "regular" education that their supporters claim. Deaf students may be placed in regular classrooms only for nonacademic courses, while taking their core curricula either in separate classrooms or at schools for the deaf to which they have to commute during school hours. Beyond sometimes being misled about the academic integrity of such programs, students with such partial integration may acquire the same kinds of stigma that students in their parents' or grandparents' generations once experienced when they went off to "remedial education classes" in their schools. Indeed, the available evidence suggests that deaf children who receive such dual-track educations have more difficulty with both social integration and academic involvement than those who are consistently taught in one setting or the other (Antia & Kriemeyer, 2003). One hears success stories of children who have made the transition from special programs to partial mainstreaming to full mainstreaming, but I have heard just as many stories about children being more successful when they go in the other direction.

Mainstream settings need not suffer from the problems of programs providing superficial integration. For some students, a mainstream classroom with appropriate academic support services can provide excellent educational opportunities. Mainstreaming is not for all deaf students, but then no one type of program is. The key is to try to identify the "right" kind of program for a child in the first place *and* closely monitor academic and social progress for signs of program appropriateness or inappropriateness. Now that parents are involved in establishing IEPs, they have a greater ability to match their children's abilities with available placements and ensure that the full range of their children's needs are addressed. Some parents of deaf children advocate for full inclusion for their children, and that needs to be an available option. Mandatory inclusion, in contrast, does not seem an appropriate response to either the needs of deaf children or the legal requirements of IDEA and NCLB. Such a policy fails to recognize that different children, whether they are deaf, hearing, autistic, gifted, or whatever, have different needs that may be best served by different educational options. Parent advocacy for quality and educational programming for deaf children has a long history (Lang, 2003), and I know many parents who have had to fight that battle more or less alone. One can only hope that innocent children will not get caught in the undertow of politics and administrative expediency and risk being overwhelmed.

Bilingual Programs

Programs that offer instruction in both ASL and English are relatively new on the deaf education scene. These programs may be housed at schools for the deaf or separate school settings, and often describe themselves as *bilingual-bicultural* (or Bi-Bi) programs. Unfortunately, there has been little formal evaluation of the extent to which students in such programs gain fluency in their two languages, are comfortable in two cultures, or evidence long-term academic benefits. To outward appearances, they usually tend to emphasize ASL rather than a balanced bilingual approach.

Several alternatives to current ASL-English bilingual programs also have been suggested. ASL might be combined with either simultaneous communication or English-based signing to provide a more effective bridge from early language (via ASL) and literacy (via English). Several programs in England have adopted such an approach to education, combining British

Sign Language and sign-supported English, but the extent of their success is unclear. Wilbur (2000) made a similar suggestion, based largely on research with deaf children of deaf parents, advocating the initial use of ASL to provide early access to language, followed by a combination of ASL and written English to promote literacy, then followed by a combination of ASL, written English, and spoken language if desired. Either of these possibilities would fit with the detailed theoretical arguments proposed by Mayer and Wells (1996) and Mayer and Akamatsu (2003), but they require implementation and evaluation to determine whether or not they work.

Postsecondary Education for Deaf Students

The days of deaf children being primarily trained in "vocational schools" for careers in manufacturing are gone, as are many of the jobs for which they once were trained. There is a now full array of educational opportunities available for deaf students in community colleges and in four-year colleges and universities. At least there should be. Section 504 of the Rehabilitation Act of 1973 and the ADA guaranteed deaf students, as well as others, full access to public and private services, including the college classroom, and the following section describes the kinds of academic services that should be provided under the ADA and other laws.

At present, there are over 31,000 deaf and hard-of-hearing students enrolled in postsecondary educational institutions in this country, roughly 93 percent of them at the undergraduate level. This is up from 15,000 when the first edition of this book was written only 10 years ago. The current number still is most likely an underestimate, as many students and colleges still are not aware of deaf students' rights to obtain support services, and it has been estimated that another 3–4 percent of college students may have an undisclosed hearing loss (Richardson, Long, & Woodley, 2004). Almost 50 percent of all 2- and 4-year institutions have identified themselves as serving at least one deaf or hard of hearing student, and among larger colleges and universities this number rises to around 95 percent. The *College & Career Programs for Deaf Students* (King, DeCaro, Karchmer, & Cole, 2001), published jointly by Gallaudet University and the National Technical Institute for the Deaf (NTID), lists over 125 and colleges and universities that provide special programs and services for deaf and hard-of-hearing students. Included in this number are four federally funded, regional Postsecondary Education Programs for Deaf Students and the two national programs, NTID and Gallaudet, which deserve special mention.

In 1965, the National Technical Institute for the Deaf was established as a college of Rochester Institute of Technology (RIT), founded in 1862. NTID opened its doors in 1968. In a unique, fully mainstreamed setting, over 1200 deaf and hard-of-hearing students at RIT are able to earn degrees in any program offered by the university, such as engineering, computer science, applied art, and photography. Courses in the college of NTID proper are taught by faculty who sign for themselves, using ASL, English-based signing, or simultaneous communication, depending on the communication preferences and needs of their students. Courses taught in other colleges of the university are supported by sign language interpreters and note takers whenever there are deaf students in a class. At present, NTID provides over 90,000 hours of interpreting and over 45,000 hours of note-taking services each year in support of deaf students cross-registered in one of the other seven colleges. The job placement rate for NTID students is about 95 percent, with approximately 80 percent of graduates finding work in business and industry.

Gallaudet University offers a wide array of undergraduate and graduate programs to its 1600 deaf and hard-of-hearing students; graduate programs are also open to hearing students. Established in 1864, Gallaudet is the only free-standing liberal arts college for deaf students in the world and, like NTID, it also serves as a research center and public service center for issues and information relevant to hearing loss. In a bilingual ASL and English setting, Gallaudet students can select from a diverse array of majors and graduate programs. Students who attend Gallaudet or NTID typically have graduation rates between 50 percent and 60 percent, although deaf students enrolled in the other colleges of RIT have a graduation rate of 70 percent. Deaf students who attend other universities have much lower graduation rates, around 35 percent from 2-year programs and 30 percent from 4-year programs. This compares to graduation rates of 40 percent at 2-year programs and 70 percent at 4-year programs among their hearing peers. Although there have not been many studies conducted to determine the precise reason for these differences, one would assume that enhanced communication, a broad array of support services, and instructors experienced in teaching deaf students are primary factors. Even when classroom support is provided at other colleges and universities, deaf students may be tacitly denied access to advising, public lectures, and other campus activities. Further, deaf students may have special needs related to their educational backgrounds prior to the college years or to multiple handicaps. Many institutions still do not know their responsibilities for providing such educational support under the ADA, and others simply are unable or unwilling to do so. Until this situation changes, special college programs for deaf and hard-of-hearing students will remain an important educational alternative.

Academic Support Services

Surprisingly, perhaps, deaf students tend to have higher academic achievement than hard-of-hearing students. This finding might seem contradictory to those who assume that more hearing is always better than less hearing. One factor likely involved here is the level of special support that the two kinds of students receive. Students who have lesser hearing losses may not be identified as easily as those with greater hearing losses, they and their parents may not know that they qualify for special services, and older students may not apply for them for personal reasons (Richardson et al., 2004). Even when such services are requested, hard-of-hearing and even some deaf students may not be able get them if they are judged "not disabled enough" by school administrators who desire to avoid costly support for only one or two students.

The primary academic support services needed by deaf students are both communication related: interpreting (for those who sign) and note taking. There are also other issues involved, including the effective use of classroom space, captioned video materials, teaching strategies, and the sensitivity of teachers and counselors to the communication needs and learning strategies of deaf students.

Interpreting

Students with mild to moderate hearing losses often can follow classroom instruction fairly well by sitting in the front row, particularly if they have the support of note takers. Nevertheless, communication can be disrupted in several ways: the teacher may talk while facing the blackboard or wandering around the room, thus reducing both the volume and the availability of mouth and other facial cues; there may be multiple conversations going on during questions and answers that require rapid switching of attention; or teachers and other students may not speak clearly enough for a deaf student to follow.[2] With greater hearing losses, following a speaking teacher is often impossible. Even when speechreading skills are sufficient for one-on-one conversations about specific topics, that strategy can quickly become swamped in a classroom, for all of the reasons cited above. True, some students with more severe hearing losses use spoken language as their primary means of communication and are able to succeed in such settings without communication support services. They are few and far between, however, and often report succeeding *despite* going to class, through the assistance of their parents, friends, and supportive teachers. Other deaf students have speech skills good enough to lead teachers to assume they have comparable abilities in speechreading—usually an erroneous assumption (Johnson, 1991).

Deaf students who are unable to survive schooling with spoken communication alone must depend on sign language interpreters. An educational interpreter is someone who has received extensive training in sign language and its variants and in special aspects of educational interpreting (as opposed to legal or medical interpreting); is certified by their state and/or the National Registry of Interpreters for the Deaf (RID); and is bound by a clear and detailed code of ethics. Under the 2004 reauthorization of the IDEA, educational interpreters are "related service providers," thus giving them the opportunity for input into children's IEPs for the first time. This is an important step forward, because interpreters are often the service providers who see individual children the most and are in the best position to identify educational needs, but they have been excluded from such discussions in the past.

Unfortunately, qualified educational interpreters are in short supply, and it is common for schools to try to make use of lesser trained individuals who can be paid less but also are less skilled (Jones, 2005; Jones, Clark, & Stoltz, 1997). Just because someone "knows" sign language does not make them competent to interpret in the classroom. Nor, for that matter, are they competent to interpret for parent-teacher meetings when one of the parties is deaf. Nevertheless, I have heard numerous stories about deaf parents going to a school meeting and requesting an interpreter, only to find that a teacher's aide or other person who has some knowledge of sign language is "interpreting" for the meeting. Those meetings are usually doomed from the outset and do not really do any good for the child, parent, teacher, or the school. One of the best outcomes is the scheduling of another meeting with a qualified interpreter, but in some cases even that may not be appropriately communicated. Some schools refuse such requests in the erroneous belief that they have met their legal and moral obligations. The increasing availability of *video relay interpreting* (*VRI*) may eliminate some of these difficulties, allowing the parties to use a remote interpreter, even if everyone else is in the same room.

Chapter 3 described some of the variety of communication systems available to young deaf children, from ASL to Signed English to spoken language, and there are interpreters for each of these.[3] In all cases, the goal of the interpreter is to faithfully communicate everything that the teacher and other students say and everything that the deaf students says (the sign-to-voice direction is sometimes referred to as *voice interpreting* or *reverse interpreting*). Usually, this occurs with the interpreter standing near the teacher, so that the student can watch both people and take advantage of the teachers' movements, facial expressions, and demonstrations. Sharing the classroom "stage" with an interpreter makes some teachers anxious, however, and teacher-interpreter cooperation is not always as good as it should be. Further, the variable language fluencies and cognitive abilities of deaf children, especially in the earlier grades, means that an educational interpreter has to know much more than just sign language. Interpreter training programs are just now starting to include courses in child development and psychology in their educational interpreting curricula.

Most interpreters will provide the deaf student with additional class-related information that they normally would be denied, such as the context of discussions, noises coming from inside or outside the room, and "tone" of communications if they are not clear. Interpreters *are not* teachers' aides, and they should not have responsibilities outside of interpreting per se. Most certified interpreters, in fact, are reluctant to step outside of their interpreter role at all, and some will deflect questions directed at them to the person for whom they are interpreting. For example, an interpreter might respond to a hearing student's question of "Who are you?" by simply signing WHO ARE YOU? and allowing the deaf student to answer the question. A similar situation arose in a meeting I attended involving 2 deaf faculty members and about 10 hearing faculty, some of whom could not sign. When we went around the room introducing ourselves, the interpreter was inadvertently left out (although I understand from interpreter friends that this is not unusual). In order to recognize the interpreter, a deaf colleague in the meeting joked, AND WHO IS THAT FAT GUY UP THERE WAVING HIS HANDS? The interpreter accordingly voiced "And who is that fat guy up there waving his hands?" to the laughter of those who understood what had happened and the puzzlement of those who did not. (The interpreter then did introduce himself!)

Note Taking

At first blush, a reader might wonder why a deaf student should have the benefit of someone to take notes for them in class—after all, hearing students do not receive such services. A deaf student has to rely on visual communication. When hearing students look down to write in their notebooks, they are able to continue to follow the lecture or classroom conversation because they can hear it. I have taught some hearing students who spend almost all of the class looking down and taking notes, but still following what was going on. Deaf students do not have that luxury, regardless of whether they rely on spoken or signed communication. Each time they look down to write something, they miss part of what is being said. The alternative of not taking notes at all puts the deaf student at a clear disadvantage, so many of them depend on classroom note takers. As deaf children move into later grades, where notes become more important in class, hearing students are often asked to volunteer to share their notes with deaf classmates. Some programs train and pay student note takers, which improves their utility for both deaf and hearing students; others may use transcripts from classroom *real-time text* technologies. As an alternative to note taking, teachers may copy their class notes or overhead transparencies for deaf students. Hearing as well as deaf students seem likely to benefit from such opportunities, and once teachers have prepared them for a deaf student, many will continue doing so for future classes.

Real-Time Text

Real-time text, or *speech-to-text service*, recently has emerged as an important classroom support for deaf students. Speech-to-text services typically involve an intermediary operator who is often (but not necessarily) in the classroom with the deaf student(s). The operator produces text as it is spoken by the teacher using a stenographic machine, automatic speech recognition, or a standard QWERTY keyboard. Students see the text displayed on a laptop computer or other screen.

Within integrated classrooms, real-time text frequently is promoted as a less expensive alternative to interpreting that also can provide greater access to the classroom for some students. Despite common assumptions, however, there is relatively little evidence that the latter assumption is true, and most of the research taken as support for the utility of speech-to-text services in deaf education has been based on student reports rather than actual performance. Such services actually appear to present a challenge for deaf students, especially younger ones, because the speed of real-time text may exceed their reading abilities (although some systems allow up to 20 lines of text to be displayed at a time). In fact, the evidence suggests that, on average, neither interpreting nor real-time text offers any generalized advantage for learning by deaf students, at least at high school and college levels (Marschark et al., 2006). Research with high school students has been inconsistent, however, as some studies have indicated that students who are better readers benefit more from real-time text.

Finally, it is important to note that using real-time text materials and visual displays (slides, computer screens) simultaneously in the classroom could actually hinder deaf students' access to information, because they cannot be looking at two sources of visual information at the same time. A similar situation may be created by classrooms which include both an interpreter and real-time text, potentially forcing deaf students to focus on one or the other at different times. Even without a third source of visual information, students in such situations risk losing the thread of a lecture, because the different information sources will be out of synchrony, and they likely will be unable to predict which source is more important at any given time. As in the case of classroom acoustics (see below), challenges to effective classroom communication for deaf students are sometimes subtle and unexpected, requiring parents and teachers to be vigilant.

Other Support Considerations

There are several other considerations important for supporting deaf students, both inside and outside the classroom. Within the classroom, deaf students' reliance on visual information makes the use of overhead transparencies, video projection, and similar teaching tools indispensable, as long as care is taken to coordinate presentations so the students are not expected to be looking at two things at the same time. In addition to possibly including a loop or FM system, as described in chapter 2, classrooms need to allow deaf students allow unhindered view of the instructor and blackboards, offer good acoustics, and reduce visual noise and window glare so children can see the entire classroom comfortably. Unfortunately, even with careful planning, visual and acoustic designs can sometimes conflict. At NTID, for example, a whole series of classrooms were designed with vertical wood slats on a sound-absorbing wall. The goal was to support spoken language communication through better acoustics, but the "visual noise" of the walls created significant eyestrain in the deaf students for whom it was intended. (The solution was painting the wood and walls the same color.) Acoustics, window glare, and visual noise are even greater problems in public school classrooms, where designs typically did not include concerns about children with hearing loss.

Outside of the classroom, deaf students benefit from the availability of tutors (either more senior students, "off-duty" teachers, or staff hired specially for that purpose), both to offset gaps in communication, and because many will be less academically prepared than their hearing classmates. Personal, academic, and career counselors also serve an important role for deaf students, who will be less likely to get such advice from hearing teachers and peers who are unfamiliar with deafness. In programs with larger numbers of deaf students, there are frequently resource rooms, advising centers, or technical assistance centers. Counselors, hearing aid technicians, and audiologists may be physically housed within these sites, or students may be directed to them by individuals who are. In many schools, electronic bulletin boards and computer "notes conferences" are increasingly popular, and users have no way of knowing which students are deaf and which are hearing (or blind or physically challenged).

Taken together, the array of support services described above help to give deaf students more equal access to the educations they have been promised and deserve. But education is not simply a matter of sitting in a classroom. Effective teaching and learning requires clear communication between students and instructors and the opportunity to ask questions and interact with other students. In addition to providing effective educational and career information, academic support services allow deaf students to be integrated into their schools and communities to an extent that would otherwise be nearly impossible. Differing school programs and differing levels of academic support therefore can lead to considerable differences in academic and social-personal success.

Educational Implications of Alternative
School Placements

A variety of investigations has examined the educational outcomes of various kinds of school programs for deaf children. In all such studies, there is a potential source of bias, and the rule of *caveat emptor,* "buyer beware," is important here. A truly fair comparison of two programs or different types of programs would need to include students who are comparable in terms of hearing losses, communication skills, academic backgrounds, family support, and so on. This kind of control happens in laboratory research, but it is not likely to occur naturally in the real world. It is therefore difficult to determine the extent to which observed differences between programs are due to something about the programs themselves or the possibility that they attract different kinds of students in the first place. This is an important issue because depending on how one views those results, they can be used to support one philosophy of schooling or another. Rather than providing hypothetical examples of this problem, let me put it in the context of actual research findings.

In light of the legal and educational issues described earlier in this chapter, there have been several recent studies comparing the academic success of deaf students attending residential school programs versus those attending mainstream programs. Several large-scale studies, however, have indicated that prior differences among deaf children are far more important than placement per se in explaining their academic achievement (Allen & Osborne, 1984; Kluwin & Moores, 1985; Powers, 1999). That is, student variables like degree of hearing loss and multiple handicaps, and family variables such as socioeconomic status, parental hearing status, and size of the family, explain more of the differences in achievement than the kind of program in which children are enrolled (see Stinson & Kluwin, 2003, for a review). Indeed, school placement has been shown to account for as little as one percent of the observed variability across deaf children in academic achievement! In part, this surprisingly low number results from the fact that better early intervention and evaluation methods today mean that deaf children are more likely to be placed in appropriate programs than they were in the past. Different school placements offer different kinds of support for deaf students, and it is no longer the case that full-time enrollment in a school for the deaf that exclusively uses sign language or a public school program that exclusively uses spoken language are the only two alternatives available to deaf children.

The small effect of school placement is also the result of deaf students' being much more heterogeneous than hearing students. Males and children with lesser hearing losses are more likely to be placed in regular school classrooms than females and those with greater hearing losses, but factors like age of hearing loss onset, previous academic experience, and even parental hearing status have much smaller effects on academic placement and achievement than is often assumed. The purported relation of parental hearing status and achievement is particularly interesting, because one can find a variety of claims indicating that deaf children of deaf parents—who are often seen as more likely to attend a school for the deaf—have higher academic achievement than deaf children of hearing parents (see also chapter 8). Most of those claims, however, are either based on weak (usually older) studies or are simply *correlational,* showing only the existence of a relationship but not its cause. Taken together, the accumulated evidence clearly points to the fact that early, effective access to fluent language is the key, regardless of the hearing status of a child's parents (see Marschark, 2005a, for a review).

If neither parental hearing status nor school placement seems to have as great an impact on academic achievement as is frequently claimed, where do we look for the determinants of success? In virtually all studies of deaf children's academic achievement, 50–75 percent of the observed differences among deaf students is unexplained, while student characteristics account for at most about one quarter of the variability observed. We thus remain at a loss in identifying any single characteristic or group of characteristics that directly influence achievement by deaf students. Various authors point out the importance of communication skills, motivation, and academic rigor, but the fact is that we are still well short of a full understanding of deaf students' academic performance, and thus are necessarily at a loss to provide specific methods for improving it.

If we ignore prior differences among deaf children, we can imagine a variety of scenarios that could result in deaf children showing higher achievement in one kind of school program or another. Deaf students in a separate program might do better because of more specialized teaching methods and better communication or do worse if they had less rigorous academic preparation or if teachers are less well qualified. They might do better in mainstream or inclusive programs that have more resources, but failure of school personnel to ensure that hearing aids and implants are functioning properly can offset potential benefits of classroom design and technology. Finally, it may be that teacher and parent expectations are higher for children in one academic setting or another. This complexity of alternatives explains why it is so important that the educational research involving a population as diverse as deaf children be conducted very carefully. Claims from inadequately controlled studies are more likely to lead to incorrect conclusions than they are to help parents in educational decision making.

Even if there is still no strong evidence in this regard, on average, deaf students with lesser hearing losses, better spoken language skills, and greater communication flexibility appear more likely to enroll in mainstream schools in the first place. Among deaf children who are enrolled in separate school programs there tend to be more students with greater hearing losses and more who have either physical or emotional problems, as compared to students who are in mainstream settings. That is, students enrolled in public school settings often are more likely to come from "advantaged" backgrounds, to have lesser hearing losses and fewer physical challenges, and to be doing better in school. Which of the first three, if any, is a cause of doing better is school is not clear. Such findings suggest that any difference in achievement between students in regular and special school programs is not caused by the school programs themselves, but by all of those individual and family factors that influence development and learning before children enter school. Finally, it is important to note again that the students who might attend particular programs favored by parents and teachers may have different expectations placed on them, and there may be a "self-fulfilling prophecy." In other words, those children might achieve just as much in other kinds of programs if the same demands were placed on them. We just do not know.

Psychological Implications of Alternative School Placements

Given the importance of factors like motivation for educational achievement and *self-esteem,* it will be worthwhile to consider possible differences in social and personality functioning as they relate to attending particular kinds of school programs. Earlier in this chapter, I described the 1992 "Notice of Policy Guidance on Deaf Students' Educational Services," clarifying some incorrect interpretations of PL 94-142 (IDEA). Part of that clarification called for the consideration of social, emotional, and cultural needs in determining the appropriate school placement for deaf children, including the opportunity for interactions and communication with peers. This provision came in response to the concern that deaf children placed in mainstream or inclusive settings would lose the normal kinds of social interactions typically available to hearing children in public schools and deaf children in residential schools.

Clearly, one aspect of education involves acquiring the roles, rules, attitudes, and values of one's society. Peer relationships are thus an essential part of social development (see also chapter 4), but the question of how best to foster the development of such relationships is not a simple matter. On the surface, one could imagine either that deaf children might benefit from being surrounded by hearing peers or that the lack of communication might result in their becoming socially isolated. In order to evaluate this issue, we have to consider deaf students' social experiences when they are in programs with hearing peers versus when they are in programs with deaf peers. Only then can we know how best to support deaf children's development of identity and integration with society. Keep in mind, however, that this is not just an issue of "having friends" or "socializing at school." Students with positive social interactions in school tend to have higher academic achievement (see chapter 8), better mental health (see chapter 9), and are more likely to succeed in their careers. Children may not be not graded on it, but they do learn a lot about social functioning in school.

Advocates of inclusion programs for deaf children argue that placing deaf children and children with disabilities in regular classes will enhance their self-esteem and sense of control, as well as foster the integration of all people with disabilities into society. Italy has been experimenting with a similar concept, in which almost all children with disabilities are placed in public school settings. As the program has been explained to me by one of its leaders, the hope is that after a generation or two of having all handicapped children in the same classrooms as nonhandicapped children, people with disabilities will no longer "seem different," and society will be more accepting of the equality of all children. While this may be a laudable goal, there appears a rather basic problem with this wholesale "inclusionist" approach. Putting deaf children or others with special needs into regular classrooms rests on the assumption that they are able to learn effectively in those settings. It is through smooth social functioning and equal performance in such classrooms that they would become part of the groups who are supposed to "accept" them. To support such efforts, Italy has a large number of special education teachers who work within the public schools as resources for children with disabilities. In the case of deaf children, however, there are essentially no sign language interpreters in schools, and relatively few of the special education teachers know Italian Sign Language. As generalists, these teachers thus have little training in how to deal effectively with the special needs of children who cannot hear—or those with other impediments to full access. Many deaf children thus are unable to benefit from the public school classroom and tend to be isolated from both peers and educators. In the interests of this grand experiment, a whole generation of deaf and handicapped children may be left out, unable to benefit fully from the school experience and with nowhere else to turn.

Several recent studies in the United States have evaluated the social-emotional consequences of placement in mainstream versus special school settings. In general, findings indicate that deaf students generally are not accepted by their hearing peers and as a result they may report feeling lonely, rejected, and socially isolated (Kluwin & Stinson, 1993). Many deaf students find themselves frustrated in their attempts to relate to or interact with their hearing classmates and thus may focus more on relations with teachers and other deaf peers—not an unusual finding for students who are excluded by their minority status. In contrast, deaf students in both the separate schools and in special programs within local public schools report feeling more emotionally secure and accepted by peers, as well as having more friendships. These findings have involved mixed groups with regard to use of hearing aids and cochlear implants. As described in chapter 2, children with implants vary widely in their reports about social interaction and social comfort in school. Because those studies have focused on students in regular public school settings, we are unable to make any comparisons between them and children with implants who are enrolled in separate school programs.

For students in partial-mainstream settings, social adjustment generally is better in interactions with deaf than with hearing peers, given equal exposure to both. Increasing the amount of mainstreaming does not improve the amount of emotional security, however. Such results suggest that, contrary to the claims of inclusion advocates, there are no clear social-emotional benefits for deaf children who attend school with hearing peers. Quite the contrary: They tend to have more problems of self-identity, emotional security, and in starting and maintaining friendships. When they do have personal interactions with hearing peers, deaf students report that their contacts are often less than positive (see Stinson & Kluwin, 2003). While it remains possible that such interactions may have some "sleeper effects" which will show up later in life, there is no way to tell whether such effects will be positive, perhaps allowing for smoother interactions with hearing society, or negative, perhaps leaving them to feel like outsiders in both deaf and hearing cultures.

Final Comments

Although most parents of deaf children want one, there is no simple and straightforward answer to the question, "What kind of school is best for my child?" If there is one message to be taken away from this chapter, it is that there must be a continuum of placements for deaf children, and parents and teachers need to collaborate to determine which is best for any particular child. Following a series of federal and state legal decisions in the United States since the 1970s, there are now several laws that protect deaf children from discrimination in education and ensure that they are fairly and appropriately evaluated, placed, and academically supported. This is not to say that there is full agreement about the best educational system for deaf children; even while the laws are being implemented, there is disagreement about what they mean and who will pay for them. Nonetheless, parents now have a central role in the planning of their deaf children's educational placement, and they need to be informed about their options and the implications of those options.

Early intervention (parent-infant and preschool) programs are available across most of the United States and in other countries. Normally funded by local school districts or schools for the deaf, these programs support the legal mandate for early testing and intervention for children who have significant hearing losses or other impediments to full educational access. Such programs provide communication instruction for both parents and children while usually providing tutoring for parents in the special needs of their children. Deaf children benefit from these programs socially as well as in communication and in educational experiences partly because they are able to interact with deaf peers and adults, often for the first time. Children who attend such programs tend to be advantaged both linguistically and socially when they enter school, and there are no disagreements about the importance of those programs.

The kind of school program a deaf child attends varies with parental hearing status, geographical location, program availability, and a variety of other factors. Deaf parents traditionally have preferred that their deaf children attend schools for the deaf. Through these schools, children gain the same kinds of early social interactions and life-long friendships that their parents experienced. In addition, they are exposed to many aspects of Deaf culture and a variety of deaf role models. Hearing parents typically are more confused and unsure about the alternatives, and they are torn between placing their children in schools for the deaf or in regular schools. The legal requirement is that there must be alternatives available across a wide range, so that parents and school systems can develop the best education plan for each child. In practice, most parents tend to lean toward regular public schools until such time as they might find their children unable to compete successfully or become integrated in the regular classroom.

Many deaf children succeed in mainstream settings with appropriate academic support services such as sign language interpreters, note takers, and appropriate advising. Success without such services is rare. Is the frequency of success enough to warrant choosing mainstream placement? Although there is no good answer to the question, there are several factors that should enter into the decision. Perhaps most obvious is a child's degree of hearing loss. If children have more residual hearing, good speech, and speechreading skills, they are more likely to succeed in a regular classroom. If the school has good support services and is knowledgeable about the needs of deaf children, they are likely to help promote achievement. In general, however, where a child is placed tends to have less impact on academic achievement than do student and family characteristics. It may be that, overall, performance of students in mainstream settings appears greater than that in separate settings, but the difference is extremely small once other factors are controlled.

Integrated classrooms of deaf and hearing students often fail to foster social development in the ways that we know are important for normal, healthy development (after all, we know how children often respond to others who are different). Deaf children often are excluded from social interactions with hearing students by virtue of communication barriers and the fact that, whether we like it or not, they are different from their hearing peers. As a result, they often feel lonely, emotionally insecure, and isolated in public school classrooms. Those students also tend to have lower academic achievement.

While emphasizing that the choice of the "right program" for a deaf child depends on many factors relevant to that particular child and her family, I would be less than honest if I did not admit that from all of my knowledge in the area, I have a good idea of how I would try to place my own deaf child if I had one. First and foremost, I would seek a quality preschool program that emphasizes sign language but also includes spoken language. I would closely monitor development in both languages and support both in order to optimize later reading and academic achievement (see chapters 3 and 7). For the school years, my decision would be based on the quality of the educational program and the availability of support services, recognizing that I might have to become an advocate for the latter. Ideally, we would include extracurricular activities, at least, at a school for the deaf if we lived near one, in order to provide opportunities for our child to interact with deaf children and adults, identify herself as a member of Deaf culture, and help her appreciate that she has a rich and supportive community in addition to her hearing family. Most importantly, I would plan to spend a lot of time in quality educationally related experiences with my child, and I would ensure that my sign language skills were as good as I could possibly make them.

7

I like reading what you write to me. Not because of what you write about. It just that I'm learning how, like when I read how you write, language, grammar. I learn and want to write like that. I hope you understand what I mean? I can't explain it. It's the writing of yours, not what you write about.
—Cheryl, age 20, writing to her English teacher

SEVEN

Learning to Read and Write

This chapter is about literacy, and specifically the kind of literacy of greatest interest to most parents and teachers of deaf and hearing children: the ability to read and write in English.[1] But there are different kinds and definitions of literacy. According to the *Oxford English Dictionary,* the original sense of the term *literacy* related to the assumption that anyone who understood the idea of combining letters of the alphabet—the basic building blocks of written language—could use it in a creative, appropriate way to get and use an education. Thus, we refer to people becoming "lettered" or acquiring "knowledge of letters," and "Doctor of Letters" is considered a prestigious, if largely ceremonial, title for the honorary college degrees conferred on politicians and celebrities.

We now use the term "literacy" in a variety of other ways as well. Educators, for example, refer to students as being computer literate or having mathematical literacy. These terms are related to the original definition of literacy in the sense of having building blocks that allow more complex and sophisticated use of the whole, but the content is no longer just language, at least in the literal sense. There is also cultural literacy, which allows an individual access to various aspects of their culture as communicated by others through art, literature, and history. Traditionally, no one was considered truly educated if they were not well versed in literature (a "collection of letters"), that is, in the documentation of knowledge within their language and culture. So, we could also talk about literacy within American Sign Language (ASL) either in the narrow sense, where the components of signs would replace letters, or in the broader sense of providing access to the cultural heritage of a Deaf community.

In this chapter, where I will be focusing specifically on the notion of print literacy, it will be important to keep in mind yet another distinction: Having some basic level of reading and writing competence may be different than having sufficient literacy skills flexible and creative enough to support educational and employment success. *Functional literacy* is the term most commonly linked to basic reading and writing abilities: The student who is functionally literate has the minimum reading and writing skills necessary to function in society. Traditionally, that minimum referred to a fourth to fifth grade level of competence—usually good enough to get a driver's license but sometimes not good enough to understand the warnings on medications or cookbook recipes, let alone the manuals that come with DVD players. Given the demands of the "information age," some educational researchers now argue that an eleventh to twelfth grade level of skill for functional literacy might be more appropriate (Waters & Doehring, 1990).

The reason that I also referred to literacy "flexible and creative enough to support educational and employment success" is that fourth- to fifth-grade functional literacy may not be sufficient for an individual to have true access to all of the educational opportunities to which they are entitled.

To most people—and certainly to parents—it seems that to be truly literate, one would have to be fluent in the language used by those who teach us, who write textbooks, and who tell us the news on television—that is, fluent in English. This issue brings us back to the education of deaf children. We can now ask whether deaf children need to be fluent in English, in ASL, or both to be considered literate. If the question seems a difficult one, consider Latino children in the United States who are fluent in Spanish but not English. Unless they learn English, they might not receive adequate educations in many parts of the United States, but they would surely be literate: They would have access to world knowledge and Latino culture through Spanish. In addition, we presume that Spanish would provide a bridge to learning English, and we would expect that Latino students who are encouraged and motivated to learn English should not have much trouble.

Consider now deaf children of deaf parents who learned ASL as their first language. Like Latino children who learned Spanish as their first language from Latino parents, those children are certainly literate: They understand the building blocks of the language (signs, sign components, and grammar), they can use them in novel and creative ways, and they have access to much knowledge of the world as well as to knowledge of both Deaf and hearing cultures. In order to gain access to the full body of knowledge available to hearing peers, however, they also will have to be able read and write (be literate) in English. This situation does not minimize the importance of ASL as a language, any more than it minimizes Spanish. It simply reflects reality: Fluency in sign language, or any minority language, is not enough for full access to the larger culture even if it is sufficient for many of the purposes of family, friends, schooling, and day-to-day life.

My reason for laying this groundwork about literacy is not to seek political correctness or claim that a deaf child can be literate even if he cannot read and write English, although that is technically true. Rather, it is to point out the fact that without special attention, deaf children frequently end up not being fully literate in either English or in sign language. Later in the chapter, we will explore the current debate concerning the best way to achieve print literacy for deaf children. Some investigators argue that initial fluency in ASL is sufficient, some claim that spoken language is necessary, and others (including me) believe that an early foundation in ASL coupled with some form of signing with English word order offers the best bridge to reading and writing.

The above description concerned deaf children of deaf parents. As we will see in the next section, those children often are described as being better readers than deaf children of hearing parents because of their early exposure to fluent language via ASL. In fact, examination of the relevant evidence indicates that this issue is not as straightforward as we once believed. But, even if deaf children of deaf parents have an advantage in print literacy, they represent barely 5 percent of deaf children in this country. What about the other 95 percent?

Compared to hearing children, most deaf children of hearing parents enter school already at a language disadvantage, regardless of whether they use spoken language or sign language and whether or not they have had the benefits of early intervention services or cochlear implants. For many children, that lag in language skills tends to increase during the school years, as deaf children of hearing parents show slower growth in language development relative to hearing children, even if both show the same general pattern of development (Geers, 2006; Newport, 1993). The important question is how we can best use the language skills they do have to build print literacy. As we will see, the available evidence indicates that being bilingual, in ASL and English for children in the United States, is the optimal situation.[2] (Note that being bilingual in ASL and English *does not* simply mean learning Signed English or any other English-sign hybrid.) Unfortunately, despite the belief of many educators that bilingual education is desirable, there has not yet been any published research validating its effectiveness.

Evidence from standardized testing in the United States indicates that 50 percent of 18-year-old deaf and hard-of-hearing students read below the fourth-grade level (equivalent to a hearing 9-year-old), compared to about 1 percent of their hearing peers (Traxler, 2000). And, notice that it is deaf *and hard-of-hearing* students who are referred to above. If one were only to consider deaf students reading levels would surely be even lower. This finding, based on the national norming of the ninth edition of the Stanford Achievement Test, immediately raises four issues of importance here. First, given that over 80 percent of deaf and hard-of-hearing children are in regular public school settings, how is it that those schools are graduating deaf students who cannot read? Second, if at least half of the deaf adults in the United States read below the fourth-grade level, how can it be that deaf children of deaf parents are supposed to be better readers? Third, if reading is such a great challenge for deaf children, why are there also many highly educated and literate deaf adults? And, fourth, why have we not made more progress in changing the situation that has plagued deaf education for more than 100 years?

What Is Reading?

Although most hearing people take reading for granted, that is only because they learned to read relatively naturally in their first language—well, it was a lot more natural than trying to learn another language as an adult. For the most part, that naturalness is created by the fact that almost everyone around a child uses the same language, and there is a one-to-one correspondence between words that people utter and what can be written or read in a book.[3] For this reason, parents' reading to their children is one of the most important facilitators of later reading skill (Andrews & Taylor, 1987; Maxwell, 1984). Not only does this activity motivate children by making reading enjoyable, but it teaches them the fundamentals of reading as well as providing them with vocabulary, world knowledge, and *metalinguistic* skills (i.e., knowledge about language). At a more general level, reading aloud seems like a literate society's equivalent to the tradition of storytelling, a natural behavior of humans that seems to run through all cultures and times.

Reading is a very complex process that is not fully understood. Consider some of the elements of reading that fluent readers typically do not have to think about. First, reading involves the ability to distinguish arbitrary marks on a background, whether stone, paper, or computer screen. Even before you know what those marks mean, if they mean anything, you have to be able to perceive those marks, for example, through the eye for print or the hand for Braille; then, you have to recognize writing as writing. Only after you discriminate one mark from another do you have to be able to discriminate one kind of mark from another (for example, in @&##&@@&) and groups of marks from other groups (for example @&# from #&@ or @@#). Up to this point, you could be looking at Chinese, English, or symbols on your typewriter, and you are doing fine, but you are not reading.

At the next level, there are two possibilities: One is that individual marks can be linked to sounds, which can be built up into larger patterns that you can say to yourself and recognize as words. In this way, you can "sound out" new words that you may have heard but have never seen or discover new words that you can pronounce but do not know. It is through this process that most readers know what *fowtuhgraf* means, even if it is written strangely. If you do, it probably means that you learned to read by what is called the "phonics method" (from *phon-* meaning "sound"): You sound out words according to what are called *spelling-to-sound rules.* If these *phonological* rules were not important, I could randomly re-arrange the letters in a word, and you would know what it is anyway.[4] Some readers, however, will have no idea what *fowtuhgraf* means. Most likely, those readers learned to read through the "whole-word method," either because that was the philosophy of the school system in which they were educated, or because they had one of many reading disabilities that made letter-by-letter reading impossible. For them, *fowtuhgraf* bears no resemblance at all to *photograph.* They also are unlikely to recognize printed words that they have heard but not seen before and thus have to make use of dictionaries more than people who learned via the phonics method.

In noting above that *phon-* refers to "sound," I demonstrated the *morphological* level of language. Although it is convenient to say that sounds combine to form words, there is actually an intermediate level in which sounds combine to form a meaningful units, sometimes syllables (e.g., *un-* or *sub-*), sometimes multisyllabic affixes (e.g., *maxi-* or *poly-*), and sometimes complete words (e.g., *dog* or *elephant*). These meaningful units are referred to as *morphemes,* and they follow particular rules in forming larger units such as *micro+organ+ism, sub+marine,* and *The+dog+chase+-ed+ the+spot+ted+cat.* Young children's earliest language, via both speech and sign, are usually described in terms of the number of morphemes in an utterance rather than the words, recognizing that multimorphemic words are more advanced than single morpheme words. Morphemes that can stand alone (as words) are referred to as *unbound morphemes* whereas those that serve as affixes are *bound morphemes.*

Assuming that a set of marks is recognized as a meaningful unit—either a bound or unbound morpheme—the next step is to link meaning to it by looking it up in some kind of *lexicon* or mental dictionary. Here, we will focus primarily on words. The hard part, especially for deaf students, is that words have many different meanings as well as different pronunciations, and which one is correct cannot be determined solely on the basis of definitions. Depending on how I count them, for example, the *Oxford English Dictionary* has either 10, 40, or 67 different meanings or senses for the word "bow."[5] These include the bow that shoots arrows, the bow in one's shoelaces, the bow one takes after a performance (just to demonstrate the variability in sound-to-spelling patterns), the bow at the front of a boat, and others. Surely I am not likely to use them all, and some, like "the stock of cattle on a farm," I have never even heard of. Nevertheless, I was able to read them in the dictionary and I would likely understand most of them in context. To do this, I have to make use of two kinds of rules.

One kind of rule that helps us select the right sense or meaning of words from our mental dictionaries and allows the construction of an infinite number of utterances in a language are *grammatical* rules or (*syntax*). People who are fluent in a particular language have internal sets of rules (grammar) that allow them to combine morphemes into words and then, in turn, into phrases, clauses, and sentences. Those rules allow us to produce completely new utterances, so we can do more than just repeat things that others have said and understand new strings of words produced by others. If grammatical rules were not important, I could randomly rearrange the words in this sentence, and it would not affect your interpretation— sentences like "Harry chased Annet" and "Annet chased Harry" would mean the same thing (see Note 4).

The grammar of English not only allows us to use the language, but it also tells us when someone else does not know how to use it, that is, when they are not using acceptable English (meaning that they do not have the correct internal rules). For example, after several years of studying Italian and French, I know enough of their grammars to understand why some people from those countries speak English the way they do: They often put English words into Italian or French grammatical structure, the same way that Signed English puts ASL signs into English grammar. Even more interesting is the fact that when I am speaking English with Italian or French colleagues, I sometimes find myself doing the same thing! Whether this is an unintentional attempt to make myself clearer or some mixing-up of the languages in my own head, I do not know, but it does seem to improve their comprehension!

So much for understanding sentences. Next is the level of *discourse structure.* It is at this level that we can identify what pronouns refer to, we combine ideas into meaningful series, and we actually understand what we read. If discourse rules were not important, I could randomly re-arrange the sentences on this page and it would not interfere at all with your comprehension. Discourse-level rules, like spelling, morphological, and grammatical rules, tell us that order does make a difference to some extent. Like grammatical rules, most children acquire discourse rules naturally by watching the correspondence between things and events and the way that people describe them.

With this brief sketch of reading out of the way, we can return to the issue of deaf children's reading skills. It is essential to keep in mind that the above language rules are learned relatively easily for most readers most of the time partly because they acquire them early. That is one of the beautiful, if still mysterious, aspects of both first- and second-language learning: As long as it happens early, before age 4 or so for first languages and through adolescence for second languages, it seems to occur with relative ease—even if it takes several years. Many adults who try to learn other languages, in contrast, find that the rules do not come so easily the second time around. Luckily, we are able to use what we know about our first language to help with the second language, and therefore languages more similar to our first language are usually easier to learn. Imagine, then, what it would be like if you did not really understand the rules of the first language when you tried to learn a second, if the letters and words on the page did not correspond to what people "said," and if you did not see the correspondence of words and events. That is the situation of the average deaf child trying to learn to read (Mayer & Wells, 1996).

What Makes Some Deaf Children (but Not Others) Good Readers?

Perhaps more than any other area, the reading and writing abilities of deaf children have been the focus of attention from educators and researchers for decades. Taken together, the results and conclusions of relevant studies provide an enlightening, if disappointing, picture of deaf children's skills in this regard.

Many of the errors that deaf children exhibit in reading and writing are the same as those made by people learning English as a second language. A variety of programs therefore has been developed to instruct teachers of deaf children in methods like those used in teaching English as a second language (Schirmer & Williams, 2003). Although their reading behaviors and their writing may look similar to second-language learners, we need to remember that most deaf children will come to school without true fluency in any language. As a result, second-language learning methods may be inappropriate or only address some of deaf students' needs. While the priority should be to ensure that deaf children acquire first language fluency during the preschool years, teachers still have to teach them to read and write in English, regardless of their prior language experience. So, we might as well face up to the issues. First, we have to take into account the variation among deaf children and the influences of early language environments, types of hearing loss, and factors like parent and child motivation. Considerable resources and effort devoted to improving deaf children's literacy have gone into trying to teach them the skills and strategies that work for hearing children, even though it is apparent that deaf and hearing children often have very different background knowledge and learning strategies (Marschark, Convertino, & LaRock, 2006). Perhaps as a result, despite decades of concerted effort, most deaf children in this country still progress far more slowly than hearing children in learning to read. This means that deaf students leaving school are at a relatively greater disadvantage, lagging farther behind hearing peers, than when they entered. At the same time, there are clearly many deaf adults and children who are excellent readers and excellent writers. What accounts for the differences?

Deaf Children of Deaf Parents

A variety of source claim that deaf children of deaf parents, on average, are better readers than deaf children of hearing parents (e.g., Chamberlain & Mayberry, 2000; Padden & Ramsey, 1998; Singleton, Supalla, Litchfield, & Schley, 1998). Why? Deaf children's relative lack of early language fluency when they have hearing parents clearly plays an important role in their reading difficulties, and several investigations have found a relationship between deaf children's ASL skills and their reading levels (e.g., Strong & Prinz, 2000; Padden & Ramsey, 2000). These studies have all been *correlational,* however, demonstrating that high or low levels of performance in one of these domains are often accompanied by similar levels in the other. Similarly, other investigations have shown a similar link between speech and literacy skills in deaf children with deaf or hearing parents who use spoken language (e.g., de Villiers, Bibeau, Ramos & Gatty, 1993; Geers & Moog, 1989). In some of those studies, the contributions of greater residual hearing and speech skill have not been distinguished, but the larger point is that early access to fluent language is central to deaf children's gaining literacy skills. For those children who are not able to benefit fully from spoken language, an early foundation in language through ASL or another natural sign language would appear to be a promising alternative. But the situation is more complex.

Earlier chapters have emphasized that there are other differences between deaf and hearing parents other than their primary mode of communication. The two groups may have very different expectations for their deaf children in terms of academic achievement. They also may differ in their ability to help their children in reading-related activities, and we know that children whose parents spend time working with them on academic and extracurricular activities are more motivated and have greater academic success (see chapter 8). Is there some reason to believe that it is parental hearing status rather than early language fluency that enable some deaf children to be better readers?

In an earlier book, *Psychological Development of Deaf Children* (Marschark, 1993b), I reviewed 30 years of studies concerning the reading abilities of deaf children of deaf parents as compared to deaf children of hearing parents. The results were surprising because I fully expected that deaf children with deaf parents would always come out on top as a result of their early exposure to language. Well, deaf children of deaf parents have been shown to be better readers than deaf children of hearing parents in some studies, but others have shown no difference. Importantly, none of the studies to date have considered the reading skills of parents, and those investigations that have included deaf parents largely have been conducted in places known for having relatively high numbers of educated deaf adults. It therefore seems likely that any generalization about a link between children's reading abilities and parental hearing status per se will be extremely limited. After all, if 50 percent of deaf and hard-of-hearing adults read below the fourth grade level, how can they be good reading models for their deaf (or hearing) children?

Indeed, it now appears that regardless of whether their parents are deaf or hearing, deaf children who are better readers turn out to be the ones who had their hearing losses diagnosed earlier, had early access to fluent language (usually via sign language), *and* were exposed to English. At the same time, having a mother who is a good signer appears to be more important than whether she is deaf or hearing or the precise age at which a child learns to sign, as long as it is early (Akamatsu et al., 2000; Strong & Prinz, 1997). Regrettably, there is no single predictor of reading success that applies to all deaf children, and the combinations of factors that positively and negatively influence reading development are not yet fully understood. It may be, for example, that different environments lead to different strengths and weaknesses (for example, big vocabularies but little grammatical knowledge) depending on when, where, and from whom children learn their first and second languages. Thus, deaf children of hearing parents tend to have better speech and speechreading abilities than deaf children of deaf parents, but those abilities do not seem linked to better reading or other academic achievement even though they would seem to support the phonological part of reading (Karchmer & Mitchell, 2003). Furthermore, while it is tempting to assume that a deaf child's early exposure to language through their deaf parents would provide a considerable advantage in learning to read, this advantage may be offset by the fact that ASL vocabulary and syntax do not parallel those of printed English (Mayer & Akamatsu, 2003).[6]

My support for the inclusion of ASL in this "language mixture" comes from the clear merits of sign language use by deaf children for social, cognitive, and linguistic purposes, as described throughout this book. ASL gives young deaf children access to what is happening in the world and provides an effective means of parent-child and teacher-child communication. In the first edition of this book, I advocated for cued speech as an English supplement in this mixture, drawing on research showing that deaf children in Belgium who are exposed to it from an early age show impressive performance in a variety of skills involved in reading (Leybaert & Alegria, 2003). As I explained in chapter 3, however, cued speech has not been shown successful for supporting literacy skills in deaf children learning English, and therefore I am no longer as enthusiastic about its potential as I was 10 years ago.

Supporters of ASL as a foundation for English literacy often argue that parents and teachers of deaf children who use simultaneous communication leave 20 to 50 per cent of what they sign out of their speech, without recognizing how much information is lost. As noted earlier, however, the little evidence there is in that regard has involved surprisingly few individuals who also were not skilled signers. It thus may be that the problem is more the fault of the language users rather than a fatal flaw with English-based sign systems. Indeed, several studies in the United States have shown that in the hands of a skillful practitioner, simultaneous communication allows deaf high school and college students to comprehend just as much as they do from ASL (Caccamise, Blaisdell, & Meath-Lang, 1977; Cokely, 1990). A similar study in Australia showed that competently signing teachers can provide fluent simultaneous communication in both signed and spoken language to children in younger grades (Leigh, 1995). Yet, the impact of *fluent* simultaneous communication on reading and other areas of deaf children's academic achievement of children has not yet been the subject of rigorous research. In addition, we need to examine the relationship of motivation, exposure to reading, and quality of teaching to literacy. Given findings that children who read more become better readers, and that better readers read more, it seems particularly important to study the effects of early exposure to reading via parents and early school environments. At present, therefore, my highest recommendation is for more research and for persistence and flexibility on the part of parents and teachers. Use whatever works!

Taking a narrower rather than a broader approach to reading, it also is important to consider the various subskills involved in reading. Deaf and hearing children, or deaf children of deaf versus hearing parents, may differ in these component skills even when their overall reading levels are the same. Alternatively, they may be similar on particular dimensions that create overall differences in reading level. Accordingly, let us spend a little more time with the three primary components of reading: phonology and spelling, vocabulary, and grammar as they relate to deaf children.

Phonological Knowledge and Spelling

One of the most central and interesting issues in this area concerns how deaf children, and especially those who have greater hearing losses, can make use of phonological information in the absence of hearing, because "phonological" normally refers to the way words sound. Hearing children who are learning to read very quickly acquire the *sound-grapheme* (sound-letter) correspondences of the language, something made much easier by orthographic regularity (homonyms like "so," "sow," and "sew" do not occur in more regular languages). It therefore is not surprising that dyslexia is more common among children learning irregular languages such as English or German than those learning regular languages such as Italian or Spanish (Paulesu et al., 2001). Such findings would suggest that deaf children learning to read English should have greater difficulty than deaf children learning to read Italian, and efforts to promote phonological skills in young deaf readers thus may be more important in English- and German-speaking countries. Comparisons of this sort have not yet been made, but it is important to take some care in making generalizations about "deaf children" (e.g., with regard to cued speech) when the spoken language a deaf child is learning may affect their potential reading abilities.

Spelling-to-sound skills, also known as *phonological* or *phonemic processing*, are enhanced in children with better speech, but we know that they are separate from speech skills and cannot be explained on the basis of articulation alone. Rather, the bases for phonological abilities in deaf children seem to involve some combination of information drawn from articulation, speechreading, fingerspelling, residual hearing, and exposure to writing, no one of which is sufficient in itself (Leybaert, 1993).[7] Several studies have indicated that the ability of deaf children to decode spelling patterns emerges by around the second grade. Skill in the use of such information does not appear directly tied to the amount of hearing loss, at least among children with severe to profound losses. Those deaf children are able to make use of phonological information, especially when words follow regular spelling patterns, although they often depend on more global characteristics such as how the word looks on the lips or on the printed page. When words are regular in their spelling, phonological strategies are most likely to be successful. The linkage of such reading strategies to writing is seen in the fact that deaf students sometimes produce phonologically accurate misspellings such as *sizzers*. Similarly, whole-word codes based on how words look may result in a greater likelihood of leaving out letters (writing *orng* for "orange") and making letter reversals (writing *sorpt* for "sport").

Phonological skill also may contribute to better grammatical skill and better comprehension, because "internal speech" has been shown to be more efficient than either visual imagery or "internal sign language" for the memory component of reading (Lichtenstein, 1998). At that level, information about words is held and accumulated until relations among words (grammatical information) and relations among events (discourse information) reveal the meaning of a phrase or sentence. Proficient reading, then, in deaf children as well as hearing children, depends on some underlying knowledge of the characteristics of individual letters. Deaf children in programs that utilize simultaneous communication programs or spoken language only tend to show more frequent use of phonological information relative to children in more sign-oriented programs, perhaps explaining some of their early advantage in reading performance. By college age, however, differences as a function of language orientation become smaller or disappear (Hanson, Shankweiler, & Fischer, 1983). While showing deaf children how words sound may be useful for speech and reading, what is especially important is showing them the link between printed words and their meanings. There is no better way to achieve this than sitting down with a child and reading to them. Books for very young children are also easy enough that they will give hearing parents a lot of good practice if they are learning to sign. Although the most popular early reading programs for deaf children have not yet been evaluated with regard to their long-term impact on reading, academic achievement, and social functioning, such daily reading shared by parents and children clearly can contribute significantly to early language and literacy development for both hearing and deaf children. One last note: It is important to remember that reading activities for children are supposed to be fun. As one of my colleagues recently pointed out: "Parents of deaf children do not have to act like teachers or trainers; they just have to act like parents!"

Vocabulary Knowledge and Knowledge of the World

Although it has been well documented that vocabulary knowledge is a primary component of reading, consideration of deaf children presents the issue in a somewhat different light. We already have seen that most deaf children have relatively limited access to fluent language. Those children accordingly have been shown to have fewer signed or spoken labels for things around them than do hearing children of hearing parents or deaf children of deaf parents. They also are less likely to gain such knowledge from reading. The two-way street of how much children read and how good they are at it suggests that we need to make special efforts to expand the vocabularies to which deaf children are exposed through print, sign, and speech. That is, the more vocabulary they encounter, the bigger their vocabularies will be; and the bigger their vocabularies, the better they will be able to deal with new vocabulary.

Compared to hearing children, deaf children are more likely to understand and use concrete nouns and familiar action verbs over more abstract or general words with which they may have less experience (Griswold & Commings, 1974). Therefore, I frequently urge teachers of deaf schoolchildren to move away from the practice of focusing primarily on practical and familiar concepts. While acknowledging that many deaf students have difficulty with basic vocabulary and related skills, parents and teachers often underestimate the language skills of children—both hearing and deaf. It is especially important to avoid this pitfall with deaf children, because the bias is even stronger than it is with hearing children. In fact, many of the vocabulary instruction practices used with both deaf and hearing students are not supported by current research, as they yield only partial knowledge of words—primarily relating to pronunciation (in spoken or sign language) and their most common meanings—with little attention to additional meanings of a word, relations to other words, or possible metaphorical or figurative usages (Paul, 1998). Perhaps as a result, deaf college students have been shown to have weaker connections among concepts in their lexicons, a likely contributor to continuing reading difficulties (McEvoy, Marschark, & Nelson, 1999).

Deaf children's vocabulary skills typically are better when words have only a single meaning or when they are presented in context rather than in isolation (the latter happens on many achievement tests). Still, in most cases, their vocabulary abilities tend to lag about a year behind their other reading subskills. This mismatch may disrupt reading by interfering with the access to word meaning that is so important for comprehension. In fact, when we observe deaf children's apparent difficulties with grammar during reading, we cannot really be sure that grammar is the problem. It could be that some children have trouble attending to grammatical information because their cognitive resources are overloaded with word-finding (Marschark, Convertino, McEvoy, & Masteller, 2004). In either case, the result would be reduced comprehension and reading speed, as well as a tendency to remember disconnected portions of texts rather than the whole picture, especially when the material is unfamiliar (Banks, Gray & Fyfe, 1990). Indeed, deaf schoolchildren have been found to focus on individual words in text, whereas hearing peers of the same age or reading level seek relations among words (Marschark, DeBeni, Polazzo, & Cornoldi, 1993).

Understanding Grammar

During the 1970s, a lot of attention was given to the grammatical skills of young deaf readers. A variety of programs tried to apply current theories of grammar to deaf children, with little success (see Paul, 1998). Deaf students generally were far more variable than hearing peers in their performance and tended to have particular difficulty with constructions that depended on keeping track of meaning across multiple events and grammatical structures in texts (Quigley, Power, & Steinkamp, 1977). Pronouns (*he, her, their, that, it*, etc.), for example, can cause difficulty because the reader has to remember the activities or characteristics of nouns in order to later understand who or what is being referred to. Such findings suggest that more global factors such as concept knowledge, cognitive style (see chapter 9), metacognition (Strassman, 1997), and memory also play important roles in deaf children's reading in ways that cannot always be distinguished from grammatical issues.

A classic research study in the field directly examined the influence of early language experience on deaf children's grammatical skill (Brasel & Quigley, 1977). In that investigation, two groups of deaf children who had hearing parents and were exposed only to spoken language were compared to groups of deaf children of deaf parents who communicated with them either via English-based signing or ASL. Overall, the children exposed to sign language consistently outperformed children who were exposed only to spoken English—a finding that is contrary to the expectations of those who support educating deaf children in spoken language only. On the other hand, children exposed to some form of signing with English word order by their deaf parents showed better grammatical skills in English than the children who learned ASL, a finding contrary to expectations of anyone who would advocate either approach alone in educating deaf children.

Another frequently cited study in the field was one that compared reading abilities in groups of deaf children who received ASL, English-based signing (SEE2), or Pidgin Signed English (PSE, see chapter 3; Luetke-Stahlman,

1990). That study is frequently cited as providing evidence that SEE2 can promote deaf children's reading, but the findings are a bit more complex. The study found that deaf children exposed to SEE2 did read better than those exposed to PSE, but so did the children exposed to ASL, and there was no difference between the SEE2 and ASL groups. Although this result might be seen as supporting English-based sign systems, it should be recalled that the whole reason for developing such systems was the belief that they would lead to enhanced literacy skills for deaf children. If, in fact, natural sign languages like ASL work just as well, there seems little reason to advocate for artificial sign systems unless they can be shown to have other benefits.

Thinking About Reading

Before leaving the components of reading, it is worthwhile considering one more higher-level skill shared by fluent readers. I noted earlier that shared reading not only provides deaf children with information about printed text, but also fosters *metalinguistic* and *metacognitive* skills. Knowledge of language and knowledge about thinking are essential components for children across academic areas, allowing them to consider alternative approaches to learning and problem solving, assess their own understanding of face-to-face communication and print, and adapt to new materials and new contexts. In general, deaf children—and hearing children who are beginning to read or who experience reading difficulties—have relatively inefficient metalinguistic and metacognitive skills. Deaf students, in particular, appear to be relatively poor at assessing their reading comprehension and often consider themselves to be good readers even when they are largely unaware of what it means to be a good reader (Ewoldt, 1986).

Perhaps because of the ways we teach them, deaf students also may demonstrate *instrumental dependence* (see chapter 9) in their reading strategies, looking to teachers and peers for explanations of text rather than attempting to determine figure out the meaning themselves. In at least one study, however, deaf adolescents were found to use a variety of independent (metacognitive) reading strategies, such as re-reading the text or looking up words in a dictionary, while their teachers appeared to encourage more dependent strategies (Ewoldt, Israelite, & Dodds, 1992). Parents, also, may inadvertently foster dependent strategies in young deaf readers, underestimating their reading abilities and demonstrating the over-directiveness often seen in hearing parents of deaf children.

Teachers and parents also appear prone to devoting so much time attempting to teach the fundamental skills underlying reading that they may overlook teaching the goals of reading. Several investigators have noted that reading and writing are labor-intensive, frustrating activities for many deaf individuals, who are thus often reluctant to engage in them for pleasure (Marschark, Lang, & Albertini, 2002; Wilbur, 1977). We know, however, that reading more helps children to become better readers (Stanovich, 1986), potentially creating a "Catch-22" situation for young deaf readers. By not reading and not having the desire to read more, deaf children may not spontaneously develop the literacy-related metacognitive skills easily acquired by many of their reading, hearing peers. Those skills can be explicitly taught (Akamatsu, 1988; Fox, 1994), but their durability is likely to be far less than if they were naturally acquired by children through their own reading.

I would be remiss if I did not include here mention of the impact of cochlear implants on deaf children's literacy skills. Having reviewed that literature recently, however, I am not confident than I can make any broad generalizations that will be helpful. There is abundant evidence that children with implants have better phonological processing skills, but we have seen that there is more to reading that that. I have been surprised, in fact, that evidence in favor of better reading by children with implants is not as strong as I had expected. Several large-scale studies have indicated little if any advantage to reading as a function of various implant characteristics (e.g., time with an implant, age at implantation; Geers, 2003, 2004). Others have suggested that a combination of cochlear implants and sign language use throughout the school years can reduce or eliminate differences between deaf and hearing children's reading comprehension scores (Spencer, Barker, & Tomblin, 2003; Spencer, Gantz, & Knutson, 2004).

If a cochlear implant does not ensure age-appropriate literacy skills (Geers, 2004), earlier implantation offers greater advantages than later implantation. Evidence from a large study in the United Kingdom recently has shown a clear relation between age of implantation and reading achievement (Archbold, Nikolopoulos, O'Donoghue, & White, 2006). Seven years after receiving their implants, 100 percent of children who had been implanted at age 6–7 years were at least a year delayed in reading achievement, compared to 81 percent of those implanted between the ages of 4 and 5 years and 44 percent of those implanted before age 3. Of those implanted at age 4–5 years, 19 percent were within one year of grade-appropriate reading levels or reading more than one year beyond grade-level, as were 56 percent of those implanted before age 3. As in other academic domains (Spencer et al. 2004; Thoutenhoofd, 2006), cochlear implants did not eliminate lags in literacy skills, but clearly had a beneficial effect. This research is just beginning, however, and many of the available studies have either lacked important controls or have not reported information necessary to be confident that their results will hold up over time.

Deaf Children's Writing

The intimate relationship of reading and writing is such that it will not come as a surprise to discover that deaf children's performance in the "input" domain of reading is mirrored in the "output" domain of writing. As in reading, deaf students vary considerably in their writing skill, and different criteria for writing may well be deemed important by different teachers at the college level as they are at the elementary and secondary levels. In a study several years ago at Gallaudet University, for example, individual faculty varied from 5 percent to 75 percent in their estimates of the number of students with "satisfactory" writing skills. Clearly, writing is a very complex skill and one that is difficult to evaluate!

Examinations of writing samples from deaf children show them to produce shorter sentences than hearing peers and to repeatedly use simple subject-verb-object sentences which give the appearance of "concrete" and literal writing. Sometimes, their sentences are not sentences at all, at least in the sense of being grammatically correct in English. Taken together, such findings have led to the general conclusion, similar to that for reading, that the average deaf 18-year-old writes on a level comparable to that of a hearing 8-year-old.

Earlier, I suggested that some characteristics of deaf children's reading and writing might be attributable to the relatively low expectations of parents and teachers. Recent research in classrooms and laboratories, however, suggests that something is missing in all of this. For example, analyses of deaf students' writing has amply demonstrated that deaf students' writing can be rich and creative, even if, as reflected in the excerpt at the beginning of this chapter, it suffers in ways that many English teachers might find unacceptable. Some of my own work similarly has demonstrated that superficial problems notwithstanding, deaf students' writing as early as elementary school is both creative and conceptually well structured. At the level where events and actions in a story are laid out and interwoven, their writing is fully comparable to that of hearing peers (Marschark, Mouradian, & Halas, 1996).

Take for example the following story written by a deaf 12-year-old. As part of a study conducted with Dr. Victoria Everhart (Everhart & Marschark, 1988), students were asked to write a story about being picked up by a UFO, what would happen, and what the aliens would be like. The following is representative of what we got and fits well with the above description of deaf children's writing.

When I get in ufo They look funny. They have long pointed ears and have round face They speak different from our. They brought strange foods and Purple beverage. When I taste it I spill [spit] and begin to cought [cough]. I [It] taste like dog food. But It was very pretty inside with many feather and clothes were very pretty. But one thing people in ufo stare at me because they never see large musclar [muscular] and can pick up Heavy thing like weight, people or table. They feel it and

said wow and start to teach me how to talk but they speak
Russian language. I hate to learn Russian language. So I stay in
ufo for 5 hours so they stop to place where they take me and
drop their and they sent me a dog with long sharp teeth and
was very tame I egan [began] to cry and miss them.

Among the other typical characteristics of deaf children's writing, one
of the most noticeable ones in this passage is the frequent omission of
words. A variety of studies and surveys have documented the fact that deaf
children use fewer adverbs, conjunctions, and auxiliary verbs than hearing age-mates, whereas the frequencies of using nouns and verbs is about
the same (note, again, the similarity to reading performance). This characteristic could be taken to indicate that they are patterning written language
on ASL, although similar errors are made by many learners of English as a
second language.

But now look again. If you ignore the spelling and grammatical errors
in this story (something English teachers and many mothers have a hard time
doing), you will see that there is a very clear and coherent story underneath
it all. The author told us what the UFO and its inhabitants would be like
and described their appearance, food, and clothing. She recounted the reaction of others to her, as well as her reactions to them. After an attempt to
communicate (through spoken language!), the aliens gave up, dropped her
off, and sent her a gift for her troubles. After all of these wonders, is it surprising that she missed them when they left? The point here is that when
we evaluated these stories on their English characteristics, the deaf students
(aged 7 to 15) were found to be writing well behind the hearing students.
When we examined the conceptual (discourse) structure of the stories, however, the two groups were functioning at comparable levels. In other words,
even if deaf children are not fluent in English spelling and grammar, they
still can demonstrate creativity and competence in writing.

Available findings thus indicate the clear parallels between deaf children's reading and writing. Although there are few studies from which to
draw conclusions about differences between deaf children of deaf versus
hearing parents, it appears likely that the writing abilities of those groups
would follow the same patterns as their reading abilities. Similarly, ex-
trapolating from reading research we would expect that the writing abilities of deaf children whose parents provide early exposure to both ASL
and English-based signing should surpass those children who are educated
in environments where they are exposed only to ASL or spoken English
(Mayer & Akamatsu, 2003). Although we do not yet have many answers in
this regard, interviews with deaf college students clearly indicate that those
who have better literacy skills had parents (hearing or deaf) who were more
involved in their children's early reading and writing activities (Toscano,
McKee, & LePoutre, 2002).

The Impact of Social and Emotional Factors on Literacy

Before leaving the topic of reading and writing by deaf children, it is worth re-emphasizing the importance of social-emotional factors, such as motivation and desire for achievement, to the development of literacy and to academic success in general. Look again at the excerpt from a student's journal at the beginning of this chapter. Despite its superficial errors, it is clear that Cheryl enjoys writing and finds it interesting to reflect on her attraction to it. In her writing about writing, she shows a motivation to succeed and reveals the importance of having good models. Having a written dialogue with a supportive teacher allows her to improve and learn about writing not by having it corrected, though that happens too, but by analyzing her own writing and the writing of others. To me, this is a true sign of academic achievement: pursuit of knowledge for the sheer joy of learning.

Studies involving hearing children have shown that academic excellence and psychosocial maturity are fostered by parents spending time with their children, facilitating their academic and extracurricular interests, and answering their questions in supportive environments. Regrettably, language barriers sometimes prevents such interactions. The challenges of deaf children's learning to read and write thus may be made even more difficult by communication issues. In addition, deaf students often appear to have relatively narrow orientations toward English as well as other academic subjects. This attitude is reflected in the fact that skills learned in one course are not used in other courses, so that, for example, the transfer of math to chemistry or biology to psychology may not occur spontaneously. The reasons for such narrow views are as yet unclear, although I believe they are partly related to the ways in which parents and teachers of deaf children often focus on the concrete and familiar rather than on exploration and discovery. Knowledge about language is very abstract, and not everyone finds language as fascinating as language researchers like me (a fact that my students have made painfully clear!). Reading and writing also may be viewed differently from the perspectives of deaf and hearing children. Deaf children may be less invested in achieving English literacy as a result of either their own values or those of their parents—or their parents may not be as good at communicating those values.

Final Comments

At several points throughout this book, I describe evidence that deaf children's language skills expressed through sign are superior to their reading and writing in English. Such findings suggest that writing skills are independent of deaf children's general intellectual abilities and should not be taken as indicators of any general language fluency or language flexibility (but see chapter 8). Those findings also suggest that literacy should be within their grasp.

The most frequently cited academic difficulty among deaf children, however, is reading. At first blush, one might expect that the hardest part of reading for deaf children would be the ability to "decode" the spelling patterns of words, a process that normally depends on knowing how letters sound. Many deaf children are surprisingly good in this regard, however, apparently making use of information combined from fingerspelling, residual hearing, speechreading, articulation, and exposure to writing. At the same time, deaf children are more likely than hearing children to use visual and whole-word strategies during reading, and the same pattern appears in comparisons of deaf children who are more oriented toward use of sign language than spoken communication.

The most well-documented areas of difficulty for young deaf readers are vocabulary knowledge and grammatical abilities. Limitations in their vocabularies reflect the influence of early nonlinguistic as well as linguistic experience, as they tend to have access to fewer language models (who name things) than do hearing peers. Slower recognition of words also may affect the ability to make use of grammar in comprehension because the "system" may be so busy trying to find word meanings that it will have less "space" to devote to understanding the larger message. Factors like vocabulary and grammatical knowledge run on a two-way street in literacy development: As they improve, children read more and more complex material, which in turns contributes to more skill development. Similarly, deaf children's beliefs about their own abilities and their desires to succeed operate in a two-way manner just as they do for hearing children, so that success breeds success! One essential aspect of academic achievement is that children have to notice that their success in school work is the result of their own efforts. This relation is consistent with the finding that children higher in intellectual achievement tend to feel that they are more in control of their own lives.

Overall, deaf children's reading difficulties do not appear to be the result of any particular orientation in their early language experience. Exactly which variables are the most important ones for predicting their reading success is unclear. At this time, it does not appear that early exposure to sign language is sufficient to provide deaf children with print literacy skills. The best deaf readers appear to be those who receive early exposure to fluent language and exposure to the language in which they will eventually learn to read. Finally, the available literature suggests that the sources of difficulty apparent in deaf children's reading performance are also found in their writing. Lags in the development of vocabulary and grammatical skill cause deaf children's writing to appear concrete and repetitive relative both to their own signed productions and to hearing children's writing (see chapter 8). At the same time, deaf children's writing is clearly well ordered and creative, showing that fluency in English and intellectual ability are at least partially separate. Nevertheless, reading and writing form an essential link to the worlds of social and intellectual interaction, and the consequences of literacy or illiteracy will have increasing impact on all realms of functioning as deaf children grow up.

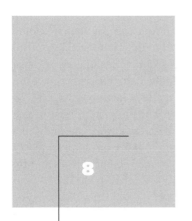

8

The education of children born deaf is essentially a war against cognitive poverty.
—R. Conrad, *The Deaf School Child* (1979)

EIGHT

Intelligence, Academic Achievement, and Creativity

For some readers, this chapter will be the "bottom line" of the book, and I suspect that a few may have skipped forward to this point seeking an answer to the question "Will deafness affect my child's intelligence or academic success?" Those who have read everything up to this point, however, will suspect (correctly) that the question is really a very complex one. As I have argued in other places, the key here will be understanding the cognitive underpinnings of learning in terms of both the knowledge and skills that deaf children bring to the learning context and what is presumably necessary in order to take advantage of educational opportunities and interventions (Detterman & Thompson, 1997).

In order to understand the foundations of deaf children's academic performance it is useful to consider the larger context of learning and intellectual functioning in the real world. In this sense, parents and teachers often ask questions about how deaf learners compare to hearing learners, an issue raised in chapter 6. Some people in our field believe that this is an inappropriate question, and we should instead focus on deaf children's strengths and perhaps variability among deaf children as a function of school placement, language skills, and so on. Such an approach might make sense if we were dealing with deaf children in isolation, but the reality of mainstream education today is such that we have to understand the ways in which deaf children learn and how their knowledge and skills differ from hearing children who share the same classrooms.

In my view, ignoring differences between deaf and hearing children is less respectful and far less academically helpful than identifying them. It is important to recognize the historical sensitivity of this issue. Investigations concerning cognitive abilities of deaf adults and children have been described as comprising three historical "stages" (Moores, 2001). The first stage, termed *the deaf as inferior,* is seen to be largely a consequence of the work in the early twentieth century by investigators of intelligence who demonstrated a variety of apparent deficits in deaf children's cognitive performance relative to hearing age-mates. Some of those results today can be seen to reflect the investigators' biases concerning the role of spoken language in human intelligence (Marschark & Spencer, 2006), but others are particularly timely and important in the current context of research concerning deaf children's learning and the goal of improving educational access and success. Indeed, many of the early findings are also obtained today, although we have a much better understanding of what they mean.

The second stage of cognitive research involving deaf individuals Moores labeled *the deaf as concrete.* During the 1960s, research on problem solving and literacy skills was interpreted to indicate that deaf children are doomed to be concrete and literal, living in the here and now, with little capability for "higher" levels of functioning. This notion was based on the assumption that a lack of hearing could change the entire psychological makeup of an individual, a position now supported by research in a variety of domains. At the time, however, most psychologists saw deaf people as having little if any language at all (see chapter 3) and failed to recognize that early language and experiential impoverishment—not hearing loss per se—was responsible for many of the findings suggesting "cognitive poverty." While deaf people are longer seen as being less capable of abstract thought than hearing people, to be fair it must be noted that educators continue to struggle with deaf children's tendencies to behave in apparently concrete ways in various problem solving, academic, and social situations.

Research conducted during the 1970s can be seen as the start of a period referred to as *the deaf as intellectually normal,* primarily because of advances and studies concerning intelligence (Moores, 2001). In a series of studies beginning in 1968, McCay Vernon, a pioneering researcher and clinical psychologist working with deaf individuals, demonstrated that given the impoverished language environments and relatively high incidence of multiple disabilities among deaf children, they did remarkably well relative to hearing peers. Vernon (1968/2005) showed that IQ scores among deaf individuals fell in essentially the same range as those of hearing individuals, and that assumptions concerning IQ differences were largely misplaced. Rather than seeing deaf children as "lacking" something, research of this sort led to a better understanding of the influences of deaf children's early language and social experiences on their development and showed that, in terms of IQ scores, they were quite normal.

We now recognize that deaf children are just as capable as their hearing peers, and that being deaf (or not being able to use spoken language) does not entail any kind of intellectual inferiority. In essence, we now realize that deaf children can be different from hearing children without being "deficient." This marks what I have elsewhere referred to as the newest stage in research concerning the intellectual abilities of deaf individuals (Marschark, 2003). In this view, deaf and hearing individuals may vary in their approaches to cognitive tasks, differ in their means of communication, and have different knowledge organized in different ways, and we do not need to assume that such differences are either good or bad. This perspective has led us to examine variability among deaf individuals and between deaf and hearing populations as a means of better understanding the intellectual development of deaf children and ways to optimize their early experiences of deaf children while avoiding political agendas.

Understanding Intelligence

From both pedagogical and psychological perspectives, as well as from the perspective of a parent of a deaf child, one simply might want to ask—bluntly—whether deaf children are as smart as their hearing peers or their hearing siblings. In order to tackle this question, we have to ask, "How much weight should we put on intelligence tests and achievement tests for deaf children?" and "To what extent do such tests really help us to understand or improve educational opportunities?" Regardless of how one approaches cognitive development, learning, and intelligence in deaf and hearing children, we first have to be clear about the kinds of characteristics we are talking about and how they are measured. Then, we can try to deal with the question and make an attempt at some answers.

To understand children's intellectual growth and their eventual successes and failures in school, we have to consider both *cognitive development* and *intelligence.* Cognitive development refers to the increasing knowledge and mental abilities that are seen in children as they get older. Over time, the mind grows in both its contents (that is, knowledge) and in the ability to understand, remember, and use those contents. Such growth results from maturation, learning, experience, and the adoption of an increasingly analytic or problem-solving approach to the world. As more complex thinking develops, mental abilities become increasingly interlinked and children are able to use them with increasing flexibility.

Thinking is only one of many cognitive skills, even if the term is often used generically. Before reading the next sentence, take a minute and try to put into words what thinking is, and you will see what I mean—but don't just think about thinking, really try to define it. As I look beyond the porch while writing this paragraph, I can "think" about the scene before me: I see the lake with trees and hills on the other side, a farm in the distance, and so on. At the same time, because I am continuing to type while I look outside, I am also thinking about what I am writing. Both of these are *conscious* levels of thinking, meaning that I am aware of them. I am not aware of the perceptual and memory skills that allow me to see in three dimensions, to recognize the trees as trees and the ducks as ducks, or to hit the right keys on the keyboard without looking at them. When we go about our everyday activities in the world, the majority of our "thinking" is at this unconscious or *automatic* level. Thinking usually is brought into awareness only when we have to solve a new problem or when we do what apparently only humans, of all animals, can do: reflect on our own thought processes.

By the time children are 5 years old, they begin to think about their thinking and recognize that others think as well. This level of sophistication likely is related to literacy in slightly older children, as reading and writing may allow them to recognize the existence of realities separate from the ones they themselves experience. Writing thus can provide both a "room" in which to explore as well as a "window" onto the thinking of others, just as we saw with regard to children's play (Spencer & Hafer, 1998), although people who cannot read or write nonetheless have very complex thought processes.

Most adults normally do not think about the development of children's thinking, but about the development of more specific aspects of cognition like memory, problem solving, mathematical skills, creativity, and language comprehension. Alternatively, some people think more globally about children's intelligence or IQ. As we take up this topic, it is important to make clear that intelligence and IQ are not the same thing, even if the terms are used that way by most people. For psychologists, the people who invented and are the sacred guardians of intelligence testing, *IQ* is defined in what seems to be a circular fashion—as whatever it is that is measured by intelligence tests. *Intelligence* meanwhile is defined a little more helpfully, as the repertoire of abilities that allow an individual to deal flexibly with novel information and situations at a particular age.

These definitions become somewhat clearer if we note that "IQ" stands for *Intelligence Quotient,* a number obtained by dividing a child's mental age, as measured on an intelligence test, by their actual or chronological age. We would not judge the intelligence of a 5-year-old by the same standards as a 25-year-old, and the intelligence quotient allows us to estimate the age level at which someone is functioning in terms of the age level at which they should be functioning using standards obtained from testing large numbers of people at each age. For example, if a child obtains a score exactly at the average for his or her age, and we divide it by their age in years (and multiply by 100 so we do not have deal with decimal points), they will have an IQ of 100: the average IQ. Scoring at a level of older children, meaning that the child's mental age is higher than her chronological age, will yield an IQ greater than 100. Scoring at the level of younger children will yield an IQ less than 100.

Finally, it is important to note that IQ is only an estimate of intelligence, one that depends of the validity of the test, the skill of the tester (especially important in the case of deaf children), and the child's understanding and following of the directions. With all of this in mind, we are now ready to reconsider the issue of intelligence and deaf children. Remember, however, that the ultimate question in all of this should not be what scores deaf children make on intelligence tests, but what they can achieve. I suggest this because it is not at all clear that intelligence tests are tapping the same things in deaf and hearing children—a topic to be discussed below.

Language, Thought, and Intelligence

In discussing intelligence in deaf children (or hearing adults or chimpanzees, for that matter), most important will be their ability to take what they already know and apply it in new ways in new situations. In this sense, intelligence depends on—or is—all of those aspects of cognitive development mentioned above: thinking, memory, problem solving, quantitative skills, and communication/language. It is the last item on this list, language, that creates the most complexity for understanding deaf children's intellectual functioning, and we need to deal with it directly. After all, most people assume that intelligence is directly related to language. How can you be intelligent without having language?

For most of the twentieth century, deaf children and sometimes deaf adults were a favorite testing group for educators and psychologists interested in intelligence, precisely because they were presumed to be "without language" (recall that signed languages were not recognized as true languages until the mid-1960s; see chapter 3). That perspective was a throwback to early psychological work in the nineteenth century, when there was a general expectation that deaf children, or anyone else without language, would be clearly deficient in intelligence or in various aspects of intelligence (e.g., Bartlett, 1850; see Marschark & Spencer, 2006, for review). One major problem with this assumption is that those investigators typically equated *language* with *spoken language.* Even now, I meet teachers and researchers in my travels who, although they deny that language and speech are the same, nevertheless do not believe that sign language is sufficient to allow "normal" intellectual functioning and therefore assume that deaf children who cannot speak must be intellectually inferior. Simply stated, they are wrong! Readers who have finished the preceding chapters are aware that the equating of language and speech is an error and that there is no reason to believe that spoken language is qualitatively better than sign language for the purposes of intellectual pursuits. These two ways of expressing language do have somewhat different characteristics and different strengths, but both can communicate essentially the same information. This statement means that children who are fluent in a spoken or signed language should have equally sophisticated (even if subtly different) intellectual abilities. "Fluent" here is meant in an age-appropriate way: Younger children generally are less fluent than older children, but hearing children of hearing parents and deaf children of deaf parents likely are equally fluent in their native languages at the same age (see chapter 5).

A more complex situation arises for young deaf children with hearing parents. Those children frequently do not share a fully accessible language with others in the family, a situation likely to affect learning in a variety of domains. The "raw material" of intelligence will be there, but those children will not be fully proficient in using language for acquiring and manipulating facts about the world. It thus becomes important to distinguish between cognitive abilities that do and do not depend on language and decide what it all means in the case of deaf children.

During the early 1900s, studies involving deaf children showed them to lag behind hearing peers in educational progress by about five years. About 40 percent of that lag was seen as due to differences in "intelligence" because deaf students scored about two years behind hearing peers on intelligence tests (this was the stage of *the deaf as inferior*). The remainder of the educational difference was presumed to result directly from a lack of language experience. During the 1920s and 1930s, therefore, psychologists developed tests of intellectual abilities that were supposedly independent from language (called *nonverbal* or *performance* tests), explicitly designed for the purpose of better evaluating the mental abilities of deaf children. Such changes notwithstanding, deaf children still generally scored lower than their hearing age-mates, even if the differences were small.

Looking back, it is now clear that many of those early nonverbal tests were not correctly constructed or used, and they may have been biased against anyone who lacked the socio-cultural experiences of hearing, white, middle-class children. That is, they were not *culture fair* for deaf children or many others who came from diverse early environments. Since that time, additional tests have been developed that are truly language-independent, meaning that they can be conducted without the necessity of understanding spoken or signed instructions, and culture-independent, at least within clearly stated limits.[1] Even now, however, when samples of deaf and hearing children are shown to have equivalent IQs according to some particular, usually nonverbal, test, the deaf children may lag behind hearing peers in school-related academic performance. Findings of this sort suggest that there are important factors other than intelligence that influence academic achievement in deaf children—seemingly an obvious conclusion. Nonverbal tests may ensure that intelligence measures are not biased by a child's fluency in a particular language, but they do not address the fact that some skills and knowledge are typically learned through language, even if they are separate from it.

Several investigators, myself included, also have suggested that because of differences in deaf children's early experience, there will be real differences between deaf and hearing children in the way that their minds and brains work.[2] These differences may result in different styles of processing information, some of which may be beneficial (for example, focusing on visual-spatial information; see below) and some of which may not (focusing on individual items rather than relations among them). Regrettably, such suggestions are often incorrectly interpreted to mean that deaf children are limited by some kind of intellectual deficiency, and the conclusions are thus dismissed out of hand. The issue is actually much more subtle, and the possibility that deaf children might have a different configuration of intellectual abilities than hearing children requires serious consideration (remember: *different does not mean deficient*). If true, these abilities might well demand particular kinds of educational experiences to optimize deaf children's academic and intellectual growth. The lack of such experiences might explain some shortcomings in the academic achievement of deaf children even when they obtain normal scores on intelligence tests. In addition to being of central importance for promoting the education of deaf children and appropriately designing instructional methods and materials, further investigation of this possibility would help us to understand the interrelations among language, cognitive development, and social functioning. But—even though we know that parents do not want to hear this—it's complicated.

Confounding Factors in Intelligence

The Language Issue

Most commonly, when deaf and hearing children's scores on intelligence tests are compared, the focus is on the manipulation or completion of test materials in ways intended to reflect abstract as well as concrete reasoning abilities. On one hand, a reliance on nonverbal tests seems eminently fair, because most deaf children with severe to profound hearing losses are not fluent in English or whatever other language in which the test is written. But if nonverbal tests provide fair and accurate assessments of intelligence, why do we persist in using verbal tests for hearing children?

The answer, I believe, is that the "verbal" parts of intelligence tests[3] tell us a lot about children's ability to deal flexibly with information because of the abstract, symbolic nature of language. Sign-language-based intelligence tests for deaf children should work just as well as spoken-language-based tests for hearing children, if they are appropriately developed and administered. (Unfortunately, because deafness is a low incidence disability, there is not much money or fame to be earned developing and publishing such tests.) Eliminating verbal abilities from assessments of deaf children requires acceptance of the fact that we are tapping only one part of intelligence as it is typically understood. Most of what is learned in school settings "comes in" through language, and thus deaf children can achieve high scores on nonverbal tests while still struggling in school. In this case, the IQ tests and the demands placed on children in school settings are different, and one may not be a predictor of the other.

If the presence or absence of various language demands in the classroom or testing situation was all that mattered, deaf and hearing children would be essentially identical in those areas which do not require language. Deaf children, however, frequently have difficulty even in nonverbal academic and problem-solving tasks, lending support to the earlier suggestion that their learning and behavioral styles may be different from those of hearing peers. Just as important as what is explicitly taught to children is the wealth of knowledge they obtain incidentally, either by overhearing (or "overseeing") the conversations of others or via informal interactions with adults and other children. Such implicit learning usually will be more frequent in hearing than deaf children because there will be more "teachers" around who share a common language.

Even when children and parents, or others in a deaf child's environment, do use the same language (sign language or speech), adults typically only take care to ensure communication when they are directly addressing the child. This situation is very different from the natural language learning environment of children who share a first language with those around them—and it is far less effective. All of this points to the importance of parents' surrounding their deaf children with language, both signed and spoken, offering them the potential to glean whatever they can from conversations around them, whether or not they are the target of that language. Eventually, with enough support, children will come to use language as a tool for learning about the world around them.

Physiological and Psychological Contributions

Another potentially confusing aspect of deaf children's intellectual skills is the possibility that any particular deaf child might have an educationally relevant disabling condition in addition to having a hearing loss. For that 50 percent of the deaf population for whom hearing loss is hereditary, such a linkage is less likely, but still possible. Chapter 2 described some etiologies of congenital and early onset hearing loss that are caused by medical conditions and which also can affect the brain. Some of these effects, however, may not become apparent until a child reaches school age. The fact that approximately 30 percent of deaf children have experienced such related medical issues means that we must be extremely sensitive to learning difficulties that cannot be attributable solely to early environments or language abilities. Early identification and attention to special needs are essential in those cases.

Meanwhile, it occasionally has been suggested that hearing loss, and especially hereditary hearing loss, might confer some intellectual advantages for deaf children (Akamatsu, Musselman, & Zweibel, 2000). Deaf children with deaf parents tend to score higher on various tests of intellectual ability than deaf children of hearing parents, presumably because they share an early language and a fully rich environment with family members and members of the Deaf community. Yet, deaf children with hereditary hearing losses also score higher than deaf children with nonhereditary losses when the effects of early environment are equated. This suggests the possibility that naturally occurring cultural or historical selection factors could have resulted in some kinds of hereditary hearing losses being linked to superior nonverbal intelligence. Another possible explanation of superior functioning by deaf children of deaf parents lies in the ways that their brains develop. Findings from a variety of studies suggest that deaf and hearing children raised in signing environments have more balanced right and left sides of their brains (less *hemispheric spe-cialization*) in terms of both language and visual abilities. The result is slightly different organizations in the brains of deaf and hearing children, which may make the best use of potential information available to each (see Note 2).

Unfortunately, such findings raise more questions than they answer, because our understanding of cognition in deaf children, like our under-standing of the relations between brain and mind, is still in its infancy. For example, we know that deaf children tend to rely on concrete experi-ence and examples more than hearing age-mates. Is this a product of their educational experiences or does it have some more basic cognitive or neu-ropsychological origin? An anecdote might make this issue clearer: Some years ago, a colleague and I were investigating problem-solving strategies used by deaf and hearing children from age 7 to 14 years (Marschark & Everhart, 1999). We assumed that the older children would perform on the task much like adults, but we tested a few deaf college students just to be sure. Although we were right in our assumption, we hit a roadblock. Our experiment focused on how students spontaneously solve problems with-

out any help or advice. Several of college our student participants, however, became agitated when we explained that we could not offer any assistance without de-feating the purpose of the experi-ment. One student even exclaimed in sign language, "You have to give examples. Deaf students always get examples!" and refused to par-ticipate. While the strength of his preference for concrete examples may not be typical, the orientation is not unusual among deaf students. The problem is that some people would attribute this attitude to the student's being deaf. I don't think so! Much more likely is that the way that he was educated, both at home and at school, led to this orientation. This student either had learned to deal with new information in a rela-tively specific manner, perhaps because of limited communication between him and his parents and teachers, or he had acquired the habit of seeking assistance in various tasks (*instrumental dependence*). In either case, he actually might have been able to perform the task just fine without any help, but he did not know that (a *metacognitive* issue) and refused to try.

This one case aside, it should be obvious that an example-bound or instrumentally dependent approach to the world would affect a child's performance in a variety of social and academic areas. At a specific level, an example-bound orientation may explain some of deaf children's apparently concrete approaches to problem solving as revealed by intelligence tests and other cognitive tasks. At a more general level, it may partially explain why deaf and hearing children frequently appear to differ in the ways they go about various tasks, even if they are equally successful in the end: It may be that the two groups have developed different cognitive styles. *Cognitive style* refers to the way in which a child approaches the organizing and processing of information in formal or informal problem-solving situations, described in terms of various dimensions such as "impulsive" versus "reflective." The issue for teachers and parents is teaching deaf children in a way that helps to enhance reflective problem solving, rather than trying to make deaf children perform more like hearing children.

I believe (or at least hope) that most educators believe that "political" and "philosophical" aspects of this issue should take a back seat to the question of what leads to better academic success for deaf children (Marschark, Rhoten, & Fabich, 2006). It does not seem to be of any service to deaf individuals to ignore the possible role of language skills, in particular, in the ability to deal effectively with problem solving either inside or outside of the classroom. Whether or not deaf children obtain intelligence scores equal to their hearing peers is not the issue. The issue is the need to determine the relative strengths and weaknesses in deaf children's abilities and to develop the means of using the former to offset the latter.

Understanding Other Minds

How does one decide what a teacher wants on a particular assignment or a parent expects us to do in a potentially awkward situation? How does a child know whether his sister is telling him the truth or not? These are questions relevant to a popular area of investigation with both deaf and hearing children concerning *theory of mind.*

Most generally, theory of mind refers to a child's understanding that they and others have mental states—thoughts, wants, ideas and so on— that are not directly observable. Interest in this area as it relates to deaf children has emerged from studies involving what is known as the *false-belief task.* The false-belief task is only one means of tapping theory of mind, but it has been used in most studies involving deaf children. The most common version of the task goes something like this: A child sees a puppet hide a marble in a basket and then "leave the room." While the puppet is gone, another puppet is seen to remove the marble from the basket and hide it in a box. When the first puppet returns, the child is asked "Where will the puppet look for her marble?" or "Where will she *first* look for her marble?" Two other questions, "Where is the marble really?" and "Where did she put the marble in the beginning?" ensure that the child actually saw and understood what happened. On the second trial, the same sequence occurs, but the marble is moved to the experimenter's pocket or some other location rather than the box, thus creating a smaller probability of the child correctly answering the question by chance.

Early studies using the false-belief task showed that children with autism had considerable difficulty with it, performing significantly worse than both "normal" children and children with Down Syndrome. Such poor performance was initially attributed to a specific neurological deficit that was assumed to be unique to autism. Other investigators, however, suggested a socially based explanation of lags in the development of theory of mind, arguing that the understanding of false beliefs and development of theory of mind normally follows from conversational interactions between parents and children (Peterson & Siegal, 1995). It was at this point that deaf children as a group became interesting to theory of mind investigators, because the frequent lack of conversational interactions between deaf children and their parents often denies them social experience and communicative feedback concerning mental states and hence the ability to attribute mental states to others. Consistent with the social-conversational explanation for theory of mind development, a variety of studies demonstrated that children who are prelingually deaf and have hearing parents usually failed the false-belief task, while hearing preschoolers passed it easily. Young deaf children who used sign language with their deaf parents and those who effectively used spoken language with hearing parents, in contrast, performed comparably to hearing peers (Courtin & Melot, 1998).

Acknowledging that communication barriers between many deaf children and their hearing parents make conversational interactions with such families challenging, does this really mean they do not understand that other people can think, want, and know? Some investigators believe so, claiming that most children who are deaf do not gain theories of mind until their teenage years, a full 10 years later than hearing children (Gray, Hosie, Russell, & Ormel, 2001). Others, however, have pointed out that the number and skill of communication partners available to deaf children, the quality of communication with those partners, and other background differences may create difficulties for interpreting results concerning their theories of mind. It also is important to note theory of mind involves much more than false-belief tasks, and predicting behavior on the basis of understanding the mental states of others is more difficult than simply knowing that others have those mental states. Consistent with this suggestion, my colleagues and I examined stories told by children deaf and hearing children and found that deaf children actually produced more statements that ascribed beliefs, doubts, desires, and other mental states to themselves or others than did their hearing age-mates (Marschark, Green, Hindmarsh, & Walker, 2000).

The success of some groups of deaf children in false-belief tasks and others on different kinds of theory of mind tasks suggests that many deaf children with hearing parents are quite capable in the domain of theory of mind—or that some experiments are better at bringing it out. Beyond the apparent ability to attribute theory of mind and recognize that beliefs influence behavior as expressed in our narrative task, there are other indicators that children who are deaf possess a full mental representation of mental states. Programs that encourage such children to reflect on each other's ideas, think about an author's intentions, and understand characters' perspectives, for example, have been found to enhance reading and critical thinking skills (Greenberg & Kusché, 1998). Deaf students also have been shown to use well-structured sequences in signing and writing stories about what they would do in novel situations, sequences including characters' goals, actions, and desired outcomes, performing just as well as hearing peers (Marschark, Mouradian, & Halas, 1994). It thus seems absurd to claim that deaf children have social cognition abilities only on par with children who have autism.

While it remains unclear why deaf children have such great difficulty with the false-belief task, there is little doubt that they have theory of mind long before their teenage years. The age at which theory of mind is acquired and expressed by deaf children is still in need of clarification, but the research area holds promise for better understanding social functioning among deaf children and the perceived lack of maturity that often seems to be expressed in academic settings. The understanding and simple attribution of some mental states develops in hearing children by around age 3, and such understanding may be found to occur just as early in deaf children, regardless of the relatively limited opportunities of linguistic interactions with their hearing parents prior to age 5. At the very least, such findings emphasize the danger in relying on a single task in deciding whether a group of children should be labeled as "deficient" in a particular domain and indicate that we are in need of further research to understand the full complexities of the false-belief task as it relates to deaf children's language fluency and theory of mind (Courtin, 2000). Otherwise, investigators will be making the same error they made with regard to deaf children's performance on other cognitive tasks, their reading and writing skills, and their performance on various IQ tests, concluding that they are cognitively lacking on the basis of a complex task that is perceived differently by deaf than hearing children.

Striving for Success

When most educators and researchers talk or write about the intellectual skills of deaf children, they tend to focus on topics like those discussed above: IQ, problem solving, language, and nonverbal performance. Noticeably lacking is any mention of a potent factor recognized by parents and teachers but not often investigated in this regard: motivation to achieve. If deaf children are to succeed academically, occupationally, and at life in general, both they and their parents have to be sufficiently motivated to overcome obstacles related directly or indirectly to hearing loss during childhood.

Studies involving hearing children have shown that parents' spending time with their children, facilitating their academic and extracurricular interests, and answering their questions in supportive environments all foster academic excellence as well as emotional maturity. Similarly, families' constant support of deaf children's endeavors has been shown to lead to higher levels of achievement in academic domains (Calderon & Greenberg, 1993), and I see the results of such support in the many successful deaf children everywhere I go. Admittedly, academic encouragement for deaf children will not be as robust in families where there are significant communication barriers, and some parents are simply unable to sustain the energy that may be necessary for meeting their deaf child's special needs. This is not to imply that those parents are bad or do not love or care about their child as much as anyone else; it is simply an acknowledgement that having a special child can be difficult. This is one reason why parents need early intervention services just as much as their children do!

Deaf children's successful experiences, whether in school, in making a cardboard box into a fort, or in a social encounter, build on each other. Discovering that they can accomplish a particular task motivates children to try similar and sometimes more difficult tasks. In this sense, success breeds success, because the emotional and physical benefits of success motivate us to strive for more. Those individuals who are more motivated therefore achieve more, and those who achieve more are more motivated. As noted earlier, an essential component of this process is that children have to notice that the outcomes of achievement-related behaviors are self-produced. This relation is apparent in the fact that intellectually achieving hearing children are more likely to believe that they have control over their academic (and other) successes, and they are more independent than hearing peers who are less successful. Achievement and independence, meanwhile, are two dimensions on which deaf children tend to vary more widely and frequently lag behind hearing age-mates, primarily because of their more varied experiences at home and in other settings during the preschool years (Marschark, 1993b).

The challenges frequently seen in deaf children's academic achievement have often been attributed to their apparent tendency to behave in a less reflective, forward-thinking manner than hearing children and to their frequent failures to generalize information learned in one context to other situations in which it is applicable. True, the "three R's" of reading, writing, and 'rithmetic involve abstract kinds of knowledge, but the benefits of having such skills also may be viewed differently by deaf children than by hearing children. Deaf students, for example, generally spend less time studying than hearing peers, but whether this difference is because they tend to have fewer demands placed on them, because they are less likely to recognize areas in which they need more work, or because they are less invested in achieving success in particular subjects remains to be determined. Most likely, there is no single answer, and we all know deaf children who do not fit such generalizations.

We do know that deaf children with more positive attitudes toward communication tend to be higher achievers. That relation could result either because they are more favorably disposed to learning in general, because they also tend to have higher *self-esteem* (higher opinions of their own abilities), or because they are more likely to have positive experiences in academic settings than children who have poorer communication skills. Deaf children who are more reflective rather than impulsive in their approaches to learning and problem solving also tend to do better in school (see chapter 9). This link is not surprising, insofar as most school learning requires problem solving of one sort or another. Impulsive behavior is unlikely to lead to long-term solutions to problems either in the classroom or on the playground, even if it works in the short-term. Most interesting, perhaps, is the way in which high self-esteem, an internal *locus of control* (feeling that you control your own life rather than having to depend on luck, fate, or others), and academic success come together when families are accepting and supportive of deaf children (Calderon & Greenberg, 1993).

Several studies have suggested that one of the most potent predictors of educational success for deaf children is the amount of individualized attention a child receives.[4] This relation was perhaps first seen in Spain during the 1600s and 1700s, when children had to be literate in order to inherit the wealth of their parents. Parents of deaf children engaged private tutors to teach their heirs how to read and write, and successful pursuits in other areas followed (Lang, 2003). Similarly, studies in the United States over the last 20 years have shown the benefits of intensive, one-on-one education for deaf students as well as hearing students. Such environments, with qualified and high-quality teachers, allow the optimal match between a student's skills and needs and their exposure to new material. Few families, however, can afford such education. The number of deaf children in the United States makes the cost of private tutors prohibitive for public schools as well. This is one reason why some parents are moving to home schooling of their deaf children, but there is not yet any sound evidence concerning the outcomes of such efforts in terms of benefits and costs.

Measuring Academic Achievement

The academic achievement of deaf children has occasionally been evaluated in terms of classroom-based information, such as grade point averages or specific examinations, but formal descriptions usually rely on standardized tests. Patterns of academic achievement among deaf children, analyzed by race and gender, closely match those of hearing children, except that Asian deaf students are less likely to surpass white deaf students at least in English-speaking countries. Similarly, deaf students from families with higher socioeconomic status and those without other disabilities tend to score higher on standardized achievement tests. The effects of socioeconomic status, however, tend to be highly dependent on setting, accounting for much less of the variance in achievement in the United Kingdom than in the Untied States, for example.

It is important to note that academic achievement for deaf children from immigrant families is especially challenging. In the United States and the United Kingdom, many such children are attempting to learn both English and ASL or BSL while having to use another language (or two) at home. Particularly in urban settings, this creates a difficult situation for teachers and schools, as a single classroom might have deaf children with almost as many home languages as there are students. For the child, parents may be less able to help with homework, and opportunities for exposure to the language of instruction may be more limited. Although there do not appear to have any specific studies on the topic, colleagues teaching deaf children in cities like Toronto, New York, and London report that their students have particular difficulties in their English literacy skills. A variety of studies during the 1970s reported that deaf children with deaf parents have more rapid language development and higher academic achievement than deaf children with hearing parents (e.g., Jensema & Trybus, 1978). Most of these studies concluded that such advantages were the result of early access to language via sign language, but that now appears not be the case. In the area of reading, for example, it appears that the children who are the best readers are those parents who early on exposed their deaf children to both sign language, establishing a firm foundation for language development, and to written/spoken language (see chapter 7). Given what we have seen in previous chapters, it should not be surprising that two of the best predictors of deaf students' academic achievement are parents' acceptance of their child's hearing loss (including a positive view of the Deaf community) and high expectations for their children (Bodner-Johnson, 1986). These two orientations typically will be higher in deaf parents than hearing parents, but they need not be. Parents of deaf and hearing children show little difference in how much time they participate in the education of their children, although parents of hearing children have been found to be more likely to volunteer to participate in classroom activities, while parents of deaf children are more likely simply to observe their children in that context. Overall, involvement and effective parent-child communication appear to be the keys; and those we can change, while parental hearing status we cannot.

As noted in chapter 6, deaf children in mainstream settings often demonstrate higher levels of achievement than those in special school settings. Few studies, however, have taken into account the many confoundings of school placement with parent preference, school availability, and persistence, that is, the fact that children who are enrolled in one kind of school setting or another are different to begin with. When such factors are taken into account, placement is seen to account for as little as one percent of the variability seen in deaf children's academic achievement (Stinson & Kluwin, 2003). Further, deaf children in mainstream settings still tend to lag behind hearing peers in achievement, and, on average, having deaf parents does not eliminate those differences.

Creativity and Flexibility

Earlier in this chapter, I suggested that one definition of intelligence is the ability to adapt to new situations. Whether we are thinking about learning physics, understanding a poem, getting along in a new school, or figuring out how to set up a new computer, intelligent people are those who can apply their knowledge in new ways in new situations and go beyond what they already know. Sometimes, the range of possible new situations will be smaller or better defined, for example, the number of ways to connect a DVD player to a television. In others, it may be larger and less well defined, for example, ways to bring peace to the world. In either case, we have to be able to reason from what is known to what is unknown or desired. That is, we have to be creative and flexible.

If creativity and flexibility are hallmarks of intelligence, they are also areas in which deaf children have traditionally been seen as lacking, at least if one reads the literature traditionally aimed at their teachers. More recently, however, a variety of books such as *Deaf Persons in the Arts and Sciences: A Biographical Dictionary* (Lang & Meath-Lang, 1995) have provided accounts of numerous deaf artists, musicians, writers, and scientists who achieved eminence in fields that demand creativity. Clearly, we need to examine the issue further if we want to understand this apparent contradiction.

What Is Creativity?

Historically, characterizations of deaf children as literal and concrete in language and cognitive functioning derived from observations indicating that deaf children tend to lag behind hearing peers in their abilities to grasp complex or abstract concepts. Most frequently, however, assessments of deaf children's "cognitive flexibility" were made using English-based materials such as written compositions or standardized tests. It therefore is unclear to what extent reported lags in such abilities reflect language-specific difficulties rather than more general limitations on cognitive development. Moreover, within some educational settings, teachers do not expect deaf children to exhibit much diversity or creativity in thinking—and not surprisingly children often live up to (down to?) those expectations.

If creativity and flexibility reflect the ability to use prior knowledge in new ways, they clearly depend on the quality and quantity of a child's experience. Deaf children have just as much experience as hearing children, but we have already seen that they may have different kinds of experience than do hearing children. These differences, in turn, may affect the ways in which they function in educational, experimental, or day-to-day settings that require flexibility and creativity. Note that "affect" does not necessarily mean "impair" here, and we have already seen the great resilience of children faced with less than ideal early environments. Thus, deaf children may have language and cognitive abilities just as flexible as hearing peers, but these qualities may not be easily tapped by the usual assessments involving the reading or writing of English. Luckily, there are a variety of nonverbal tests of creativity available, and for various reasons (some of them based on the misguided equating of speech and language) they have been used extensively with deaf children (Marschark & Clark, 1987).

Among researchers who study creativity, there is some debate over exactly what it is; whether it can be learned; and whether it is an ability, an achievement, a disposition, or a strategy. For the present purposes, these issues are largely irrelevant, and I will simply accept two definitions of creativity. First is the psychological definition, one that fits nicely with the definition of intelligence adopted above: Creativity is the process of becoming aware of a need for objects or information, searching for solutions, and producing a result. Second is the artistic kind of creativity: Creativity is the expression of emotion, beauty, or new ideas through the invention of new things or the novel rearrangement of old things.

Nonverbal Creativity of Deaf Children

As we found earlier in the discussion of intelligence, nonverbal measures of creativity generally indicate that deaf children are more competent than is suggested by language-based measures. Recent evidence, for example, indicates that young deaf children show considerable creativity and imagination in their play, an area that is popular in studies of hearing children's creativity and intellectual flexibility and an important predictor of later language and academic achievement (Spencer & Hafer, 1998). Communication abilities of deaf children and their parents seem to be an important predictor of success in play settings, even when nonverbal behavior is observed. That is, investigations have suggested that hearing children, as a group, show somewhat more creative and imaginative play than deaf children as a group. However, when only those deaf children with good mother-child communication are considered, the difference disappears (Meadow-Orlans, Spencer, & Koester, 2004). This result could have several causes, but they all relate to the fact that better communicating mother-child pairs will have engaged in more complex and creative play than mothers and children who do not communicate well.[5] Those children thus become more "skilled" in play and are likely to transfer their learning to situations in which they play with others. At the same time, play teaches children a lot about rules, about causes and effects, about objects that are played with, and about other peoples' perceptions and beliefs (theory of mind). Play clearly can be creative, and creative play leads to increased creativity!

Mothers also affect their deaf children's creativity by taking or giving up control during play. Recall that hearing mothers of deaf children were described earlier as more controlling and less permissive than deaf mothers of deaf children or hearing mothers of hearing children. These characteristics can be seen when they are playing with their deaf children, as hearing mothers may try to direct activities and games where they would not do so with hearing children. In those situations, mothers also tend to be less flexible, less encouraging, and less imaginative than they are when playing with hearing children. Better educated mothers, however, are more likely to treat deaf and hearing children equally during play.

In addition to studies of play, deaf children's nonverbal creativity also has been investigated using standardized creativity tests, similar to the tests used to measure intelligence. When we weed out those studies that appear to have been correctly conducted and interpreted from the many that have not, deaf children are seen to do quite well, even though the tests were originally designed with hearing children in mind. Some studies even suggest that deaf children, at least in the 11–12 year old range, are more flexible in their nonverbal thinking (for example, in construction tasks) than hearing age-mates. Others have indicated that deaf children can learn to be more creative within particular testing situations. The extent to which such learning occurs in "natural" contexts and the characteristics of the setting that make such learning more or less likely remains to be determined.

Verbal Creativity of Deaf Children

Because of the importance given to the link between language and learning, much more research has been conducted concerning verbal than nonverbal creativity. Nonetheless, it is still surprising how little attention has been given to deaf schoolchildren's verbal creativity, especially in books intended for parents and teachers. This is likely due to the common assumption that deaf children have little verbal creativity to evaluate, but that assumption is clearly wrong. Conclusions about deaf children's lack of creativity in language largely have been based on observations of their flexibility within English. Although the need for literacy is a laudable goal for an educational system that seeks quality instruction for deaf children, drawing conclusions about their cognitive and language abilities on the basis of their performance in written or spoken language is likely to underestimate of those abilities. Assessment of deaf children's verbal creativity thus should be seen as a somewhat different enterprise from assessment of their capabilities within any particular language. That means we need to consider their comprehension and production capabilities in sign language as well as English.

Studies of deaf children's verbal creativity based on their skills in English have found that those children with better English skills, spoken or written, appear more creative. On average, however, deaf children will lose out to hearing children on English-based tests of creativity, if only because hearing children have much more experience (and greater fluency) in the language than deaf peers. Certainly, there are exceptions to this assertion, but the generalization is as valid as it is obvious. Similarly, I know that I am not seen as very creative when I write in Italian, and would never dream of writing anything other than scientific papers, which tend to be rather dry and stuffy anyway.

One alternative means of evaluating deaf children's verbal creativity involves examination of their comprehension and production of figurative language—expressions like "dry and stuffy." Do deaf children, or hearing children or deaf adults, understand such phrases? Figurative language is assumed by educators and psychologists to reflect both verbal and nonverbal flexibility, as well as a general ability to consider the world from alternative perspectives—again, an essential component of intelligence. More specifically, figurative language abilities depend on the ability to see abstract relations across different domains. If deaf children were as cognitively rigid as some investigators have reported, they would not be expected to either comprehend or produce figurative language. Consistent with that view, studies conducted during the 1970s found that deaf children did not understand English expressions like "knowing it by heart" or "looking a gift horse in the mouth" (remember *the deaf as concrete*). Notice, however, that most children learn these kinds of figurative expressions from their families, teachers, or peers; they normally would not have to figure them out for themselves. The spontaneous use of such expressions is a sign of fluency in English, or whatever language the expression is drawn from, and does not really tell us very much about deaf children's verbal creativity per se. More recent studies, therefore, have looked at deaf children's use of figurative language within sign language (see Marschark, 2005b, for a review).

Usually, such studies have examined the stories that deaf children tell on fantasy themes like what it would be like if animals and people "changed places," but similar results are obtained when they describe common everyday events. At the outset, such studies are interesting because they have shown deaf children to be very skilled in telling stories within sign language, even if some of them have trouble with writing stories in English. In fact, both their signed stories and their written stories generally include all of the elements that make up "good" stories (see chapter 7). At least from 8 years of age onward, deaf and hearing children's written stories are fully comparable in this sense, even if they differ in the quality of their English vocabulary and structure (Marschark et al., 1994).

Deaf children's signed stories are interesting not only because they have good structure, but also because they contain a wealth of figurative language. We now have recorded stories told by dozens of deaf and hearing children, and time after time we find that the deaf children are at least as creative as their hearing peers, and sometimes more so. Part of this creativity comes from the fact that deaf children are more skilled with the creative tools of sign language than they are with the creative tools of English. They use gestures, pantomime, and creative modifications of existing signs much more frequently than hearing children use gestures, pantomime, and creative modifications of words. Just as importantly, deaf children use and create the same kinds of "figures of speech" as hearing children, but they do it in sign language (Marschark et al., 1986). For example, we have seen deaf children refer to people as being like birds, insects, machines, and monsters, and they do so just as often as hearing children. In short, as in other areas, deaf and hearing children show different kinds of verbal creativity, but the two groups are more similar than they are different. Deaf children do not appear any less creative than their hearing peers when they are evaluated in ways that are unbiased with respect to their language and experience.

Do Deaf Children Have Special Visual Skills?

One domain in which people often expect deaf children to be more flexible and creative than hearing children has to do with visual and spatial skills. A variety of findings—and much more speculation—has suggested that deaf individuals may have enhanced visual abilities relative to hearing peers as a result of their reliance on the visual modality. Most obvious, perhaps, is the suggestion that deaf individuals would have more acute vision, especially in the periphery, as a consequence of the necessity of attending to visual (including linguistic) signals that occur outside of central visual fields. Typically, this belief goes along with the assumption that blind people should have more acute hearing than sighted people, simply because they depend on it more. In fact, several studies conducted during the 1980s and 1990s demonstrated that deaf children and adults—at least those who depend on sign language rather than spoken language—are more sensitive to movement in the visual periphery. More recently, there is some suggestion that this visual sensitivity is more the result of auditory deprivation at an early age rather than language modality (Proksch & Bavelier, 2002), but the issue is complex because sometimes skilled hearing signers have been found to have such visual advantages, and sometimes they have not.

Other visual-spatial benefits have been found to accrue to deaf individuals who are fluent signers. For example, both deaf and hearing individuals who acquired ASL as their first language have been found to be faster than nonsigning individuals in generating and manipulating complex (but not simple) mental images (see Marschark, 2003, for a review). For simplicity, first imagine a map of the United States with all of the individual states outlined rather than just the shape of the country (generation); then turn it upside down and see if you can still identify the shapes of individual states (manipulation). On average, deaf signers would be better at that than us mere mortals. Advantages among deaf signers also have been demonstrated with regard to discriminating one face from another, as long as the differing facial features are those involved in carrying grammatical information in ASL. Thus far, these abilities appear to be more the result of skill in sign language that lack of hearing, but we have not yet identified the ways in which such skills can provide benefits in the classroom or in everyday problem-solving situations. Just as "difference" does not imply "deficiency," it also need not imply "advantage" (Marschark, Pelz, Convertino, Sapere, Arndt, & Seewagen, 2005).

Final Comments

Early investigations of deaf children's thinking skills routinely found them to lag behind hearing peers by several years. The tests used in those studies often required comprehension of English, however, and many confused language and intelligence. More recently, a variety of intelligence tests and other tests of cognitive ability have been developed that depend only on nonverbal, "performance" measures. Although there are still *differences* observed between deaf and hearing children, these often are more qualitative than quantitative.

The question of whether language is independent of intelligence or IQ scores is made more confusing rather than clearer by the evaluation of deaf children. The problem is that those deaf children who are most lacking in language abilities are also likely to be different from other deaf children and hearing children in other ways, including the diversity of their early experiences and the quality of parent-child and peer-peer relationships. Carefully constructed performance tests sometimes have eliminated differences between deaf and hearing children, but in other cases differences have remained. Such findings indicate that there are factors beyond communication that contribute to children's intellectual development.

This chapter considered a variety of evidence concerning verbal and nonverbal flexibility of deaf children. In general, in both nonverbal and verbal areas, deaf children appear just as creative as their hearing peers. Factors negatively impacting deaf children's creativity and flexibility, however, include overcontrol by adults, lack of communication and interaction with teachers and parents, and less diversity in early experiences relative to hearing age-mates. Deaf children do appear less creative than hearing children when they are evaluated using printed materials. When evaluated in terms of their sign language production, however, signing deaf children are found to be just as creative as their hearing peers. These findings support the hypothesis that deaf children have great intellectual and creative potential that may not be easily tapped by testing in English or other spoken-written languages.

Because individual differences among deaf children are so large, we need to be very cautious in making any generalizations about their intellectual development or creative processes. What evidence is available nonetheless strongly indicates that they are far more capable than earlier books and reports suggest. Although the charge of being more concrete in their thinking than hearing peers may be warranted for some deaf children in some domains, the reason for that characteristic is likely due more to how they have been educated than to anything directly related to their being deaf.

9

I never met a deaf adult when I was a kid, so I always assumed that I would be able to hear when I grew up. I was shocked when I started at a school for the deaf and saw teachers and houseparents with hearing aids! Wow! They were just like me! It really changed the way I thought of myself and about being deaf.
—Marvin, a Deaf accountant (MBA)

NINE

Deaf Children to Deaf Adults

Chapters 1 and 4 explored the beginnings of social development in deaf children during the first months of life. The focus there was primarily on the early interactions between infants and their parents, which also were shown to have a role as a foundation for later social development. The present chapter moves beyond early childhoodand the influences of particular individuals to consider the ways in which deaf children develop socially and emotionally as they pass through the school years and into adulthood. In this context, we can look at the influences of early social interactions on later social behavior, but we also have to consider the skills and preferences that children acquire during the early years—characteristics that help to make up their personalities. Throughout the chapter it will be useful to keep in mind that we are discussing general observations and broad but imprecise statements about social-emotional development and other kinds of psychological functioning. Not all deaf children will fit these stereotypes and they are not meant to be prescriptive for any particular child or family. Similarly, because children and families vary widely, the rules, customs, and behaviors learned in the home will not always apply to social situations outside of the home, and those learned in the immediate neighborhood may not apply at school. This situation may be even more true for deaf children.

Differences in the generality or relevance of social rules for deaf and hearing children can result from the fact that deaf children may have fewer playmates during the early years, from their parents having more restrictive rules for behavior, or from parents and peers not being as able to fully communicate expectations about social interactions. For example, it is common to see a teacher or parent react to one hearing child hitting another by saying something like "Jane, don't hit Jonathan. How does it feel when someone hits you? It hurts, doesn't it? You wouldn't like it if Jonathan hit you, would you?" This kind of response is more likely to lead to positive changes in behavior than spanking or yelling "Stop that!" at the child, and it begins the process of internalizing the rules and expectations of the society (see the discussion of theory of mind in chapter 8). In order to be successful, however, there must be effective communication.

Parents who do not share a common, fluent language with their children cannot engage in such "moral teaching" as effectively as parents who do. Their children are not as likely to learn the reasons for social rules at home. This is not to say that deaf children need to be any less polite or well behaved than hearing children or that parents need to have any special tools for bringing up their deaf children. Quite the contrary: Deaf children should learn about social interactions and will develop personality characteristics in precisely the same way as hearing children. The important issues are who their teachers and role models will be, and how those children see themselves as part of the social world. Growing up is hard enough when it comes to friends, social pressure, falling in love, and "doing the right thing." Growing up deaf adds some extra dimensions to it.

Personality and Emotional Growth
During the School Years

Deaf children from deaf families often are more comfortable socially than deaf children coming from hearing families. Those children are likely to have had a wider range of social interactions, due in part to having more effective communication skills and proximity to the Deaf community, and they likely will have experienced greater understanding and acceptance from others (who are deaf) inside and outside the family. Deaf children of deaf parents also may be more likely than those with hearing parents to have experienced consistent parenting behaviors and effective communication from an early age. Social interactions with deaf individuals outside of the immediate family thus are more likely to be similar to those within the family. Partly as a result of this consistency, deaf children of deaf families tend to have relatively greater social confidence, self-esteem, and a greater sense of being in control of their own lives (Ritter-Brinton, 1993). This latter characteristic, known as *locus of control,* is an important predictor of social as well as academic and career success and has surfaced at various points in other chapters. Deaf children of hearing parents can be just as confident and secure as those of deaf parents, but it may require more conscious planning by hearing parents to ensure that their children have the right kind of personality-building experiences.

As young children become more social, the variety of their relationships with family, peers, and other adults (including teachers) increases far beyond that established with their parents and other family members. Most children will naturally be attracted to other people who will serve both emotional and practical roles in their lives. That is, all children have a need to be liked and emotionally close to others, and so they seek approval and affection from both adults and, later, from peers. At the same time, they often depend on others to help them or show them how to achieve their goals. Both of these kinds of attention seeking are referred to as *dependence* (*emotional dependence* and *instrumental dependence,* respectively), and they are normal and healthy parts of children's personalities. Even children who are said to be *independent* still display appropriate dependence, but they blend dependent behavior in some situations with self-reliance and assertiveness—for example, attempting some new acrobatic trick—but wanting someone to be watching. Children who are overly dependent on others may not feel in control of their own lives and are said to have an external locus of control. Children who blend independent and dependent behavior and feel in control are said to have an internal locus of control.

Children who are linguistically, physically, or psychologically challenged may encounter difficulties in establishing their independence. In
part, their need for more assistance from others is a real one, with the kinds
and extent of such help varying with the nature of the child's challenges.
Nonetheless, the frequent overprotection of children with disabilities by
well-meaning adults creates further barriers to social independence and
physical competence, as those children are often able to perform a variety
of tasks that others typically do for them. Social immaturity may be one
result, although it could have been avoided. As Kathryn Meadow-Orlans,
a pioneer researcher in the field once noted:

> Parents generalize from the narrow range of tasks that the
> handicapped child actually cannot do, and assume that there is
> a much larger spectrum of tasks of which he is incapable.
> Eventually, the assumed inability becomes a real inability
> because the child does not have the opportunity to practice
> tasks and develop new levels of expertise. In addition, it takes
> more patience and time for handicapped children to perform
> the trial-and-error process of skill acquisition—time and
> patience that parents may not have or be willing to give. For
> deaf children with deficient communication skills, it takes
> additional time and patience merely to communicate what is
> expected, required, and necessary for the performance of even a
> simple task. (Meadow, 1976, p. 3)

Meadow-Orlans's suggestion concerning the importance of effective
communication between deaf children and their parents and peers is supported by observations of researchers and teachers in a variety of settings.
Because they typically receive (or understand) fewer explanations for the
causes of other people's social and emotional behaviors, deaf children
may have more difficulty controlling their own behavior and learning
from social experience. Communication barriers also may result in deaf
children and adolescents having less knowledge about social rules, and
their lack of social skills in turn may impede the development of independence and self-esteem (Vaccari & Marschark, 1997a). Yet another
hurdle for social development is the fact that deaf children often lack
social role models with whom they can identify and communicate. All
of these factors would lead us to predict the observed greater social maturity of deaf children of deaf parents, as compared to those with hearing parents, and of deaf children enrolled in school programs with other
deaf children, as compared to those who are the only deaf child in a
mainstream school setting. Nonetheless, we have to remember that descriptions of whole groups as "socially mature" or "socially immature"
are broad generalizations, and that there is no reason why deaf children

cannot be just as socially and behaviorally adjusted as hearing children of the same ages.

As in other areas, some children are faster or slower social learners. Some will have families that are more or less "instructive" with regard to social interactions outside of the home. Deaf children are often seen to be more involved with their families than are hearing children in hearing families. In some sense, family interactions are more important for deaf children than for hearing children because a greater percentage of their social experience happens with family members than with others outside the home. This situation makes family members very important as role models. *Role modeling* plays an important part in development, helping children to learn about different social roles, about their cultural heritage, about the values and morals of their family and community, and about more specific things like religion, politics, preferences for particular sports teams, and favorite foods. The ability to identify with others and to model their behavior first depends on a child believing that they are similar to the model. Boys, for example, learn "how to act like boys" by watching their fathers and other boys, not by watching their mothers and older sisters. As children discover ways they are like others, they try to act like them and think like them, eventually developing similar likes and dislikes. Finding that their parents have the same last name as they do or that they look like one of their parents can contribute to this development in the same way that sharing cultural or ethnic characteristics often makes children act more like others with similar backgrounds.[1]

Perhaps a real-life example will help to make the general point: When I was growing up, my family did not have a strong distinction between "girl" things and "boy" things. We were all involved in cooking, cleaning, painting, and so on. It was primarily my father who taught me to sew and to cook, and with him as my role model, both activities became very natural for me (I now do both more often, if not better, than my wife). A colleague of mine was eager to have his two daughters grow up the same way, and so he made a point of having them build things with him, work on the family car, and help him paint the house. It did not work. Why? Probably because it was their father who always did the "boy things" with the girls. If their mother had built the bird houses with them and their father had taught them to cook, perhaps the gender roles would have seemed more flexible. As it is, they are both wonderful young women, but they are not very interested in the kinds of activities that we think of as being done by males.

Modeling plays an important role in giving children a sense of identity, both as individuals and as part of a larger community. By sharing characteristics with others in their family or their community, they come to see themselves as part of a group, as *belonging* (see the quote at the top of this chapter and Note 2). Deaf children in hearing families will have a sense of family identity, but their sense of being part of the larger community often will be colored by whether or not they know other deaf people. Deaf children normally learn about Deaf culture only by being around Deaf children and Deaf adults, and that is why schools for the deaf are seen as so important from the perspective of the Deaf community.

Living With Parents, Peers, and Siblings

Early language experience for deaf children has been shown to have a significant impact on their personality and emotional development, just as it does with hearing children. Most research in this area has focused on the benefits of early exposure to sign language, but the important thing is to have consistent two-way communication, regardless of whether it is spoken or signed. For example, studies have shown that children enrolled in preschool intervention programs utilizing total communication are more likely to respond appropriately to their mothers' requests and use far more communication with them during play than children enrolled in spoken language programs (Greenberg, Calderon, & Kusché, 1984; see chapter 6). Those interactions tend to be longer, more relaxed, and more gratifying on both sides. Deaf children who have established good communicative and social relationships within the family thus will be better equipped to venture out into the social world (Meadow-Orlans, Spencer, & Koester, 2004).

Thinking back to the school years and our social lives during that time, many adults agree that they were "the best of times and the worst of times." There are many fond memories of friends and events, but it also was a time when there were conflicting pressures, and most people say they would not want to go through them again. We were supposed to act like individuals, but we also wanted to fit in with the crowd; we were supposed to be successful in academics, but also to be liked by others. As school and our school friends became major social influences, we started to accept the values of our peers and our role models, sometimes even when those values were in conflict with the values of our families. During the school years, we had to face problems of self-esteem, gender identity, and of trying to figure out who we were and what we wanted. Sometimes, it seemed that our parents were not much help.

Deaf children encounter all of the same social problems and find the same social solutions as other children. Depending on their environments, they also might face additional challenges. In a public school setting, for example, being deaf makes them different, and the parent who thinks being different in school does not matter is forgetting a lot about his own youth. In a residential school or day school program, deaf children find others who are like them, but the hearing world is still all around them. Chapter 6 described the impact of different school settings on deaf children's social adjustment. In general, the evidence indicated that those students in mainstream programs tended to feel more isolated and lonely than students in schools for the deaf (Stinson & Whitmire, 1992).

When children share common characteristics and attitudes with others, when they are part of a group, it contributes to their self-esteem. A variety of studies have examined the self-esteem of deaf children and identified factors that promote or hinder its development. Although there have been some mixed findings, it now appears that neither hearing status nor school placement have a large effect on self-esteem (see Stinson & Kluwin, 2003). Nevertheless, deaf children whose parents are better and more consistent signers have been seen to have higher self-esteem than children whose parents do not sign as well, and when families use both signed and spoken language deaf children have higher self-esteem than when they are exposed to spoken language only (Desselle, 1994). Still to be determined is whether such findings are a consequence of communication skill per se or improved social relations that are due to having more flexible communication skills.

The lack of acceptance that deaf students frequently find in public school classrooms may not affect their self-esteem, but it does affect

their comfort and satisfaction with public school settings (Stinson, Whitmire, & Kluwin, 1996). Many individuals thus continue to believe that schools for the deaf are a potential source of social growth for deaf children, and available findings support that view. Hearing proponents of mainstreaming and inclusion sometimes argue that the "artificial" nature of separate school programs might result in a narrow view of social responsibility and social interaction, but there is no support from existing research for such a position. Moreover, the fact that many hearing parents do not have fluent communication with their deaf children means that the socialization they receive at home also can be rather narrow, and it is difficult to know which situation would be better or worse for any particular child.

The apparent advantages of schools for the deaf or other separate programs for deaf children in terms of social development do not deny their need for a secure family life. Nevertheless, those special programs offer a fertile ground for social interactions with peers and deaf adults that go beyond what is available in most homes and preschool programs. In that setting, deaf children will have more playmates and more communication during play than in public schools. They also will be less overprotected and intruded upon by well-meaning adults. Some of the benefits of the larger social circle gained in residential or day school settings may seem trivial: things like going to the mall with a group of friends, telling jokes in the hallway, and flirting on the playground. But, I think that the importance of those behaviors for "normal" social and personality development during the school years cannot be ignored. This kind of experience leads directly to children's acquisition of an accurate assessment of their personal strengths and weaknesses (*self-image*), leadership skills, and self-esteem. These characteristics, in turn, play an important role in children's desire for achievement and eventual success in academic and social settings.

Clearly, the most important part of raising a deaf child is trying to give them as normal a childhood as possible. Social, language, and educational experiences all enter into the "normal" mix, but "normal" does not mean "business as usual." As I noted earlier, having a deaf child affects the whole family, and a deaf child in a mainstream setting affects the entire class. This means that some day-to-day activities may have to change if deaf children are to have access to the experiences and opportunities available to hearing children. (No one ever said raising a deaf child was going to be easy!)

Interactions With Peers

Interactions with peers are an essential component in children's development of the social skills necessary for the establishment and maintenance of friendships. Those interactions also facilitate the growth of perspective-taking ability, as children come to understand their peers' preferences, goals, and emotions. Ultimately, they also will play a role in educational settings. As noted earlier, there have been numerous studies of communication interactions between deaf children and their deaf and hearing mothers and some research concerning communication among peers during the preschool years. Until relatively recently, however, rather less was known about how school-aged deaf children interact with deaf and hearing peers. The issue has become particularly important as most deaf children have moved into mainstream school settings, and the social needs of deaf students is one factor that legally has to be considered in deciding what constitutes a "least restrictive environment" (see chapter 6).

At this point, there are some general findings concerning social interactions of school-age deaf children, but social relations in the classroom are so complex that we do not yet fully understand the causes of those findings nor what can be done to ameliorate those we would like to change. For example, deaf and hard-of-hearing students enrolled in regular school classrooms are seen by hearing peers as less likeable and are less likely to be preferred as social companions. Both deaf and hearing children and adolescents generally prefer companions of the same hearing status (Capelli, Daniels, Durieux-Smith, McGrath, & Neuss, 1995; Minnett, Clark, & Wilson, 1994). If such qualitative differences are fairly consistent, results are mixed with regard to the quantity of social interactions that deaf students have relative to hearing classmates. In elementary school, it appears that deaf and hard-of-hearing children interact less frequently with peers than do hearing children, regardless of whether their classmates are deaf or hearing and regardless of whether they are in a regular classroom or a resource room with only deaf students (Antia, 1982; Antia & Dittilo, 1998). In other words, simply having deaf and hard-of-hearing peers available for interaction does not necessarily increase the frequency of social interactions.

It is important to note here that deaf children's communication skills are likely to be an important predictor of their success or failure in the social domain. Studies have shown, for example, that young hearing children are more likely to ignore deaf children's attempts at social interaction than the reverse. Deaf and hearing children also appear to initiate social interactions with peers in very different ways. Social initiations by deaf children often oblige their playmates to respond, by explicitly asking for information or action, whereas hearing children are more likely to initiate social interactions with comments that do not require a response but "invite" a playmate to interact (McKirdy & Blank, 1982). Such patterns of interaction demonstrate a link between social experience and communication, but the precise nature of that interaction has received relatively little attention.

Given that deaf children tend to rely more heavily on nonlinguistic communication than hearing peers, it is not surprising that the two groups develop different patterns of social interaction which may clash in the classroom or on the playground. Even in preschool settings, deaf children with better language skills are more likely than children with poorer language skills to play with multiple peers at one time, to interact with teachers, and to use and receive more language from their play partners (Lederberg, 1991). One might expect that older deaf and hard-of-hearing children who have better spoken language skills would have more frequent and rich social interactions with hearing peers than others with lesser spoken line or skills. That assumption has received some support from research in which deaf and hard-of-hearing students were asked about their communication preferences and about how often they interact with their peers (Stinson & Whitmire, 1992). Teens who preferred to use spoken language reported more frequent interaction with hearing peers than deaf and hard-of-hearing peers, while those who preferred sign language reported more interactions with deaf peers. A recent study we conducted with college students, however, showed that when we actually watched interactions among deaf students playing Trivial Pursuit, those who used sign language understood each other better than students who used spoken language (Marschark, Convertino, Macias, et al., 2006).

Whether such conflicting findings indicate a difference between high school and college-aged students or a difference between student perceptions and reality is unclear and awaits further investigation. At the same time, is important for us to understand how interactions among students affect learning and not only social behavior. Classroom discussion becomes more important in higher grades, and we have very little information concerning the extent to which deaf students have access to peer communication and exchanges between classmates and teachers. Given the popularity of mainstream educational placements and cochlear implants, this issue is becoming even more complicated. We cannot wait any longer to gain an understanding of classroom communication and to determine methods to optimize it.

Influences of Brothers and Sisters

Most people who have brothers or sisters recognize that siblings have an effect on each other's personalities and development. In general, siblings are less emotionally tied to each other than they are to their parents, and they thus can serve as confidants and behavior-modifying critics for one another. Siblings observe and evaluate each other in ways that can contribute to social growth and maturity. They also learn from each other and share resources in a variety of contexts. They can protect each other from emotional or physical harm and serve as a buffer between each other and the parents or outside world. They can make life simpler or more complex, more comfortable or more difficult.

We actually know very little about how sibling relationships might be affected when one child is deaf. Some changes will be subtle, others not so subtle, and all will vary depending on the parents' ability to adjust to having a deaf child. When the parents accept their deaf child, they are more likely to help their other children come to an acceptance of their deaf sibling. Hearing siblings of deaf children, nonetheless, sometimes become angry and resentful toward their deaf siblings. In addition to normal sibling rivalry during childhood, hearing siblings may be frustrated at the lack of communication in the family and at first may not understand what it means to be deaf. Hearing siblings may be jealous of the increased attention that a deaf child receives from their parents and upset at sometimes having to act like caregivers, explaining to people outside of the family that their brother or sister is deaf. At other times, the relationship may be "seamless," and deaf and hearing siblings may have especially warm feelings for each other. Positive relationships among deaf and hearing siblings provide deaf children with social and emotional support as well as encouragement in dealing with the implications of their hearing losses outside of the home. Hearing siblings, for example, can serve as helpful resources in social as well as academic contexts. Deaf children with hearing siblings thus often show better social skills than deaf children with no hearing siblings.

With regard to the effects of siblings on deaf children's communication abilities, it is important to note that there will be considerable difference in quality and quantity of communication in a family with only one deaf child compared to a family with more deaf children. Consider first the most common situation, in which there is only one deaf child in an otherwise hearing family.[2] On average, there appears to be more active communication between deaf children and their hearing siblings than with their hearing parents. Hearing siblings are often more likely to use signed and non-sign gestural communication than their hearing parents, who often try to focus on spoken communication. Hearing siblings thus may serve as intermediaries between a deaf child and her parents as well as with people outside of the family. Their possible interpreter role aside, older siblings will provide models of language use and someone with whom deaf children can "practice" communicating. Deaf children accordingly would be expected to achieve higher communicative functioning when they have older siblings, either deaf or hearing (see Vaccari & Marschark, 1997a).

If the situation in which deaf and hearing siblings share some mode of communication (either spoken, signed, or a combination) has positive consequences for both deaf children and their families, the absence of a common language between siblings can lead either to negative consequences or to the failure to benefit from a potentially positive situation. For example, it may be too difficult for hearing children to explain to their deaf siblings what is going on in a particular context, how to play a game, or why there is an argument between them. Hearing siblings thus may cut short or avoid more complex social interactions, even if they are on good terms with their deaf siblings. This reduced interaction will not only have a direct effect on social interaction, but it will also affect the learning of social skills and the ability to resolve conflicts.

Consider now the situation where there is more than one deaf child in the family. Such families are likely to have histories of deaf members, indicating hereditary causes of hearing loss (see chapter 2). Those families not only will tend to be more accepting of people who are deaf, but they are more likely to accept gestural and signed communication, and may have considerable sign skills. In the promotion of social growth, there is likely to be a considerable difference between a hearing family with only one deaf child—who will tend to be the center of family attention—and a family with several deaf children—where the family will function more naturally. Growing up with deaf siblings provides a rich environment for modeling and all of the typical characteristics of sibling relationships. Although more research needs to be done, what we know so far indicates that those relationships have only positive effects on deaf children, both socially and cognitively.

Understanding the Feelings and Values of Others

The ability to consider the feelings of other people is intertwined with both social and cognitive development (see chapter 8). Over time, children learn to balance social roles, the feelings and goals of others, and the values that their family and culture place on different kinds of behavior. To behave in a socially appropriate way, children have to consider alternative perspectives in social situations, and role taking therefore is an essential component of mature social functioning.

Historically, deaf individuals, and deaf children in particular, have been described as having difficulty taking the perspective of others, thus making them emotionally egocentric,[3] lacking in empathy, and insensitive to the needs of those around them (e.g., Bachara, Raphael, & Phelan, 1980). Such reports are common in the literature, but they often overlook the fact that role-taking ability is strongly related to children's language skills. That is, children who have the benefits of early communication are better able to consider the perspectives of others in social situations, probably because they have gotten more explanations of the causes and effects of behavior (Peterson & Siegal, 1995). Among such children, any delays observed in their role-taking ability during the preschool years tend to disappear by the middle-school years.

A child's understanding of the perspectives of others and of their culture is an important part of deciding what is right and what is wrong. *Moral development* requires that children understand the reasons for avoiding "bad" behaviors and performing "good" behaviors. Punishment and rewards also can accomplish this at some superficial level, but unless the values of the family and society are internalized, the generality of the effects are limited and often short-lived. When children truly understand how others view their behavior, they are more likely and more able to try to follow societal rules. Moral development thus is related to role taking and, more generally, to children's cognitive development and theory of mind.

Research studies have shown that deaf children lag behind hearing children in their abilities to judge other people's behavior in terms of their intentions rather than the outcome (Kusché & Greenberg, 1983). For example, they might see a child who accidentally breaks a dish while trying to help in the kitchen as being just as bad as the child who intentionally breaks a dish in a fit of anger. Deaf children also are more likely to behave out of fear of punishment rather than because they understand the principles underlying appropriate behavior. As a result, they may be more likely than hearing age-mates to be disruptive in school or to get into trouble if they think they can "get away with it," an attitude even found among deaf college students (DeCaro & Emerton, 1978). Unfortunately, for reasons cited earlier, deaf children also may be more likely than hearing children to misjudge their chances of getting caught.

Any explanation of the above behaviors needs to take into account the social and cultural context in which they occur. For example, hearing parents may have fewer opportunities to directly teach their deaf children the family's rules or the culture's morals. They also tend to give in to their deaf children's demands when they lack sufficient communication skill to explain the reasons for delays or for denying children something they want. Those children will experience inconsistency in responses to their actions when behavior permitted at home is not allowed in school or neighborhood play settings. Such inconsistency often leads to resistance to parental values by the time children reach the middle-school years, thus accelerating the movement to identification with peers (regardless of whether those peers model acceptable or unacceptable conduct). The resulting behavior will further affect socialization and may be interpreted as indicating underlying psychological problems if it is consistently negative. While there are certainly many more factors that go into the mental health of either deaf or hearing children, the ways they behave in interpersonal interactions are often a primary indicator of psychological well-being or psychological difficulties from the perspectives of concerned parents and teachers.

Mental Health

In the previous section, we saw that deaf children may lag behind hearing children in their recognizing the reasons for other people's behavior. This was seen to be related in part to communication, as deaf children are less likely than hearing peers to receive explanations for other people's social behaviors. As a result, deaf children might not always understand why people respond to them the way they do.

One might expect that because deaf children rely heavily upon visual information, they would develop particular sensitivity to the underlying meanings of facial expressions. There are at least two reasons why this would not be the case, however. First, the emotional state underlying a facial expression or even a verbal description of one's feelings is considerably more abstract than behaviors associated with them. Moreover, although interpretation of facial expressions of emotion generally is considered to be a nonverbal skill, it usually develops within linguistic contexts. Given the relative lack of fluent communication between deaf children and hearing adults around them, it is likely that the making of such connections is delayed relative to hearing children. Second, but not unrelated, is the difficulty that many deaf children exhibit in relational processing, in this case, linking observed events to individuals' behaviors and facial expressions (see chapter 8). Consistent with this suggestion, an early study of social-emotional development in deaf children showed that 7- to 8-year-olds were less successful than hearing peers in matching faces showing different emotions with emotionally related scenes (Odom, Blanton, & Laukhuf, 1973). Deaf children understand and can name the emotions on faces (Gray, Hosie, Russell, & Ormel, 2001), but they have trouble connecting the emotions with the right contexts.

Findings of this sort suggest that deaf children might sometimes behave inappropriately or misunderstand others' behavior in ways that might appear to be the result of emotional difficulty, when the roots actually lie in cognitive development. For example, deaf children (and adults) have been described as tending to act more immaturely or aggressively than hearing peers. In particular, deaf children are often said to be more disruptive and more impulsive in school, whereas deaf adults are sometimes described generally as oversensitive, depressed, or even paranoid (Vaccari & Marschark, 1997b).

Is there any truth to these descriptions? The research findings with regard to deaf children are scant and mixed, and the conclusions we draw may depend on the assumptions we have about deaf people in general. Caution is necessary, especially when considering older literature, because there is a long history of misdiagnosing hearing loss in children as mental retardation, autism, or other psychological disturbances. "Mistakes" like these are disgraceful and potentially devastating for deaf children and their families, but they do occur. Clearly, they reflect a lack of information about hearing loss on the part of parents, pediatricians, and teachers. Beyond such confusions, however, there is a variety of factors that may put deaf children at risk for psychological stress.

It might be argued that if deaf individuals do have greater emotional difficulties than hearing people, it would be understandable. After all, some deaf children grow up in homes where there is little acceptance of their hearing losses and less understanding of their special needs, even if early identification and intervention appear to be reducing the frequency of such situations. Surely they would be expected to have some anger or to show other effects of such a situation. Even in more accepting families, there may be emotional consequences that follow from a lack of effective communication between parents and children (Wallis, 2006). In stressful situations, deaf children may not fully understand what is happening, what is wrong, who was bad, or what their role is in the episode. Similarly, the constant frustrations of not being able to communicate with the hearing-oriented worlds of education and business surely must have some impact on deaf adults, especially when they are the only deaf person in a company or a small community.

It is surprising that better statistics on mental health and deaf individuals are not available, but as better assessment tools have become available there also has been a shift in the social-political landscape. As we saw in the case of cognitive development, there is reluctance among many investigators to point out differences between deaf and hearing individuals (especially when most investigators are themselves hearing), and thus some questions simply are not being asked. There are also misconceptions by health professionals concerning deaf people that may lead to erroneous conclusions about psychological functioning, and difficulties of diagnosis because of communication barriers are well documented (see Leigh & Pollard, 2003). Relatively few qualified therapists are fluent signers, and most deaf people who want counseling or therapy need a sign language interpreter to optimize communication between them and the therapist. Some years ago, a deaf acquaintance pointed out to me that it is difficult enough to discuss serious personal problems with a psychotherapist, but sharing them at the same time with an interpreter who may be a neighbor and who works with all of your friends can be very intimidating. Certified interpreters have a strict code of ethics about such matters, but the situation still can be an awkward one.

Research has shown that the quality of a therapist's sign language skills can directly influence the range of psychological symptoms identified in deaf children and adolescents. In addition to the simple language barrier, most psychotherapists are unfamiliar with deaf people and Deaf culture and may not understand social and emotional differences between them and hearing clients. This situation can result in the failure of a deaf person to benefit from the therapeutic situation, but it occasionally will lead to misdiagnoses as well. For example, a doctoral student in clinical psychology once came to me concerning a deaf adolescent girl with whom he was working. He was beginning to think that the girl was paranoid, because she reported that her hearing parents were talking about her "behind her back." She also apparently refused to make eye contact with the graduate student therapist during their sessions. This was the student's first deaf client, and he was seeking some books or articles on mental health in deaf people, but I sent him back to the girl rather than to the library. As I suggested to him at the time, he eventually discovered that the girl's parents really were talking about her when she was present. It turned out that neither parent could sign very well, and they had never really discussed their daughter's future with her. Often, however, she would do something that would start the parents talking about their plans and hopes for her future. They would look at her during those conversations, but when she would ask what they were talking about, they would say "nothing." Apparently, they were trying to avoid having to explain their parental concerns (or were unable to), and they never realized how much anxiety they were causing their daughter. As for not making eye contact, moving the interpreter to a seat beside the therapist solved that problem!

Recognizing that there have been few studies in which we can have confidence, what do we know about the incidence of psychiatric problems in the deaf population? Perhaps the most famous study about mental health among deaf people was the statewide survey in New York in the early 1960s (Rainer, Altshuler, Kallman, & Deming, 1963). The "New York Project" suggested that the more severe forms of mental illness, such as psychoses, bipolar (or manic-depressive) disorder, and schizophrenia, are equally frequent among hearing and deaf populations. That finding has been confirmed several times since in both the United States and England (Leigh & Pollard, 2003). At the same time, because linguistically accessible mental health services are rare, those deaf individuals who do seek mental health care tend to have more serious needs. As a result, estimates of severe mental illness within the deaf population appears greater than that in the hearing population when based on the number of individuals receiving inpatient services (i.e., those who are hospitalized; Black & Glickman, 2006; Vernon & Daigle-King, 1999).

Other studies have suggested that deaf people may be less likely than hearing people to suffer from more severe forms of depression (Leigh & Pollard, 2003), but at least one study has indicated that deaf college students are more likely than hearing students to report mild depression (Leigh, Robins, Welkowitz, & Bond, 1989). This finding is particularly interesting because both deaf and hearing students who reported that their mothers were more overprotective during their childhoods were more likely to report being depressed as young adults. Insofar as we know that hearing mothers of deaf children tend to be relatively overprotective, the greater incidence of mild depression among the deaf students perhaps follows quite naturally. We have already seen that more effective communication between parents and their deaf children can reduce the incidence of mental health problems later, during the teenage years, but we need to recognize that deaf children are still at risk. Such results can serve as reminders to parents of the need for "normal and natural" parenting of deaf children.

The finding that deaf college students might experience mild depression more frequently than hearing college students is consistent with findings suggesting that deaf students in mainstream settings may feel isolated and lonely compared to students in special programs (most of the students in the above study came from regular public schools; see chapter 6), and are much more likely to self-report mental health difficulties than hearing peers (Wallis, 2006). Deaf adults and adolescents, for example, may be prone to more posttraumatic stress disorders. For those deaf people who are not engaged with a larger deaf/Deaf community, there may be considerable social isolation that leads to difficulty when parents or other people who are close die or move away. These feelings may be reflected in either depression or posttraumatic stress reactions. Generally speaking, however, although deaf children might have more frequent behavior problems than hearing children, these do not appear to be related to any serious, long-term psychological effects. Parents might take some consolation in such findings, but there is still a variety of practical issues to make raising a deaf child a challenge for most parents.

One final note: In searching for information concerning mental health in deaf children, I have come upon some research beyond what is described above. Most of that work, however, appeared questionable, either because of the size and composition of the samples studied or because they were lacking comparisons of hearing children of the same age. Given that I had little confidence in the few results I was able to find, I have omitted them here for fear of creating even more misunderstanding and confusion. Research in this area is sorely needed, as without fully understanding the psychological challenges faced by deaf children we cannot optimize services and educational opportunities available to them. Nevertheless, there are two areas in which somewhat more information is available: impulsivity and learning disability.

Are Deaf Children Impulsive?

Perhaps the most common psychological problem attributed to deaf children is impulsivity. The term "impulsivity" has two closely related meanings. Normally, we apply the word "impulsive" to people who seem to act without thinking, usually behaving in a way that seems to satisfy their immediate desires without concern for others or for long-term implications. Considering this everyday kind of impulsivity, educators and researchers have claimed that deaf children's behavior often shows a desire for immediate gratification. This need is reflected either in an inability to wait for what they want or a willingness to settle for less if they get it sooner rather than getting what they really want later.

In deaf children, impulsive behavior often is attributed to the lack of early language interaction with hearing parents and teachers, who may not understand what a deaf child is asking for or may not be able to explain why children cannot have what they want when they want. Although other possible explanations for impulsive behavior are considered below, hearing parents of deaf children frequently do yield to their demands for attention, assistance, or objects in order to avoid the possibility of temper tantrums. Mothers of deaf children, for example, appear over six times more likely than mothers of hearing children to invariably respond to demands for attention, a situation that is habit-forming for both mothers and children (Gregory, 1976). Part of the problem is that once such an episode starts, parents might not have sufficient communication skill to be able to stop it.[4] That is, without enough language proficiency to relate the present to the past and to the future, parents unintentionally might be teaching their children that dependence and demands will be immediately rewarded (Vaccari & Marschark, 1997b). This attitude then may be carried over into the classroom, where deaf children are more likely than hearing children to "act up" and get in trouble.

So much for the common use of "impulsive." When psychologists use that term to describe a child, they normally are referring not to how children behave on the playground, but to the way they solve problems. From the psychological perspective, impulsivity is one end of an impulsivity-reflectivity dimension, one of several dimensions that comprise a child's *cognitive style.* Although the standard tests of impulsivity-reflectivity examine cognitive or academic problem solving, the underlying dimension also relates to social problem solving. Impulsivity and reflectivity are most easily seen in the trade-off between speed and accuracy in doing a task or in decision making. Tests for younger children generally involve choosing which of several pictures is the "same" or "different" as a target picture. For preschoolers, this might involve a target picture of a bear and a child's having to choose from among pictures of another bear, a horse, a cat, and a mouse. Children in the second grade might be asked to choose from among several clown pictures and pick the one that has exactly the same pattern of striped clothing as the target. Children who make their choices quickly and with frequent errors will fall into an impulsive range, whereas those who take more time to consider the alternatives before making (more often correct) decisions will fall into a reflective range. Similarly, when older children are asked to trace through mazes printed on paper, those who take longer but "stay in the lines" are rated as more reflective than those who go more quickly, but "bump into" lines and have to backtrack out of "dead ends."

Despite all of the stories about impulsivity in deaf children, relatively few research studies have been conducted to determine whether or not they are really more impulsive than hearing peers in any formal sense. This question is important in part because we know that for both hearing and deaf children, those who are more reflective tend to have better academic achievement scores in school than those children who are more impulsive. The few studies that have been done in this area have suggested that deaf children of deaf parents may be more reflective than deaf children with hearing parents, that deaf children enrolled in early intervention programs will show better impulse control than those without such intervention (see chapter 6),[5] and that deaf children who learn sign language earlier in life may be less likely to be impulsive than those who learn to sign later. There is no evidence that I am aware of, however, linking reflectivity or impulsivity to the presence or absence of hearing. In the one study I know of which actually compared deaf and hearing children, no differences in impulsivity-reflectivity were found between the deaf and hearing aged 7 to 14 years (Marschark & Everhart, 1999).

It is difficult to say whether impulsive behavior on school tasks results in poor performance, or poor performance and frustration in school lead to impulsive behavior (or both). In any case, given the evidence showing positive relations between (1) early language experience and reflective problem solving, (2) parental involvement with children and academic success, and (3) reflectivity and academic success, it seems safe to conclude that effective communication and involvement of parents in their deaf children's schooling are important for avoiding impulsivity. Impulsivity is not a consequence of hearing loss, but there are avoidable hurdles in growing up deaf that can lead to impulsive behavior in some children and may have implications for later psychological functioning. The goal should be to prevent such situations in childhood before they occur.

Learning Disability

The issue of the frequency of learning disability among deaf children often arises in contexts similar to impulsivity. If it appears that some deaf children have advantages by virtue of their use of sign language or genetics (Akamatsu, Musselman, & Zweibel, 2000), there is also some evidence that they also may be at risk for various learning disabilities. I approach this topic with some caution, as in the past many deaf children were classified as learning disabled solely on the basis of their hearing losses or their lack of spoken language skill. Perhaps as a result, the dual classification of deaf children as having both a hearing loss and a learning disability is now not even considered, even though there has been some evidence that deaf children may more likely to display the symptoms of attention deficit disorder (ADD) and related disorders. In fact, the *Education of All Handicapped Children Act* (PL 94-142) in the United States explicitly stated that the classification of a learning disability "does not include children who have learning problems which are primarily the result of visual, hearing, or motor handicaps; mental retardation; emotional disturbance; or environmental, cultural, or economic disadvantages." It therefore is difficult to obtain accurate numbers concerning the frequency of learning disability among deaf children. Most studies estimate that around 6–7 percent of deaf children have educationally relevant learning disabilities, although surveys of teachers of deaf children have yielded estimates as high as 23 percent (Mauk & Mauk, 1998).

The lack of definitive findings in the area has created difficulties for parents and professionals seeking support for deaf children. It also creates a challenge for educators and investigators seeking to clarify the complex situation involved in educating deaf children. In general, however, recent research suggests that there likely is a greater incidence of learning disability in deaf children than hearing children. Although the *nature versus nurture* origins of that risk are unclear, essentially all of the common etiologies of hearing loss described in chapter 2 are also associated with learning disabilities, even if there is not necessarily a causal connection.

Because estimates of the prevalence of learning disability among deaf children vary so widely, offering numbers from specific studies here would only contribute to the misunderstanding and confusion that already exist in the field. One colleague, however, has suggested that given the fact that deaf children's academic achievement scores lag behind their IQ scores (one definition of learning disability), "we would have to classify the majority of deaf children as learning-disabled by the time they reach mid-elementary school" (Calderon, 1998, p. 2). Such findings should be taken not as an indication of a general deficit in the population of deaf children but as a call to better understand the early contexts of development that would lead to this result and to disentangle the factors that really matter from those that do not. Only then can we improve our educational methods and our assessment tools.

The same issue arises when we consider that the demonstration of impulsive-like behavior by some deaf children may result from a developmental delay with its origins in early language deprivation. Impulsive behavior does not reflect any neurological or biological foundation, but may be based on the interaction of language and interpersonal functioning in early childhood. This is not to suggest that there are no physiological correlates of impulsivity in deaf children, but that they are the product rather than the cause of some common causal factor. The fact that deaf children rely on various visuospatial strategies in problem-solving tasks, for example, can lead to incorrect diagnoses of ADD by psychologists unfamiliar with deaf individuals.

As in the case of impulsivity, widely divergent estimates of the prevalence of learning disability, attention deficits, and hyperactivity among deaf children leave us unable to make any accurate statements in that regard. However, it appears that the diagnoses of attention deficit and hyperactivity disorder (ADHD), as well as impulsivity, have been inflated by inappropriate assessment tools and a lack of necessary and appropriate language fluencies on the part of both test administrators and deaf children. Indeed, it has been suggested that a large number of misdiagnoses of ADHD and related disorders could result from misunderstandings about deaf children's communication problems, different perceptions of behavioral or learning style, confounding medical disorders, and inappropriate school placements (Hindley & Kroll, 1998, p. 66). Although distractibility and restlessness sometimes might indicate a mood or anxiety disorder, they also can be the product of histories of boredom and frustration in the absence of effective communication.

It is possible that deaf children sometimes appear to have learning disabilities simply because they "march to a different tune," that is, they have different learning styles and ways of interacting in the classroom in academic settings (Mauk & Mauk, 1998). Importantly, these different styles also include specific strengths which, with appropriate instructional methods and support, allow deaf children to fulfill their potential even if in different ways than hearing children (Marlowe, 1991; Marschark & Lukomski, 2001). Sometimes these "different tunes" may have their origins in hidden, or not so hidden, learning disabilities, but there has been limited research on the relatively small proportion of deaf children among the population of learning disabled youth. Further, as is the case with regard to intelligence testing, there are considerable difficulties in determining whether assessments used to evaluate learning disability among deaf children are valid and reliable. When I was involved in the (largely fruitless) search for information for this section, one investigator of learning disability among deaf adults suggested:

> No one is doing any research on learning disability in deaf children. Some schools are interested in research, but there isn't anyone with research and discipline credentials who cares to or has the freedom and resources to enter that thorny field. The real repository of existing knowledge about deaf kids is not the journals or textbooks, but rather the experienced brains of school psychologists in deaf education settings. They know a great deal. For example, they know how to compensate for invalid norms and test content on tests that they need to use for learning disability assessment but that were never validated on deaf kids. They probably know a great deal more about how to spot and help deaf kids with learning disability. But, the fundamental research that needs to be done before learning disability in deaf kids is understood is not being undertaken.

So, to begin with, there is little research available that would shed light on learning disability and deaf children. Further confounding both research and education is the fact that children may have additional handicaps that obscure or delay correct identification. Because hearing loss is more easily identified than learning disability, there is a tendency to place deaf students who are suspected as having learning disabilities in programs for the deaf rather than the mainstream "and hope that the strategies developed for teaching the deaf will be effective with any other suspected problems" (Roth, 1991, p. 391). In the complex challenges of dealing with deaf children who have multiple handicaps, learning disabilities may not become apparent until educational delays are so pronounced as to be difficult to remedy. While the relegating of learning disabilities to a "second class" category of concern among deaf children may be inappropriate, it also may be that specific instructional strategies appropriate for children with learning disabilities might be generally helpful in the teaching of deaf children (i.e., rather than the reverse).

Even if deaf children do not experience learning disabilities at a much greater rate than hearing children, educational methods aimed at them might be enhanced by the borrowing of strategies that have been used effectively in educating hearing children with learning disabilities (Marschark & Lukomski, 2001). Such techniques tend to involve direct instruction, encourage processing of information in multiple levels, and use of pictorial materials, repetition, and incorporation of multisensory information, all features that seem likely to facilitate learning by deaf children. This does not mean that deaf children should be viewed as though they all are learning disabled, but rather that we should examine carefully the utility of methods which already have been shown to be effective in other domains. Thus far, this suggestion has been viewed negatively by many, as though some "guilt by association" with learning disability might brand all deaf youngsters. Nevertheless, such methods have been used to improve deaf children's reading (Ensor & Koller, 1997), and I believe the field of learning disabilities might have something to offer us.

Final Comments

Childhood and adolescence are a time of social and personality growth, emerging from interactions of children with others in their environments. Regardless of whether children are deaf or hearing, they seek the same kinds of emotional and practical support, learn the same kinds of behaviors, and are influenced by the same kinds of factors. Communication plays an important role during these years, as children learn their roles as members of a family, a gender, a community, and a culture. Deaf children who have access to other people's interactions and explanations for behaviors better understand social dynamics (and also have advantages in cognitive development). Those who have access to social rules and can consider the perspectives of others develop the moral codes of others who they try to emulate.

In early childhood, parents are the primary source of implicit and explicit teaching about social expectations. As children get older, siblings, playmates, and adults outside of the home take on greater roles in this regard. During the school years, deaf and hearing students seek to be accepted by their peer groups and adopt the values, preferences, and behaviors of children and adults who are their role models. Modeling teaches children about appropriate (and inappropriate) ways of behaving. Children are more likely to model people who are perceived as similar to them and over time become more like those models. Having higher self-esteem and a sense of control better enables children to think for themselves and make good decisions about how to act and whom to emulate.

Families play a relatively larger role in deaf children's socialization than in hearing children's socialization, if for no other reason than that deaf children are likely to have a relatively greater proportion of their social interactions with family members than are hearing children. Siblings generally have an important role in childhood, providing a safe opportunity to try out new roles and get feedback on behavior. Deaf children, in particular, benefit from siblings both emotionally and in terms of communication skills. Deaf peers in schools for the deaf or public school classrooms can play similar roles, and such social networks provide deaf children with life-long friends and social-emotional support. Schools for the deaf and separate programs do not lead deaf children away from their families, but provide them with an important kind of social support that they cannot get at home. There, they find children of various ages who are like them and who accept them as brothers and sisters. Meanwhile, deaf adults who work in schools for the deaf can serve as important role models, much like aunts and uncles, promoting accurate self-images and higher self-esteem.

Deaf students often show more behavior problems in school than hearing students. These can result from inconsistent social experiences, misunderstandings about social rules, and frustration with lack of communication. Behavior that might be referred to as impulsive, however, should not be confused with the psychological sense of impulsivity referring to problem-solving strategies. Contrary to many unsubstantiated claims, there is no evidence to suggest that deaf children or adults are any more likely than hearing peers to have impulsive cognitive styles. At the same time, better communication skills and consistent parenting seem to lead to more reflective, successful social problem solving.

Deaf children and adults also do not appear much different than hearing peers in terms of the incidence of mental health problems. More serious illnesses are equally frequent in deaf and hearing populations. Deaf people may be slightly more prone to some mild disorders, but they appear to be less prone to others. Meanwhile, full access to competent mental health services is difficult for deaf people, usually requiring the services of a sign language interpreter in addition to the barriers faced by hearing people. Perhaps most importantly, mental health professionals need to become better informed about social and cultural differences between deaf and hearing people if they are to provide effective services and avoid misdiagnoses and lost opportunities.

Acknowledgment

The 1997 version of this chapter was written in collaboration with Dr. Cristina Vaccari.

Fate takes by the hand he who will follow.
—Italian Proverb

TEN

Where Do We
Go From Here?

The preceding chapters have discussed what it means to be deaf technically, practically, and culturally. They have examined a variety of issues confronting children who grow up deaf, as well as their parents and teachers. In discussions of everything from language to laws and from education to cochlear implants, the emphasis has been on providing deaf children with access to all that they need for normal and successful lives. Beyond this, however, there is much more.

Deaf children deserve more than just text pagers, captioned films, and classes they can understand. They deserve the commitment of people around them to give them every opportunity to achieve excellence in their own ways, in their own chosen careers. They have the right to a free and appropriate public education, but they also have just as much right as hearing children to be involved in decisions that affect them. For that, they need access. I once heard an interview with the world-famous violinist Itzhak Perlman, who had polio as a child and now walks with leg braces and crutches. He was discussing access and lamented that even now he sometimes has to take freight elevators or struggle up flights of steps to reach the stage of concert halls in which he is performing. Perlman said that, for him, true access would be the freedom to walk into a public place with his family and friends when they do and through the same entrance. Understandably, he resents having to call ahead to arrange for a security guard to unlock a back door for him. Perlman asked simply for "access with dignity." Is this a society that will deny him that? How can we continue to deny such access for the millions of deaf adults and children who are deaf?

In several chapters, I have discussed past and current opportunities and hurdles encountered by people who are deaf. Although generalizations are dangerous and deaf children vary even more widely than hearing children, we have seen that most deaf children enter school already at a disadvantage relative to hearing children in language proficiency and in the knowledge that contributes to social and cognitive development. In part, these hurdles have their origins in early childhood, when late discovery of hearing losses, parents' emotional confusion, and lack of objective information can result in barriers to effective communication and to many kinds of early childhood experiences. If deaf children's needs are met, differences between them deaf and hearing children that might affect personal and academic success disappear as they get older. If those needs are not met, deaf children will face a long and uphill struggle.

Overall, deaf children are similar to hearing children in many more ways than they are different. To the extent that there are real differences, most of them relate more to issues of communication and experience than having a hearing loss. Deaf children who have early exposure to language turn out to be those who are most successful in school and in their quality of life. Throughout the book, I have placed considerable emphasis on the need for early and effective access to language. To some extent, it might appear that I have a bias toward sign language. If so, it is not a bias in favor of sign language instead of spoken language. I strongly support deaf children acquiring either mode of communication—or ideally both—depending on their early successes and circumstances. At the same time, the simple fact is that spoken language is largely inaccessible and unattainable for many young deaf children. The overwhelming preponderance of research evidence indicates that deaf children exposed to sign language from an early age are more likely to be academically and socially successful than those exposed only to spoken language. For those children who do acquire intelligible spoken language and speechreading skills, they may indeed find it a bit easier to navigate the ways of a largely hearing society. Nevertheless, most parents will assume that their child is one of those deaf children who will achieve spoken language sufficient for educational purposes, and thus language delays are all too common. Throughout the preceding chapters, I have tried to impress on readers the importance of *natural* language. In the case of children in the United States, my own reading of the available literature has led me to conclude that a combination of American Sign Language (ASL) and English are necessary to optimize the opportunities for deaf children. It does not appear that artificial systems like Signed English are sufficient to provide deaf children with access to all of the information they need to fully achieve their social and educational potentials, even if some children do very well with such systems. ASL *and* some form of English-based signing or ASL *and* cued speech seem much more likely to succeed, but the key is consistency. Unfortunately, we cannot produce both ASL and either English or cued speech at the same time. Therefore, I have suggested an emphasis on ASL first, later supplemented by other systems to facilitate reading and speech skills when children are ready for them (see Mayer & Akamatsu, 2003, for discussion with regard to the impact of such a model on literacy). Contrary to some honest misconceptions and some ill-informed claims, there is *no evidence at all* to suggest that learning sign language interferes with deaf children's learning of English or their potential for using spoken language. Children who learn sign language early generally are more, not less, competent in English reading and writing skills and more socially and emotionally competent and confident. Most importantly, parents and children need to be able to communicate effectively with each other.

Being a Parent of a Deaf Child

Throughout this book, I have described the social, language, and cognitive growth of deaf children. At every age level, we have seen that the context for learning and growth plays an essential role in making children who they are. That context will determine whether a deaf child will be satisfied with short-term success or will strive for a lifetime of excellence. Who decides what the context will be? We do. It is parents, teachers, politicians, and educational administrators who will either provide deaf children with access to excellence or deny it to them.

Generally speaking, we have seen that those children whose parents are more actively involved with them will have better success in language learning, social interactions, and academic performance. This is not just true for deaf children; it is true for all children. Similarly, virtually all children will benefit from preschool programs that provide enriched language and social experiences. I have argued for the importance of early intervention and preschool programs for deaf children and indicated that there is considerable evidence in support of them. The goal of such programs is to start as early as possible to give deaf children the kinds of experiences they need and to ensure that parents are able to be full participants in their children's growth and education. This kind of opportunity may be especially important for deaf children of hearing parents, who are less likely than other children to have such experiences at home. Language is not the only issue here, although I have argued that it is perhaps the most important one. Self-esteem, learning strategies, and social skills are also promoted in good preschool programs, and their importance should not be underestimated.

Perhaps above all else, I have argued for the need to make the educational and other experiences of deaf children as normal as possible. This conclusion is not a call for mainstreaming deaf children into regular classrooms. Concerns about the appropriateness of a separate, special environment for deaf education have been with us for over 100 years, and they are likely to be with us for some time to come. The Individuals with Disabilities Education Act (IDEA; see chapter 6) mandated that deaf children and all those with disabilities should be educated in local school classrooms to the greatest appropriate degree. But, it also recognizes that regular classrooms may be inappropriate for some deaf children. Being in a regular classroom does not necessarily provide deaf children with the same education as hearing peers. Quite the contrary; in the absence of comparable early environments and appropriate accommodations, many deaf children will be unable to gain from either the content or the context of a regular public school classroom.[1] Such a setting would be neither "normal" nor helpful.

Public school thus needs to be one option within a range of educational opportunities for deaf children. As affirmed by the United States Department of Education, the decision of which kind of school program is best for any particular child has to include a variety of considerations, some directly related to school curricula and some related to social development. Parents need to be informed and supported through that decision process, not preached to or bullied. If laws like IDEA and the Americans with Disabilities Act are to be fruitful for deaf children and deaf adults, I believe that the focus of attention must be placed prior to the classroom on early detection of hearing loss (see chapter 2), support for parents (chapter 1), availability of instruction in sign language as well as spoken language (chapter 3), and a better understanding of the skills and strategies that young deaf children will eventually bring to the classroom. The challenges facing deaf children go beyond their inability to hear, or speak, or read. Most of those problems did not develop during the school years and it is unlikely that they can be easily resolved there.

A search of the World Wide Web or the public library will yield a list of organizations and programs that might be of help or interest to parents or others involved with deaf children and to people who are deaf themselves. One would expect that organizations like the American Society for Deaf Children (www.deafchildren.org), Hands and Voices (www.handsandvoices .org), the Alexander Graham Bell Association of the Deaf and Hard of Hearing (www.agbell.org), or the National Association of the Deaf (www.nad .org) would be obvious resources for parents of deaf children. Unfortunately, they may be discovered only after a period of time in which parents did not know their child was deaf and then a longer time still while they cast around looking for good advice from people who seemed to know what they were talking about. Along they way, they will be pulled by those favoring one language orientation or another and one educational philosophy or another. Occasionally, they will be misled by those who, as the biochemist Sam Pennington once said, "may be wrong but are never uncertain."

Being a parent of a deaf child may not be easy. Particularly for first time or younger parents, changes in family life when a child is born take considerable adjustment. Finding out that your child is different from others or will have special needs can be daunting, but having a deaf child will be no less rewarding, less enjoyable, or less exciting than having a hearing child. There are some emotional and practical issues that parents will need to resolve, but they do get resolved, and we move on. Dealing with those matters requires both professional information and sharing of experiences with others who are in similar situations. For parents, such support can come from parent-infant (early intervention) programs and preschools within the community as well as from national organizations. For teachers and other professionals, such support can come from workshops and various professional development opportunities that focus on the needs of deaf students. Meanwhile, it is essential that both "basic" and "applied" research relating to deaf children continue to ask the hard questions and help to establish an agenda for change.

Recognizing that deaf children are in some ways different and in some ways the same as hearing children is an important step for educators and parents. As much as we might want them to be like hearing children, forcing deaf children into that mold does them no service and may do them harm. If deaf children are to receive help in those areas in which they need it, they must be appreciated in their own right; and we should recognize that they might need more or different educational experiences to derive the same benefits. Similarly, if they are to be allowed to develop on their own in areas in which they do not need help, we must try to allow deaf children all of the freedoms and experiences of hearing children without being overly controlling of their behavior either at home or at school. It therefore is important to keep in mind that methods for understanding the competencies of hearing children might not always be appropriate for deaf children. Deaf children are not hearing children who cannot hear, but *differences* should not be equated with *deficiencies.*

Looking back, the two themes I have most tried to emphasize are the need for early and consistent exposure to language and the importance of flexible learning strategies. Together, these tools will promote deaf children's abilities to interact with and gain from interactions with the world. This was found to be true in social as well as cognitive domains, both of which are enhanced by natural and normal experiences with other deaf adults and children, hearing adults and children, and members of their families. Both explicitly and implicitly, I have placed much of the responsibility for these needs on parents and teachers. Throughout the book, I have urged them to take an active and proactive role in deaf children's educations. Flexibility, patience, and communication skill are essential for the parents and teachers of any child. Deaf children may require a greater quantity of each of these, but the quality of the stuff is essentially the same.

Notes

Chapter 1

1. Henceforth, for convenience in writing, "English" and "American Sign Language" are used generically to refer to any spoken language and the corresponding natural sign language used in the same country or region. There is no evidence that other established sign languages have any fundamental differences that would affect children's development (although there are linguistic differences of interest to those who study languages) any more than do different spoken languages. There are some cognitive differences between children (deaf and hearing) who grow up with signed versus spoken language, and those will be of relatively minor interest here, discussed in chapter 8 and elsewhere. Issues relating to literacy and flexibility in using language are considered in chapters 7 and 8, respectively.

2. There have been several books published about the Deaf community, some written by deaf individuals and others by hearing people within the community or close to it. These works provide valuable insights into a diverse subculture that otherwise might be inaccessible to hearing people. In their book *Deaf in America,* for example, Padden and Humphries (1988) provided some of the first insights into the vibrant Deaf culture. Tucker (1995) provides a very different perspective in *The Feel of Silence,* that of a deaf person who grows up entirely within hearing culture.

3. Disagreement over issues like use of the term *deafness* reflects some of the political disagreement within the Deaf community itself. There are prominent Deaf people known for

being particularly radical, and others are known for being not "Deaf enough." Such differences of opinion are present in any group (and especially in minority groups), and for the most part I avoid dealing with them in this book. However, just as I fault some hearing professionals for not always informing parents of deaf children about the full range of options available to them, I can fault some Deaf professionals for doing the same thing.

4. It is interesting to speculate on why boys often tend to be later talkers than girls. There does not appear to be any clear biological or physical reason for this to occur. The answer might lie in the different ways in which adults treat boys and girls. Parents tend to talk to their baby girls more than their baby boys and to let the boys cry longer than the girls before trying to soothe them with soft words. Boys, in contrast, appear to have the advantage in early physical activity, and parents are more likely to playfully move their sons' arms and legs around than is the case with their ("more delicate"?) daughters. Perhaps herein lie the beginnings of gender-related differences in talkativeness and rough-and-tumble play.

5. The preference for mother's smell is an ability seen only in infants who are breast fed; bottle-fed babies do not seem to learn that distinction. Importantly, the evidence for babies being able to recognize their mothers by sight comes from hearing babies who might take advantage of the correspondence between mother's familiar voice (see chapter 4) and her appearance. It is unknown whether deaf babies show the same ability.

Chapter 2

1. Rochester's large deaf population originally derived from the presence of the historic Rochester School for the Deaf and, later, the National Technical Institute for the Deaf, a college of Rochester Institute of Technology. With such a large presence, the area is particularly "deaf-friendly" and has an active Deaf community known around the world.

2. There are a few other cities in the United States with proportionally large deaf populations, such as Riverside, California, and Hartford, Connecticut—the examples I use are those with which I am personally familiar.

3. Clearly, hearing loss is a frequent problem for older people. Thirty to 35 percent of Americans between 65 and 75 years of age, and over 40 percent of those over 75, have some degree of hearing loss, but this book is not about them.

4. Sound also can be carried through the bones of the body via *bone conduction* just as it can through solid materials outside of the body (remember the hero in old western movies putting his ear to the railroad tracks to listen for the train?). Most fetuses thus are able to hear their mothers' but not fathers' voices during the last part of pregnancy, when their heads are resting on their mothers' pelvises (see chapter 4). To demonstrate bone conduction of sound for yourself (unless you are deaf), try tapping on your teeth with the soft end of a finger.

5. The availability of such systems varies widely. While working on this chapter, for example, I discovered that Heathrow Airport in London does not have a loop system, but the Travelex currency exchange booth there does!

6. Much of the material in the following section is drawn from Spencer and Marschark (2003).

7. Unfortunately, many deaf people cannot get the full effect of large-screen films in theaters. Deaf moviegoers used to be able to pay half price for admission to a theater, on the assumption that they missed half of the film's content by not hearing the dialogue and music. Theater owners have largely abandoned that practice in the United States (although not in other countries, like Taiwan), arguing that deaf patrons take up a full seat just like hearing patrons. Several new technologies have been developed that allow deaf people to see closed captioning in movie theaters during regular film showings, but they are not yet cost-effective enough to be coming any time soon to a theater near you.

Chapter 3

1. It is noteworthy that this debate, and the suppression of gesture and sign in some settings, has been going on in deaf education for over 100 years. It is fascinating to read both sides of the argument in early issues of the *American Annals of the Deaf*, then called the *American Annals of the Deaf and Dumb* (see especially, Alexander Graham Bell's (1898/2005) classic articles on the sign-spoken language issue). Clearly, the debate is sometimes less about facts than strong beliefs about what is in the best interests of deaf children.

2. Note that this description is necessarily limited to deaf children who make use of hearing aids or do not use any assistive listening devices, because evidence concerning academic achievement and literacy in children with cochlear implants is just now emerging (see chapter 2). Preliminary data suggest that those children with implants who also sign have higher reading achievement scores than peers with implants who use only spoken language.

3. Deaf parents who use spoken language as their primary means of communication typically do not teach their deaf children to sign, but there apparently is no research available concerning the development of deaf or hearing children in such settings.

4. Saying that signs are arbitrary means that, like words, they bear no relation to the things they represent. Some words do sound like what they represent (*onomatopoetic* words like "gurgle" or "swish") and some signs look like what they represent (*iconic* signs like CAMERA or FISHING), but these are not as common as typically believed. Most units of language, however, mean what they do only by social agreement, and therefore they are different in each language. Recent studies of sign language development indicate that iconic properties underlie many early language productions, but they play a relatively minor role in language learning itself.

5. The origins of ASL in French Sign Language means that a deaf person from the United States would be more likely to understand a signer in France than in England. I experienced this when a deaf friend and I visited the French National Institute for the Deaf, in Paris. We could converse in sign fairly well with hearing and deaf people there, even though our French left much to be desired.

6. The linkage of a sign language like ASL to fingerspelling may seem a rather odd situation, because it combines a language that is explicitly not English with an English "back-up" system. This may be an indicator of the merging of ASL and its English "host," although the relevant studies have not yet been done. The use of fingerspelling also varies across both languages and geographic regions, with both ASL and Rochester, New York, being known in the Deaf community as more reliant on fingerspelling than other signed languages and places (Padden, 2006).

7. Throughout this book, English "gloss" (translations) of signs are indicated by capital letters (e.g., WORD). Fingerspelled words are indicated by hyphenated capital letters (e.g., W-O-R-D).

8. Note that I used "system" rather than "language" here. That is because such systems are not really languages in the technical (linguistic) sense. They also differ from true languages in the way they are acquired by children (taught, not learned naturally from their parents).

9. Admittedly, the NTID situation is somewhat awkward, given the documented difficulties of using spoken English and sign at the same time. NTID believes in the rights of deaf students to make their own communication choices, however, and requiring oral deaf students to sign seems no more fair than requiring signing deaf students to speak.

10. At one level, it is obvious that language is not the same as speech (witness sign language). At another, however, it is important to note that language development is not the same as spoken language production or reception. A young child may be able to speak and hear despite being in only the early stages of language development. Similarly, a deaf child may be able to speak but still be delayed in language development, or vice versa.

11. Some "oral programs" are successful because they often only accept children who appear likely to acquire spoken language. This should not be seen as dishonest, but simply an appropriate effort to help those children most likely to benefit from their methods.

12. Information in this section derives largely from several conversations with Rod G. Beattie of the Royal Institute for Deaf and Blind Children and his chapter "The oral methods and spoken language acquisition" (Beattie, 2006).

Chapter 4

1. To date, no one has provided detailed studies of deaf mothers who use spoken language, so we do not know how interactions with their young children are structured or how it affects various aspects of development.

2. One example of this occurred when a well-known televangelist and faith-healer visited Greensboro, North Carolina, while I was living there. During a revival, he brought a deaf boy and his hearing parents up on the stage to "cure him of his affliction." The preacher fired a pistol (loaded with blanks) behind the boy's head; and when he jumped, the boy was declared "healed." The child left the stage just as deaf as when he stepped onto it. If every window in a house would vibrate to a gunshot, why would the child not be expected to feel it?

3. According to an advertisement I saw in *News of the World*, an expensive mixture of garlic and honey is an effective cure for hearing loss. While I would like to joke about it, people actually buy such products. Others have their deaf children flown around in rapidly ascending and descending airplanes. So, I suppose I have to point out that such methods do not work!

4. Differences in the number of adults with whom deaf children interact can have implications far beyond social interaction. Research on hearing children's language development, for example, has shown that the variety of their experience with adults is a better predictor of vocabulary size than the variety of experience with other children (Nelson, 1973). This relation primarily reflects the fact that adults are better language models than children.

Chapter 5

1. One of the more convincing lines of argument for the pre-eminence of manual communication is that the human (or pre-human) brain developed to the point of controlling the fine muscle movements involved in use of the hands before those necessary for spoken communication. Most likely, the earlier development of hand coordination was for grasping and tool use, but eventually the predominance of tools required that the hands be freed, and manual forms of communication were replaced by simple oral forms. (Mouth tools would have been a bit harder to develop than hand tools!)

2. Pointing gestures remain in deaf children's vocabularies after they learn language, just as they remain in the vocabularies of hearing children. The important conceptual issue here is that there are two different kinds of pointing available to sign language users, one (a sign) within the language and one (a gesture) that supplements language. In the normal course of language development, however, this distinction may be of lesser importance to parents than it is to language researchers.

3. Parents who complain that their children use "baby talk" at an age when they should have already grown out of it usually have only themselves to blame. If children continue to hear such language, it will be "accepted" and will persist.

4. Examples given here are from ASL. Other sign languages may have signs for these same concepts that are more or less related to what they represent. In British Sign Language, for example, the sign CHURCH is made by showing the movement of pulling a bell-ringing rope—quite different from the more arbitrary ASL sign.

5. Even if they were not recognized by linguists as true languages until the 1960s, sign languages have been used in schools for over 200 years. Even Alexander Graham Bell, a staunch advocate of spoken language for most deaf and hard-of-hearing children, recognized that sign language might be more appropriate for children with severe to profound losses (Bell, 1898/2005).

6. Several CODAs I know report using a spoken CODA language that sounds like a spoken ASL among themselves. They also claim that it sometimes intrudes in their writing, but as far as I can tell, no investigations of this "CODA language" have been undertaken.

Chapter 6

1. Of course, those parents do not mention the fact that there are "normal" children who are equally or more disruptive in the classroom.

2. Deaf and hard-of-hearing students who have had to deal with non-interpreted classes also report suffering from related eye strain and headaches, as well as severe bouts of frustration.

3. Interpreters for spoken language, usually called "oral interpreters," provide clear and well-articulated mouth movements for students who might have reduced visual acuity or others who depend on clear and consistent oral cues for speechreading. The use of oral interpreters eliminates many potential problems in the classroom (e.g., teachers can move around more), but relatively few deaf students find them useful.

Chapter 7

1. As in previous chapters, "English" is used here only for convenience and refers to whatever spoken and written language is used by the community in which a deaf child lives. Similarly, most references to "American Sign Language" in this chapter could appropriately be replaced by any other sign language.

2. True bilingualism is rare, and most people who use ASL and English, or any two languages, are really more proficient in one language than the other. That issue does not concern us here, and the term *bilingual* will be used in its usual sense meaning relatively competent in two languages.

3. Actually, the exact correspondence between spoken and written words is illusory. The breaks between spoken words are often shorter than breaks within words, for example, making speechreading and the develop-ment of accurate speech-to-print "translation" systems extremely difficult. Issues like this create interesting problems for psychologists who study language and language learning, but they can be ignored for the present purposes.

4. Because all languages have limited numbers of elements, rearranging them is the method used to create new words. Rearranging the letters in TAP, for example, does more than just change the way the word looks and sounds (PAT, APT, PTA). The same constraint holds for words in sentences and may hold for sentences in paragraphs.

5. The many dictionary meanings of words do not include the fact that words also can be used in novel, figurative ways and still be understood by competent users of the same language. That topic is somewhat outside of the current discussion, but deaf children's use and comprehension of figurative language is described at length in chapter 8. With regard to the literal meanings of words like "bow," multiple meanings create additional problems for artificial English/sign language systems (see chapter 3).

6. As noted in chapter 3, one problem in combining ASL with either Signed English or cued speech is that you cannot be doing both at the same time. It therefore is important to carefully identify which contexts are better served by one way of communicating or another. Thus far, it appears that ASL is a better

(and more natural) route for everyday communication during the early years, while signing with English word order may be more helpful later, as a bridge to reading and writing.

7. Phonological skill also is related to the "inner voice" that we sometimes notice when we are reading. A friend who lost his hearing as a teenager tells me that he still "hears" his "inner voice." Although this issue has been investigated with regard to young adults who are deaf, there have been no studies relating to deaf children or its role in reading.

Chapter 8

1. To clarify what is meant by *culture fair* tests, consider the following example. One might expect that tests that involve the rearrangement of geometric shapes or construction of objects using blocks would be universally appropriate for testing the intelligence of young children. However, there are cultures in the world where there are very few right angles, in which geometric shapes have little relevance, and in which children do not have experience with things like Tinker Toys, Lego, or bricks. Tests involving such materials therefore would not be measuring the same things for these children as they would for children living in New York City. Thus, the tests may not be culture fair for individuals without particular experiences.

2. The suggestion that "deaf" and "hearing" people's brains may be different is not meant metaphorically. We know, for example, that rats raised in "rich" environments with objects and places to explore have many more interconnections in their brains than rats that are raised in relatively "sterile" environments. Similar differences would be expected in human brains. In addition, different parts of the brain will be used more or less in particular situations depending on the kinds and amounts of information they have encountered in the past, and differing brain activity in some areas has been identified bewteen individuals raised with spoken versus signed languages.

3. "Verbal" should not be confused with "vocal" here. The use of "verbal" in "verbal intelligence" refers to language.

4. The important ingredient here most likely is not the one-on-one situation per se, but its promotion of greater "time on task" activity. Traditionally, in-depth, continued attention to communication and educational topics was maximized for deaf students through personal tutors. Computers in education now may provide a far less expensive alternative.

5. Sorry, dads, there is nothing wrong with you, it is just that almost all the research has involved mothers because they typically have the greater care-giving responsibility.

Chapter 9

1. Identification and modeling are the sources of behaviors that underlie stereotypes: The more a child feels like an X, the more she will try to act like an X and seek out other Xs to socialize with and have as friends.

2. Nationally, almost 80 percent of deaf children have hearing siblings only, while almost 10 percent have both deaf and hearing siblings.

3. "Egocentric" here is meant in the psychological sense of being self-oriented. When used in its everyday sense, it implies arrogance or vanity. In its developmental sense, it refers to young children's frequent inability to understand that the world may look different to other people. Thus they often cannot consider the feelings of others or even understand that a visual scene looks different from different vantage points. The simplest way to demonstrate this is to show a 2-year old both sides of a card that has, for example, a dog on one side and a cat on the other. If you hold it up so that the dog is facing him, he can tell you that he sees the dog; but when you ask what *you* see, he often will say "dog" as well (see also the discussion of *theory of mind* in chapter 8).

4. As difficult and embarrassing as temper tantrums might be in a public place, most psychologists suggest simply removing the child from the situation for a "time out." Punishing a child who is already "wound up" usually makes the situation worse. Ignoring the child might work, but parents' embarrassment often pushes them to the point where they resort to physical punishment anyway.

5. As described earlier, there are a variety of differences between those deaf children who are involved in early intervention programs and those who are not (Calderon & Greenberg, 1997). We therefore should not draw any simplistic conclusions from these findings.

Chapter 10

1. Interestingly, in American Sign Language, "public school" is signed HEARING SCHOOL; the adjective "hearing" literally is signed SPEAKING (near the mouth, whereas the verb HEARING is signed near the ear).

References

Akamatsu, C. T. (1988). Instruction in text structure: Meta-cognitive strategy instruction for literacy development in deaf students. *ACEHI/ACEDA, 14,* 13–32.

Akamatsu, C. T., Musselman, C., & Zweibel, A. (2000). Nature vs. nurture in the development of cognition in deaf people. In P. Spencer, C. Erting, & M. Marschark (Eds.), *Development in context: The deaf child in the family and at school* (pp. 255–274). Mahwah, NJ: Erlbaum.

Aldersley, S. (2002). The courts and "least restrictive environment." *Journal of Deaf Studies and Deaf Education, 7,* 189–199.

Alegria, J., & Lechat, J. (2005). Phonological processing in deaf children: When lipreading and cues are incongruent. *Journal of Deaf Studies and Deaf Education, 11,* 122–133.

Allen, T. E., & Osborne, T. (1984). Academic integration of hearing-impaired students: Demographic, handicapping, and achievement factors. *American Annals of the Deaf, 129,* 100–113.

Americans With Disabilities Act, P.L. 101–336, 42 U.S.C. §12101 *et seq.*

Anderson, D., & Reilly, J. (2002). The MacArthur Communicative Development Inventory: Normative data for American Sign Language. *Journal of Deaf Studies and Deaf Education, 7,* 83–106.

Andrews, J., & Taylor, N. (1987). From sign to print: A case study of picture book "reading" between mother and child. *Sign Language Studies, 56,* 261–271.

Antia, S. D. (1982). Social interaction of partially mainstream hearing-impaired children. *American Annals of the Deaf, 127*, 18–25.

Antia, S. D., & Dittillo, D. A. (1998). A comparison of the peer social behavior of children who are Deaf/hard of hearing and hearing. *Journal of Children's Communication Development, 19*, 1–10.

Antia, S. D., & Kreimeyer, K. (2003). Peer interactions of deaf and hard of hearing children. In M. Marschark & P. E. Spencer (Eds.), *Oxford handbook of deaf studies, language, and education* (pp. 164–176). New York: Oxford University Press.

Antia, S. D., Stinson, M. S., & Gaustad, M. G. (2002). Developing membership in the education of deaf and hard of hearing students in inclusive settings. *Journal of Deaf Studies and Deaf Education, 7*, 214–229.

Archbold S. M., Nikolopoulos T. P., O'Donoghue G. M., & White, A. (2006, April). Reading abilities after cochlear implantation. Paper presented at the British Cochlear Implant Group annual academic meeting, London.

Armstrong, D. F. (1999). *Original signs: Gesture, sign and the sources of language.* Washington, DC: Gallaudet University Press.

Arnos, K. S., & Pandya, A. (2003). Advances in the genetics of deafness. In M. Marschark & P. E. Spencer (Eds.), *Oxford handbook of deaf studies, language, and education* (pp. 392–405). New York: Oxford University Press.

Bachara, G. H., Raphael, J., & Phelan, W. J., III. (1980). Empathy development in deaf preadolescents. *American Annals of the Deaf, 125*, 38–41.

Banks, J., Gray, C., & Fyfe, R. (1990). The written recall of printed stories by severely deaf children. *British Journal of Educational Psychology, 60*, 192–206.

Bartlett, D. E. (1850). The acquisition of language. *American Annals of the Deaf and Dumb, 3(1)*, 83–92.

Bates, E., Benigni, L., Bretherton, I., Camaioni, L., & Volterra, V. (1977). From gesture to the first word: On cognitive and social prerequisites. In M. Lewis and L. A. Rosenblum (Eds.), *Interaction, conversation, and the development of language* (pp. 247–308). New York: Academic Press.

Beadle, E. A. R., McKinley, D. J., Nikolopoulos, T. P., Brough, J., O'Donoghue, G. M., & Archbold, S.M. (2005). Long-term functional outcomes and academic-occupational status in implanted children after 10 to 14 years of cochlear implant use. *Otology & Neurotology, 26*, 1152–1160.

Beattie, R. (2006). The oral methods and spoken language acquisition. In P. E. Spencer & M. Marschark (Eds.), *Advances in the spoken language development of deaf and hard-of-hearing children* (pp. 103–135). New York: Oxford University Press.

Bell, A. G. (1898/2005). The question of sign-language and the utility of signs in the instruction of the deaf. Washington, DC: Sanders Printing Office. Reprinted in *Journal of Deaf Studies and Deaf Education, 10*, 111–121.

Bertram, B. (2004). Cochlear implantation for children with hearing loss and multiple disabilities: An evaluation from an educator's perspective. *Volta Review, 104*, 349–359.

Bilingual Education Act, 20 U.S.C. §3001–3304.

Black, P. A. & Glickman, N. S. (2006) Demographics, psychiatric diagnoses, and other characteristics of north american deaf and hard-of-hearing inpatients. *Journal of Deaf Studies and Deaf Education, 11*, 303–321.

Bodner-Johnson, B. (1986). The family environment and achievement of deaf students: A discriminant analysis. *Exceptional Children, 52,* 443–449.

Brasel, K., & Quigley, S. P. (1977). Influence of certain language and communicative environments in early childhood on the development of language in deaf individuals. *Journal of Speech and Hearing Research, 20,* 95–107.

Brown, P. M., & Nott, P. (2003). Family-centered practice in early intervention for oral language development: Philosophy, methods, and results. In P. E. Spencer & M. Marschark (Eds.), *Advances in the spoken language development of deaf and hard-of-hearing children* (pp. 136–165). New York: Oxford University Press.

Caccamise, F., Blaisdell, R., & Meath-Lang, B. (1977). Hearing impaired persons' simultaneous reception of information under live and two visual motion media conditions. *American Annals of the Deaf, 122,* 339–343.

Calderon, R. (1998). Learning disability, neuropsychology, and deaf youth: Theory, research, and practice. *Journal of Deaf Studies and Deaf Education, 3,* 1–3.

Calderon, R., & Greenberg, M. T. (1993). Considerations in the adaptation of families with school-aged deaf children. In M. Marschark and M. D. Clark (Eds.), *Psychological perspectives on deafness* (pp. 27–48). Hillsdale, NJ: Erlbaum.

Calderon, R., & Greenberg, M. (1997). The effectiveness of early intervention for deaf children and children with hearing loss. In M. J. Guralnik (Ed.), *The effectiveness of early intervention* (pp. 455–482). Baltimore: Paul H. Brookes.

Calderon, R., & Greenberg, M. (2003). Social and emotional development of deaf children: Family, school, and program effects. In M. Marschark & P. E. Spencer (Eds.), *Oxford handbook of deaf studies, language, and education* (pp. 177–189). New York: Oxford University Press.

Capelli, M., Daniels, T., Durieux-Smith, A., McGrath, P. J., & Neuss, D. (1995). Social development of children with hearing impairments who are integrated into general education classrooms. *Volta Review, 97,* 197–208.

Chamberlain, C., & Mayberry, R. I. (2000). Theorizing about the relationship between ASL and reading. In C. Chamberlain, J. Morford & R. I. Mayberry, (Eds.), *Language acquisition by eye* (pp. 221–260). Mahwah, NJ: Erlbaum.

Christiansen, J., & Leigh, I. (2002). *Cochlear implants in children: Ethics and choices.* Washington DC: Gallaudet University Press.

Cokely, D. (1990). The effectiveness of three means of communication in the college classroom. *Sign Language Studies, 69,* 415–439.

Cole, E., & Paterson, M. (1984). Assessment and treatment of phonologic disorders in the hearing-impaired. In J. Castello (Ed.), *Speech disorders in children* (pp. 93–127). San Diego, CA: College Hill Press.

Cone-Wesson, B. (2003). Screening and assessment of hearing loss in infants. In M. Marschark & P. E. Spencer (Eds.), *Oxford handbook of deaf studies, language, and education* (pp. 420–433). New York: Oxford University Press.

Conrad, R. (1979). *The deaf school child: Language and cognition.* London: Harper & Row.

Cornelius, G., & Hornett, D. (1990). The play behavior of hearing-impaired kindergarten children. *American Annals of the Deaf, 135,* 316–321.

Courtin, C. (2000). The impact of sign language on the cognitive development of deaf children: The case of theory of mind. *Journal of Deaf Studies and Deaf Education 5,* 266–276.

Courtin, C., & Melot, A. M. (1998). Development of theories of mind in deaf children. In M. Marschark & M. D. Clark, (Eds.), *Psychological perspectives on deafness, Vol. 2* (pp. 79–102). Mahwah, NJ: Erlbaum.

DeCaro, P., & Emerton, R. G. (1978). *A cognitive-developmental investigation of moral reasoning in a deaf population.* Paper Series, Department of Research and Development, National Technical Institute for the Deaf, Rochester, New York.

DeCasper, A. J., & Spence, M. J. (1986). Prenatal maternal speech influences newborns' perception of speech sounds. *Infant Behavior and Development, 9,* 133–150.

Desselle, D. D. (1994). Self-esteem, family climate, and communication patterns in relation to deafness. *American Annals of the Deaf, 139,* 322–328.

Detterman, D. K., & Thompson, L. A. (1997). What is so special about special education? *American Psychologist, 52,* 1082–1090.

deVilliers, J., Bibeau, L., Ramos, E., & Gatty, J. (1993). Gestural communication in oral deaf mother-child pairs: Language with a helping hand? *Applied Psycholinguistics, 14,* 319–347.

Education of All Handicapped Children Act, 20 U.S.C. §1400 *et seq.*

Einstein, A. (1948). Foreword. In L. Barnett, *The universe and Dr. Einstein.* New York: William Morrow.

Emmorey, K. (2002). *Language, cognition, and the brain.* Mahwah, NJ: Erlbaum.

Ensor, A. D., II, & Koller J. R. (1997). The effect of the method of repeated readings on the reading rate and word recognition accuracy of deaf adolescents. *Journal of Deaf Studies and Deaf Education, 2,* 61–70.

Everhart, V. S., & Marschark, M. (1988). Linguistic flexibility in signed and written language productions of deaf children. *Journal of Experimental Child Psychology, 46,* 174–193.

Ewoldt, C. (1986). What does "reading" mean? *Perspectives for Teachers of the Hearing Impaired, 4,* 10–13.

Ewoldt, C., Israelite, N., Dodds, R. (1992). The ability of deaf students to understand text: A comparison of the perceptions of teachers and students. *American Annals of the Deaf, 137,* 351–361

Fox, S. (1994). Metacognitive strategies in a college world literature course. *American Annals of the Deaf, 139,* 506–511.

Francis, H., Koch, M., Wyatt, R., & Niparko, J. (1999). Trends in educational placement and cost-benefit considerations in children with cochlear implants. *Archives of Otolaryngology Head and Neck Surgery, 125,* 499–505.

Gallaudet Research Institute. (December, 2003). *Regional and national summary report of data from the 2002–2003 annual survey of deaf and hard of hearing children and youth.* Washington, DC: GRI, Gallaudet University.

Gallaudet Research Institute. (2006). How many deaf people are there in the United States? http://gri.gallaudet.edu/Demographics/deaf-US.php (retrieved August 1, 2006).

Geers, A. E. (2003). Predictors of reading skill development in children with early cochlear implantations. *Ear & Hearing, 24*, 59–68.

Geers, A. E. (2004). *Speech, language, and reading skills after early cochlear implantation. Archives of Otolaryngology—Head and Neck Surgery,*130, 634–638.

Geers, A. E. (2006). Spoken language in children with cochlear implants. In P. E. Spencer & M. Marschark (Eds.), *Advances in the spoken language development of deaf and hard-of-hearing children* (pp. 244–270). New York: Oxford University Press.

Geers, A. E., & Moog, J. S. (1989). Factors predictive of the development of literacy in profoundly hearing-impaired adolescents. *Volta Review, 91,* 69–86.

Gray, C. D., Hosie, J. A., Russell, P. A., & Ormel, E. A. (2001). Emotional development in deaf children: Facial expressions, display rules, and theory of mind. In M. D. Clark, M. Marschark, & M. Karchmer (Eds.), *Context, cognition, and deafness* (pp. 135–160). Washington, DC: Gallaudet University Press.

Greenberg, M., Calderon, R., & Kusché, C. (1984). Early intervention using simultaneous communication with deaf infants: The effect on communication development. *Child Development, 55,* 607–616.

Greenberg, M. T., & Kusché, C. A. (1998). Preventive intervention for school-age deaf children: The PATHS curriculum. *Journal of Deaf Studies and Deaf Education, 3,* 49–63.

Gregory, S. (1976). *The deaf child and his family.* New York: Halsted Press.

Griswold, L. E., & Commings, J. (1974). The expressive vocabulary of preschool deaf children. *American Annals of the Deaf, 119,* 16–28.

Hamzavi, J., Baumgarner, W. D., Egelierler, B., Franz, P., Schenk, B., & Gstoettner, W. (2000). Follow-up of cochlear implanted handicapped children. *International Journal of Pediatric Otorhinolaryngology, 56,* 169–174.

Hanson, V. L., Shankweiler, D., & Fischer, F. W. (1983). Determinants of spelling ability in deaf and hearing adults: Access to linguistic structure. *Cognition, 14,* 323–344.

Henggeler, S. W., Watson, S. M., & Cooper, P. F. (1984). Verbal and nonverbal maternal controls in hearing mother-deaf child interaction. *Journal of Applied Developmental Psychology, 5,* 319–329.

Hindley, P., & Kroll, L. (1998). Theoretical and epidemiological aspects of attention deficit and overactivity and deaf children. *Journal of Deaf Studies and Deaf Education, 3,* 64–62.

Hurwitz, T. A., & Hurwitz, V. T. (2004, August). Creating a language-rich environment: The experiences of deaf parents raising one hard-of-hearing child and one deaf child. Paper presented at the Prague English Conference, Budapest.

Individuals With Disabilities Education Act, 20 U.S.C §1400 *et seq.*

Jensema, C. J., & Trybus, R. J. (1978). *Communication patterns and educational achievement of hearing impaired students.* Washington, DC: Gallaudet College Office of Demographic Studies.

Johnson, K. (1991). Miscommunication in interpreted classroom interaction. *Sign Language Studies, 70,* 1–34.

Johnston, T. (2005). In one's own image: Ethics and the reproduction of deafness. *Journal of Deaf Studies and Deaf Education, 10,* 426–441.

Jones, B. E. (2005). Competencies of K-12 educational interpreters: What we need versus what we have. In E. A. Winston (Ed.), *Educational interpreting: How it can succeed* (pp. 113–131). Washington, DC: Gallaudet University Press.

Jones, B. E., Clark, G., & Stoltz, D. (1997). Characteristics and practices of sign language interpreters in inclusive education programs. *Exceptional Children, 63*(2), 257–268.

Karchmer, M. A., & Mitchell, R. E. (2003). Demographic and achievement characteristics of deaf and hard-of-hearing students. In M. Marschark & P. E. Spencer (Eds.), *Oxford handbook of deaf studies, language, and education* (pp. 21–37). New York: Oxford University Press.

King, S. J., DeCaro, J. J., Karchmer, M. K., & Cole, K. J. (2001). *College and career programs for deaf students* (11th ed.). Washington, DC: Gallaudet University Press.

Kluwin, T., & Moores, D. F. (1985). The effect of integration on the achievement of hearing-impaired adolescents. *Exceptional Children, 52,* 153–160.

Knoors, H., & Vervloed, M. P. J. (2003). Educational programming for deaf children with multiple disabilities: Accommodating special needs. In M. Marschark & P. E. Spencer (Eds.), *Oxford handbook of deaf studies, language, and education* (pp. 82–94). New York: Oxford University Press.

Koester, L. S., Brooks, L., & Traci, M. A. (2000). Tactile contact by deaf and hearing mothers during face-to-face interactions with their infants. *Journal of Deaf Studies and Deaf Education, 5,* 127–139

Kusché, C. A., & Greenberg, M. T. (1983). Evaluative understanding and role-taking ability: A comparison of deaf and hearing children. *Child Development, 54,* 141–147.

Lane, H. (2005). Ethnicity, ethics, and the Deaf-World. *Journal of Deaf Studies and Deaf Education, 10,* 291–310.

Lang, H. G. (2000). *A phone of our own: The deaf insurrection against Ma Bell.* Washington, DC: Gallaudet University Press.

Lang, H. G. (2003). Perspectives on the history of deaf education. In M. Marschark & P. E. Spencer (Eds.), *Oxford handbook of deaf studies, language, and education* (pp. 9–20). New York: Oxford University Press.

Lang, H. G., & Meath-Lang, B. (1995). *Deaf persons in the arts and sciences: A biographical dictionary.* Westport, CT: Greenwood Press.

LaSasso, C. J., & Metzger, M. A. (1998). An alternative route for preparing deaf children for BiBi programs: The home language as L1 and cued speech for conveying traditionally-spoken languages. *Journal of Deaf Studies and Deaf Education, 3,* 265–289.

Lederberg, A. R. (1991). Social interaction among deaf preschoolers: The effects of language ability and age. *American Annals of the Deaf, 136,* 35–59.

Lederberg, A., & Mobley, C. (1990). The effect of hearing impairment on the quality of attachment and mother-toddler interaction. *Child Development, 61,* 1596–1604.

Lederberg, A. R., Prezbindowski, A. K. & Spencer, P. E. (2000). Word learning skills of deaf preschoolers: The development of novel mapping and rapid word learning strategies. *Child Development, 71,* 1571–1585.

Leigh, G. R. (1995). *Teachers' use of the Australasian Signed English system for simultaneous communication with their hearing-impaired students.* Unpublished doctoral dissertation, Monash University, Melbourne, Australia.

Leigh, I. W., & Pollard, R. Q., Jr. (2003). Mental health and deaf adults. In M. Marschark & P. E. Spencer (Eds.), *Oxford handbook of deaf studies, language, and education* (pp. 203–215). New York: Oxford University Press.

Leigh, I. W., Robins, C. J., Welkowitz, J., & Bond, R. N. (1989). Toward greater understanding of depression in deaf individuals. *American Annals of the Deaf, 134,* 249–254.

Leybaert, J. (1993). Reading in the deaf: The roles of phonological codes. In M. Marschark & M. D. Clark (Eds.), *Psychological perspectives on deafness* (pp. 269–310). Mahwah, NJ: Erlbaum.

Leybaert, J., & Alegria, J. (2003). The role of cued speech and language development of deaf children. In M. Marschark & P. E. Spencer (Eds.), *Oxford handbook of deaf studies, language, and education* (pp. 261–274). New York: Oxford University Press.

Lichtenstein, E. (1998). The relationships between reading processes and English skills of deaf college students. *Journal of Deaf Studies and Deaf Education, 3,* 80–134.

Luetke-Stahlman, B. (1990). Types of instructional input as predictors of reading achievement for hearing-impaired students. In C. Lucas (Ed.), *Sign language research* (pp. 325–336). Washington, DC: Gallaudet University.

Marlowe, B. (1991). Learning disabilities and deafness: Do short-term sequential memory deficits provide the key? In D. S. Martin (Ed.) *Advances in cognition, education, and deafness* (pp. 279–288). Washington DC: Gallaudet University Press.

Marmor, G., & Petitto, L. (1979). Simultaneous communication in the classroom: How well is English grammar represented? *Sign Language Studies, 23,* 99–136.

Marschark, M. (1993a). Origins and interactions in language, cognitive, and social development of deaf children. In M. Marschark & M. D. Clark (Eds.), *Psychological perspectives on deafness* (pp. 7–26). Hillsdale, NJ: Erlbaum.

Marschark, M. (1993b). *Psychological development of deaf children.* New York: Oxford University Press.

Marschark, M. (1994). Gesture and sign. *Applied Psycholinguistics, 15,* 209–236.

Marschark, M. (2003). Cognitive functioning in deaf adults and children. In M. Marschark & P. E. Spencer (Eds.), *Oxford handbook of deaf studies, language, and education* (pp. 464–477). New York: Oxford University Press.

Marschark, M. (2005a). Developing deaf children or deaf children developing? In D. Power & G. Leigh (Eds.), *Educating deaf students: Global perspectives* (pp. 13–26). Washington, DC: Gallaudet University Press.

Marschark, M. (2005b). Metaphor in sign language and sign language users: A window into relations of language and thought. In H. Colston & A. N. Katz (Eds.), *Figurative language comprehension: Social and cultural influences* (pp. 309–334). Mahwah, NJ: Erlbaum.

Marschark, M., & Clark. M. D. (1987). Linguistic and nonlinguistic creativity of deaf children. *Developmental Review, 7,* 22–38.

Marschark, M., Convertino, C., & LaRock, D. (2006). Optimizing academic performance of deaf students: Access, opportunities, and outcomes. In D. F. Moores & D. S. Martin (Eds.), *Deaf learners: New developments in curriculum and instruction.* Washington, DC: Gallaudet University Press.

Marschark, M., Convertino, C. M., Macias, G., Monikowski, C. M., Sapere, P., & Seewagen, R. (2006). Understanding communication among deaf students who sign and speak: A trivial pursuit? Manuscript submitted for publication.

Marschark, M., Convertino, C., McEvoy, C., & Masteller, A. (2004). Organization and use of the mental lexicon by deaf and hearing individuals. *American Annals of the Deaf, 149,* 51–61.

Marschark, M., De Beni, R., Polazzo, M. G., & Cornoldi, C. (1993). Deaf and hearing-impaired adolescents' memory for concrete and abstract prose: Effects of relational and distinctive information. *American Annals of the Deaf, 138,* 31–39.

Marschark, M., & Everhart, V. S. (1999). Problem solving by deaf and hearing children: Twenty questions. *Deafness and Education International, 1,* 63–79.

Marschark, M., Green, V., Hindmarsh, G., & Walker, S. (2000). Understanding theory of mind in children who are deaf. *Journal of Child Psychology and Psychiatry, 41,* 1067–1074.

Marschark, M., Lang, H. G., & Albertini, J. A. (2002). *Educating deaf students: From research to practice.* New York: Oxford University Press.

Marschark, M., Leigh, G., Sapere, P., Burnham, D., Convertino, C. M., Stinson, M., Knoors, H., Vervloed, M. P. J., & Noble, W. (2006). Benefits of sign language interpreting and text alternatives to classroom learning by deaf students. *Journal of Deaf Studies and Deaf Education, 11,* 421–437.

Marschark, M., LePoutre, D., & Bement, L. (1998). Mouth movement and signed communication. In R. Campbell & B. Dodd (Eds.), *Hearing by eye II: The psychology of speechreading and auditory-visual speech* (pp. 243–264). London: Taylor & Francis.

Marschark, M., & Lukomski, J. (2001). Understanding language and learning in deaf children. In M. D. Clark, M. Marschark, & M. Karchmer (Eds.), *Cognition, context, and deafness* (pp. 71–86). Washington, DC: Gallaudet University Press.

Marschark, M., Mouradian, V., & Halas, M. (1994). Discourse rules in the language productions of deaf and hearing children. *Journal of Experimental Child Psychology, 57,* 89–107.

Marschark, M., Pelz, J., Convertino, C., Sapere, P., Arndt, M. E., & Seewagen, R. (2005). Classroom interpreting and visual information processing in mainstream education for deaf students: Live or Memorex? *American Educational Research Journal, 42,* 727–762.

Marschark, M., Rhoten, C., & Fabich, M. (2006). Ethics and deafness in the 21st century: Research, pedagogy, and politics. In M. Hintermair (Ed.), *Ethik und Hörschädigung: Reflexionen über gelingendes Leben unter erschwerten Bedingungen in unsicheren Zeiten* [*Ethics and deafness: Reflections on living a life under difficult conditions in insecure times*]. Heidelburg: Median-Verlag.

Marschark, M., & Spencer, P. E. (2006). Understanding spoken language development of deaf and hard-of-hearing children. In P. E. Spencer & M. Marschark (Eds.), *Advances in the spoken language development of deaf and hard-of-hearing children* (pp. 3–21). New York: Oxford University Press.

Marschark, M., West, S. A., Nall, S. L., & Everhart, V. (1986). Development of creative language devices in signed and oral production. *Journal of Experimental Child Psychology, 41,* 534–550.

Masataka, N. (2003). *The onset of language.* Cambridge: Cambridge University Press.

Massaro, D. W. (2006). A computer-animated tutor for language learning: Research and applications. In P. E. Spencer & M. Marschark (Eds.), *Advances in the spoken language development of deaf and hard-of-hearing children* (pp. 212–243). New York: Oxford University Press.

Mauk, G. W., & Mauk, P. P. (1998). Considerations, conceptualizations, and challenges in the study of concomitant learning disabilities among children and adolescents who are deaf or hard of hearing. *Journal of Deaf Studies and Deaf Education, 3,* 15–34.

Maxwell, M. (1984). A deaf child's natural development of literacy. *Sign Language Studies,* 44, 191–224.

Mayer, C., & Akamatsu, C. T. (2003). Bilingualism and literacy. In M. Marschark & P. E. Spencer (Eds.), *Oxford handbook of deaf studies, language, and education* (pp. 136–147). New York: Oxford University Press.

Mayer, C., & Wells, G. (1996). Can the linguistic interdependence theory support a bilingual-bicultural model of literacy education for deaf students? *Journal of Deaf Studies and Deaf Education, 1,* 93–107.

Mayer, C., & Wells, G. (1996). Can the linguistic interdependence theory support a bilingual-bicultural model of literacy education for deaf students? *Journal of Deaf Studies and Deaf Education, 1,* 93–107.

McEvoy, C., Marschark, M., & Nelson, D. L. (1999). Comparing the mental lexicons of deaf and hearing individuals. *Journal of Educational Psychology, 91,* 1–9.

McKirdy, L. S., & Blank, M. (1982). Dialogue in deaf and hearing preschoolers. *Journal of Speech and Hearing Research, 25,* 487–499.

Meadow, K. P. (1976). Personality and social development of deaf people. *Journal of Rehabilitation of the Deaf, 9,* 1–12.

Meadow-Orlans, K. P., Spencer, P. E., & Koester, L. S. (2004). *The world of deaf infants.* New York: Oxford University Press.

Meier, R. P., & Newport, E. L. (1990). Out of the hands of babes: On a possible sign advantage in language acquisition. *Language, 66,* 1–23.

Minnett, A., Clark, K., & Wilson, G. (1994). Play behavior and communication between deaf and hard of hearing children and their hearing peers in an integrated preschool. *American Annals of the Deaf, 139,* 420–429.

Mitchell, R. E., & Karchmer, M. A. (2004). Chasing the mythical ten percent: Parental hearing status of deaf and hard of hearing students in the United States. *Sign Language Studies, 4,* 138–163.

Moeller, M. P. (2000). Early intervention and language development in children who are deaf and hard of hearing. *Pediatrics, 106*(3), 1–9.

Mohay, H., Milton, L., Hindmarsh, G., & Ganley, K. (1998). Deaf mothers as communication models for hearing families with deaf children. In A. Weisel, (Ed.), *Issues unresolved: New perspectives on language and deaf education* (pp. 76–87). Washington, DC: Gallaudet University Press.

Moores, D. F. (2001). *Educating the deaf: Psychology, principles, and practices.* Boston: Houghton Mifflin.

Musselman, C., & Churchill, A. (1993). Maternal conversational control and the development of deaf children: A test of the stage hypothesis. *First Language, 13,* 271–290.

National Institutes of Health (1995). *National research strategic plan.* Washington, DC: National Institute on Deafness and Other Communication Disorders.

Nelson, K. (1973). Structure and strategy in learning to talk. *Monograph of the Society for Research and Child Development, 38*(149).

Newport, E. L. (1993). Maturational constraints on language learning. In P. Bloom (Ed.), *Language acquisition: Core readings* (pp. 543–560). Cambridge, MA: MIT Press.

No Child Left Behind Act, 20 U.S.C. §6301 *et seq.*

Notice of Policy Guidance on Deaf Students' Educational Services, 57 Fed. Reg. 49274–49276 (October 30, 1992).

Odom, P. B., Blanton, R. I., & Laukhuf, C. (1973). Facial expressions and interpretation of emotion-arousing situations in deaf and hearing children. *Journal of Abnormal Child Psychology, 1,* 139–151.

Office for Civil Rights (2006). Deaf students education services. *http://www.ed .gov/about/offices/list/ocr/docs/hq9806.html.* (Retrieved August 4, 2006.)

Oller, D. K. (2006). Vocal language development and deaf infants: New challenges. In P. E. Spencer & M. Marschark (Eds.), *Advances in the spoken language development of deaf and hard-of-hearing children* (pp. 22–41). New York: Oxford University Press.

Orlansky, M. D., & Bonvillian, J. D. (1984). The role of iconicity in early sign language acquisition. *Journal of Speech and Hearing Disorders, 49,* 287–292.

Oxford English Dictionary (2nd ed.). (1989). Oxford: Clarendon Press.

Padden, C. (2006). Learning to fingerspell twice: Young signing children's acquisition of fingerspelling. In B. Schick, M. Marschark, & P. E. Spencer (Eds.), *Advances in the sign language development of deaf children* (pp. 189–201). New York: Oxford University Press.

Padden, C., & Humphries, T. (1988). *Deaf in America.* Cambridge, MA: Harvard University Press.

Padden, C. A., & Ramsey, C. (1998). Reading ability in signing deaf children. *Topics in Language Disorders, 18*(4), 30–46.

Padden, C. A., & Ramsey, C. (2000). American Sign Language and reading ability in deaf children. In C. Chamberlain, J. P. Morford, & R. I Mayberry (Eds.), *Language acquisition by eye* (pp. 165–190). Mahwah, NJ: Erlbaum.

Paul, P. (1998). *Literacy and deafness: The development of reading, writing, and literate thought.* Boston: Allyn and Bacon.

Paulesu, E., Démonet, J.-F., Fazio, F., McCrory, E., Chanoine, V., Brunswick, N., et al. (2001). Dyslexia: Cultural diversity and biological unity. *Science, 291,* 2165–2167.

Peterson, C. C., & Siegal, M. (1995). Deafness, conversation, and theory of mind. *Journal of Child Psychology and Psychiatry, 36,* 457–474.

Petitto, L. A. (1987). On the autonomy of language and gesture: Evidence from the acquisition of personal pronouns in American Sign Language. *Cognition, 27,* 1–52.

Power, D., & Hyde, M. (1997). Multisensory and unisensory approaches to communicating with deaf children. *European Journal of Psychology and Education, 12,* 449–464.

Power, M. R., Power, D. & Horstmanshof, L. (2007). Deaf people communicating via SMS, TTY, relay service, fax and computers in Australia. *Journal of Deaf Studies and Deaf Education, 12.*

Powers, S. (1999). The educational attainments of deaf students in mainstream programs in England. *American Annals of the Deaf, 144,* 261–269.

Proksch, J., & Bavelier, D. (2002). Changes in the spatial distribution of visual attention after early deafness. *Journal of Cognitive Neuroscience, 14,* 687–701.

Quigley, S. P., Power, D., & Steinkamp, M. (1977). The language structure of deaf children. *Volta Review, 79,* 73–84.

Rainer, J. D., Altshuler, K. Z., Kallman, F. J., & Deming, W. E. (1963). *Family and mental health problems in a deaf population.* New York: New York State Psychiatric Institute.

Rehabilitation Act (as amended), 29 U.S.C. §701 *et seq.*

Richardson, J. T. E., Long, G. L., & Woodley, A. (2004). Students with an undisclosed hearing loss: A challenge for academic access, progress, and success? *Journal of Deaf Studies and Deaf Education, 9.* 427–441.

Risley, B., & Hart, T. R. (1995). *Meaningful differences in the everyday experience of young American children.* Baltimore: Paul H. Brookes.

Ritter-Brinton, K. (1993). Families in evaluation: A review of the American literature in deaf education. *Association of Canadian Educators of the Hearing Impaired, 19,* 3–13.

Roth, V. (1991). Students with learning disabilities and hearing impairment: Issues for the secondary and postsecondary teacher. *Journal of Learning Disabilities, 24,* 391–397.

Sass-Lehrer, M., & Bodner-Johnson, B. (2003). Early intervention: Current approaches to family-centered programming. In M. Marschark & P. E. Spencer (Eds.), *Oxford handbook of deaf studies, language, and education* (pp. 65–81). New York: Oxford University Press.

Schick, B. (2003). The development of American Sign Language and manually coded English systems. In M. Marschark & P. E. Spencer (Eds.), *Oxford handbook of deaf studies, language, and education* (pp. 219–231). New York: Oxford University Press.

Schick, B. (2006). Acquiring a visually motivated language: Evidence from diverse learners. In B. Schick, M. Marschark, & P. E. Spencer (Eds.),

Advances in the sign language development of deaf children (pp. 102–134). New York: Oxford University Press.

Schick, B., Williams, K., Bolster, L. (1999). Skill levels of educational interpreters working in public schools. *Journal of Deaf Studies and Deaf Education, 4,* 144–155.

Schirmer, B. R., & Williams, C. (2003). Approaches to teaching reading. In M. Marschark & P. E. Spencer (Eds.), *Oxford handbook of deaf studies, language, and education* (pp. 110–122). New York: Oxford University Press.

Siegel, L. (2002). The argument for a constitutional right to communication and language. *Journal of Deaf Studies and Deaf Education, 7,* 258–266.

Singleton, J. L., Supalla, S., Litchfield, S., & Schley, S. (1998). From sign to word: Considering modality constraints in ASL/English bilingual education. *Topics in Language Disorders, 18,* 16–29.

Spencer, L. J., Barker, B. A. & Tomblin, J. B. (2003). Exploring the language and literacy outcomes of pediatric cochlear implant users. *Ear & Hearing, 24,* 236–247.

Spencer, L. J., Gantz, B. J., & Knutson, J. F. (2004). Outcomes and achievement of students who grew up with access to cochlear implants. *Laryngoscope, 114,* 1576–1581.

Spencer, L. J., & Tomblin, J. B. (2006). Speech production and spoken language development of children using "total communication." In P. E. Spencer & M. Marschark (Eds.), *Advances in the spoken language development of deaf and hard-of-hearing children* (pp. 166–192). New York: Oxford University Press.

Spencer, P. E., & Deyo, D. A. (1993). Cognitive and social aspects of deaf children's play. In M. Marschark and M. D. Clark (Eds.), *Psychological perspectives on deafness* (pp. 65–92). Hillsdale, NJ: Erlbaum.

Spencer, P. E., & Hafer, J. C. (1998). Play as "window" and "room": Assessing and supporting the cognitive and linguistic development of deaf infants and young children. In M. Marschark & M. D. Clark (Eds.), *Psychological perspectives on deafness, Vol. 2* (pp. 131–152). Mahwah, NJ: Erlbaum.

Spencer, P. E., & Marschark, M. (2003). Cochlear implants: Issues and implications. In M. Marschark & P. E. Spencer (Eds.), *Oxford handbook of deaf studies, language, and education* (pp. 434–448). New York: Oxford University Press.

Stanovich, K. (1986). Matthew effects. *Reading Research Quarterly, 4,* 360–406.

Stinson, M. S., & Kluwin, T. N. (2003). Educational consequences of alternative school placements. In M. Marschark & P. E. Spencer (Eds.), *Oxford handbook of deaf studies, language, and education* (pp. 52–64). New York: Oxford University Press.

Stinson, M. S., & Whitmire, K. (1992). Students' views of their social relationships. In T. Kluwin, M. Gaustad, & D. Moores (Eds.), *Toward effective public school programs for deaf students* (pp. 149–174). New York: Teachers College Press.

Stinson, M. S., Whitmire, K., & Kluwin, T. N. (1996). Self-perceptions of social relationships in hearing-impaired adolescents. *Journal of Educational Psychology, 88,* 132–143.

Strassman, B. (1997). Metacognition and reading in children who are deaf: A review of the research. *Journal of Deaf Studies and Deaf Education, 2,* 140–149.

Stokoe, W. C. (1960/2005). *Sign language structure: An outline of the visual communication system of the American deaf.* Studies in Linguistics, Occasional Papers 8. Buffalo, NY: Department of Anthropology and Linguistics, University of Buffalo. Reprinted in *Journal of Deaf Studies and Deaf Education, 10,* 3–37.

Strong, M. & Prinz, P. (1997). A study of the relationship between American Sign Language and English literacy. *Journal of Deaf Studies and Deaf Education, 2,* 37–46.

Strong, M., & Prinz, P. (2000). Is American Sign Language skill related to English literacy? In C. Chamberlain, J. P. Morford, & R. I Mayberry (Eds.), *Language acquisition by eye* (pp. 131–142). Mahwah, NJ: Erlbaum.

Summerfield, A. Q. (2004, summer). Current issues in cochlear implantation. National [UK] Cochlear Implant Users Association Newsletter.

Thoutenhoofd, E. (2006). Cochlear implanted pupils in Scottish schools: Four-year school attainment data (2000–2004). *Journal of Deaf Studies and Deaf Education, 11,* 171–188.

Tomkins, W. (1969). *Indian sign language.* New York: Dover.

Toscano, R. M., McKee, B., & Lepoutre, D. (2002). Success with academic English: Reflections of deaf college students. *American Annals of the Deaf, 147,* 5–23.

Traxler, C. B. (2000). Measuring up to performance standards in reading and mathematics: Achievement of selected deaf and hard-of-hearing students in the national norming of the 9th Edition Stanford Achievement Test. *Journal of Deaf Studies and Deaf Education, 5,* 337–348.

Tucker, B. P. (1986). *The feel of silence.* Philadelphia: Temple University Press.

Vaccari, C., & Marschark, M. (1997a). Communication between parents and deaf children: Implications for social-emotional development. *Journal of Child Psychology and Psychiatry, 38,* 793–802.

Vaccari, C., & Marschark, M. (1997b). Il controllo dell'impulsività nei bambini sordi: L'influenza della inabilitá linguistica del bambino e suoi genitori [Impulsivity in deaf children: The effects of lacking effective communication between children and parents]. *Psicologia Clinica dello Sviluppo, 1,* 173–187.

Vernon, M. (1968/2005). Fifty years of research on the intelligence of deaf and hard of hearing children: A review of literature and discussion of implications. *Journal of Rehabilitation of the Deaf, 1,* 1–12. Reprinted in the *Journal of Deaf Studies and Deaf Education, 10,* 225–231.

Vernon, M., & Daigle-King, B. (1999). Historical overview of inpatient care of mental patients who are deaf. *American Annals of the Deaf, 144,* 51–61.

Volterra, V., Iverson, J., & Castrataro, M. (2006). The development of gesture in hearing and deaf children. In B. Schick, M. Marschark, & P. E. Spencer (Eds.), *Advances in the sign language development of deaf children* (pp. 46–70). New York: Oxford University Press.

Waters, G. S., & Doehring, D. G. (1990). Reading acquisition in congenitally deaf children who communicate orally: Insights from an analysis of component reading, language, and memory skills (pp. 323–373). In T. H. Carr & B. A. Levy (Eds.), *Reading and its development.* San Diego, CA: Academic Press.

Wilbur, R. B. (1977). An explanation of deaf children's difficulty with certain syntactic structures in English. *Volta Review, 79,* 85–92.

Wilbur, R. B. (2000). The use of ASL to support the development of English and literacy. *Journal of Deaf Studies and Deaf Education, 5,* 81–104.

World Health Organization (1992). *International statistical classification of diseases and related health problems, 10th revision.* Geneva: WHO.

Yoshinaga-Itano, C. (2006). Early-identification, communication modality, and the development of speech and spoken language skills: Patterns and considerations. In P. E. Spencer & M. Marschark (Eds.), *Advances in the spoken language development of deaf and hard-of-hearing children* (pp. 298–327). New York: Oxford University Press.

Young, A., & Andrews, E. (2001). Parents' experience of universal neonatal hearing screening: A critical review of the literature and its implications for the implementation of new UNHS programs. *Journal of Deaf Studies and Deaf Education, 6,* 149–160.

Index